ALSO BY WILLIAM GOLDMAN

FICTION
The Temple of Gold (1957)
Your Turn to Curtsy, My Turn to Bow (1958)
Soldier in the Rain (1960)
Boys and Girls Together (1964)
No Way to Treat a Lady (1964)
The Thing of It Is . . . (1967)
Father's Day (1971)
The Princess Bride (1973)
Marathon Man (1974)
Magic (1976)
Tinsel (1979)
Control (1982)
The Silent Gondoliers (1983)
The Color of Light (1984)
Heat (1985)
Brothers (1986)

NONFICTION
The Season: A Candid Look at Broadway (1969)
The Making of "A Bridge Too Far" (1977)
Adventures in the Screen Trade:
A Personal View of Hollywood and Screenwriting (1983)
Wait Till Next Year (with Mike Lupica) (1988)

SCREENPLAYS
Masquerade (with Michael Relph) (1965)
Harper (1966)
Butch Cassidy and the Sundance Kid (1969)
The Hot Rock (1972)
The Great Waldo Pepper (1975)
The Stepford Wives (1975)
All the President's Men (1976)
Marathon Man (1976)
A Bridge Too Far (1977)
Magic (1978)
Mr. Horn (1979)
Heat (1987)
The Princess Bride (1987)

PLAYS
Blood, Sweat, and Stanley Poole
(with James Goldman) (1961)
A Family Affair
(with James Goldman and John Kander) (1962)

FOR CHILDREN
Wigger (1974)

HYPE AND GLORY

VILLARD BOOKS   NEW YORK   1990

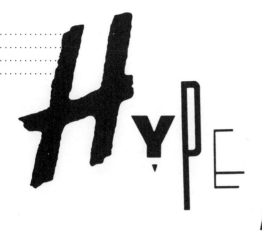

WILLIAM GOLDMAN

Library of Congress Cataloging-in-Publication Data
Goldman, William.
    Hype and glory/by William Goldman.
      p.   cm.
    ISBN 0-394-58432-5
  1. Goldman, William. —Journeys.   2. Cannes Film Festival.
  3. Miss America Pageant, Atlantic City, N.J.   4. Authors,
  American—20th century—Journeys.   I. Title.
  PS3557.0384Z467   1990
  814'.54—dc20   89-27125

Manufactured in the United States of America
9 8 7 6 5 4 3 2
First edition

Book design by Debbie Glasserman

For my future . . .
on the blithe assumption that it exists

CONTENTS

. . . returns . . .

I WENT BACK TO CANNES yesterday, wandered. It seemed the proper time. The film festival had been in May. The Miss America Contest was to be in September.

It was July now.

Midway.

Early evening. A light wind. The sun was deciding to go down, the mist was rising to cover the not-so-distant mountains. The beach was emptying. In the harbor, the pirate ship was making long, then longer, shadows. It had been built for a film directed by Roman Polanski, entitled, logically enough, *Pirates*. I was told it had been sailed to Cannes during the festival to publicize the movie.

Few films have ever lost more money. The extent of the carnage is hard to put precisely: people connected with a calamity tend to be the least bit skittish on the subject, since they're panicked they'll be tarred forever with red ink. (Only buffs associate Michael Cimino first with *The Deer Hunter* nowadays; like it or not, he's the guy who gave us *Heaven's Gate*.)

Pirates is in that league. It was weirdly financed—some say the prince of Tunisia, assuming there is such a creature, went on the hook for it. One top Hollywood executive told me, "We are talking a movie Edsel here. Lost fifty million easy. But then, look at the casting—Walter Matthau starring in an *action* picture? In 1986? How about doing *The Chuck Norris Story* with John Candy?"

This is not a book about money, but probably it's not unwise to try to remember why movie people have kept the tranquilizer business booming: after a debacle, it's hard to get work; after two, it's hard to get television.

Whether it was the failure of the flick or not, no one seems to know—there may have been nothing left in the coffers for vehicle removal—but the pirate ship is still there, bobbing on the waters. This masted hulk, now darkening, as the day disappeared.

I turned away from the Mediterranean, crossed the street to the Majestic Hotel, where I'd stayed during the festival. The concierge was alone behind his desk. In the two months since I'd seen him, he seemed to have lost ten years. There was a spring in his step; he was actually smiling.

"Quieter than the festival," I said.

He nodded with much enthusiasm. "Everything is quieter than the festival. Look," and he gestured around. "It is truly possible to see the lobby."

Truly possible indeed.

The pillars were there, unscathed. As were the startling bouquets of flowers. The proportions of the space were somehow tranquil now.

During the festival, tranquillity was in hibernation. The lobby was sardined with movie people. The pillars were nailed over with posters. *Action Jackson*, most notably. Everywhere you looked, there was Carl Weathers (the reason, say I, for the success of the first *Rocky*) standing with a gun in his hand watching you with killer's eyes.

The movie posters simply dominated the town. It seemed as if every tree, wall, building side, was laden with giant blowups of movies you didn't want to see.

Now, in the Majestic, the concierge turned to take care of the needs of a mother and child. One final glance back to me. "No crowds," he said, making it seem like poetry. "No crowds at all."

During Festival Fortnight, this cannot be said. People are standing, thousands of them, in front of the Palais, where the pictures are shown. They're there in the morning, stay all day, hoping for just one thing: that a star will amble by. This, of course, is not possible. Cannes is filled with movie stars, but they don't take constitutionals. They don't dare.

SCHWARZENEGGER: "In 1978, when I first went there, it was the key thing for me to be in town and to be seen. People asked for my autograph and I liked it because it was such a new thing for me. I would think, People know me. That was nice. I had come, of course, from bodybuilding, and the recognition on an international level gave me pleasure.

"Now in the ten years, a lot of things have happened, good things for my career. Now, being in town would have been impossible. This year, I was in a limo in town and we were stopped in traffic and I was spotted by a photographer. He began taking pictures. Now, fifteen other photographers ran over because they saw the first one taking pictures, and they all began taking pictures. And then the people on the sidewalk saw the commotion and they ran over, and in seconds, literally within seconds, the car was surrounded by two, maybe three hundred people, and the car started rocking and we couldn't go anywhere until the police came. . . ."

I left the Majestic, stopped for a moment by their pool. Amazing: *people were actually in it*. The area around the pool was empty, but the pool was full.

Why amazing? Because during the festival—my room overlooked the pool and I clocked the phenomenon—the surrounding area was totally jammed with people trying to make deals, and no one ever, *ever*, went into the water.

I left the pool, went to the corner where every morning I'd buy my *USA Today* for sports statistics.

On that walk, something even more amazing happened: I heard people speaking French. Don't even dream about that when the festival's on—English is the language of choice. Cannes, of course, is in France, but if you closed your eyes, there was no way of knowing that. The words "profit" and "gross" were much more used than, say, *"bonjour"* or *"au revoir."*

There is a continuing ambivalence about the south of France revolving around one unignorable constant: the crowds. We are talking about one of the most famous and fashionable places on earth—at least, so the media insists—the Riviera.

What, if anything, makes it special?

The restaurants, yes, the sea, of course, the light, exceptional; even the climate's not much worse than the travel agent's promise.

But there's more. I went for the first time back in the seventies, and I stayed at a lovely hotel that was on the water. So, bright and early, I hotfooted it down to the beach—

—someone had stolen it. That was my first reaction, because for someone who thinks of California or Long Island when the word "beach" is mentioned, the Riviera is in a very low minor league. Sand is at a premium. Mostly, if there's anything, there are pebbles. When you do find sand, you will have exactly as much square footage of it as your towel covers. "Shoulder to shoulder," as Nelson Eddy once sang.

So I am trying to locate the hotel beach, but then the lifeguard—his job was to patrol this rocky area by the water—pointed up a few steps toward the pool—

—no one had taken the pool, it was there. It was also the size of a puddle. This was a top hotel, understand, and large. Disgruntled the least bit, I lay down on the cement—there were no beach chairs—and started reading a Ross Macdonald. I was alone at puddleside, and I could see the Mediterranean, which was only slightly less blue than Lake Michigan.

What, I wondered, was the big deal?

Macdonald was, for me, the master of the mystery novel, and once I was hooked, it took a lot to make me let go, so I didn't pay much attention as these two Frenchwomen came down in their robes with their towels and chose cement spots not far from me.

They took off their robes—built like boys, more or less. I am not, you will be thrilled to discover, much taken with Frenchwomen, because they are as close to an anorexic nation as we've yet produced. Italian peasant women are more my style. (I don't think I've ever met any, but I'm sure I'm right.) Anyway, they're both in string bikinis, and one of them says something like *"Avez-vous la crème à mamelon?"* or whatever, and the other one nods, and then I'm back with Macdonald. But when I hit a chapter break, I put the book down—and one of these two ladies is creaming her nipples.

Now, she hands the tube of—I can only assume it was nipple cream—to her friend, and chattering away, she begins to squirt the stuff on the tips of *her* boobies.

Dissolve, as they say in Magic Town. By late morning, the pool area is filled with ladies, all of them topless, most of them nipple-creamed, sunning away. We didn't tan like this back outside Chicago while I was growing up.

There were maybe two or three other men. Maybe two or three dozen other women, some old and sagging, some old and perky (it's definitely possible), most of them young and worth a detour.

I am not saying that the Riviera is what it is in our consciousness because of nude sunbathing. But there was one other person poolside. A kid, maybe eleven or twelve. He was at one end of the pool area. And from his angle, what he sees is first his mother, half-naked, chatting with a friend. But he ignores them.

He is staring at this aisle of flesh, most of it fit and bronzed, and to this day I don't think I've ever seen wider eyes. As I watched him watching them, I knew, yes, it was the high point of his life. And sure it would be downhill, at least in his mind, from then on.

Because, I like to think, he was seeing something he didn't know till then was possible. Something magical.

That's the special gift of the Riviera—the promise of magic. Financial—the song was about the man who broke the bank at Monte Carlo, remember, not the man who broke the bank at Trop World. Sexual—never forget what Miss Bardot's bottom did for the then unknown town of St.-Tropez. (I was once told that when she was young, she roomed, however briefly, with Ursula Andress. To those who don't remember, they were the two best bodies in the world then, and I used to wonder what it must have been like if two guys on a blind date came knocking on their door and it opens and there they are and—and that way madness lies. Anyway, I don't know if the roommates story is true, but I do know that if it is, they had to have shared rent not in Hoboken, New Jersey, but on the Riviera.)

At any rate, the masses kept coming. Because the magic might touch them. And the natives gripe. But this isn't an eighties dilemma. *Phoenicians* went to the area for the beauty and the climate. Saracens too. The Romans built villas there, and probably bitched to their neighbors that they couldn't find a place to park their chariots. The love/hate that seems to linger permanently in the beloved-by-painters light has been discussed by many, but perhaps none more clearly than this man who lived here a lot of his life:

D. H. LAWRENCE: "Yes, the weather, the sun, the light, are lovely. Man is everywhere vile. They are just beginning to mess this coast up—but the messing seems to proceed rapidly once it starts. . . .

"... when the morning comes, and the sea runs silvery and the distant islands are delicate and clear, then I feel again only man is vile. But man, at the moment, is very vile."

On the other hand:

D. H. LAWRENCE: "I still love the Mediterranean; it seems young as Odysseus, in the spring. . . ."

Now, as the sky darkened, I moved slowly along the walk that parallels the beach. A sculptor with wild eyes was making Jesus busts out of wood. Two young blacks with long robes were having a religious argument in French. A white Rolls convertible was parked with a large FOR RENT sign dominating its windshield. A solitary portrait painter was looking around urgently for work—as examples of his talent, he had charcoals of Hitchcock, Bogart, and Monroe surrounding him. Four children came racing by, two of them on motorbikes with two more on skateboards clinging to their shirts. During the festival, they would have killed people. Now, no one to obstruct the contest.

I sat on the seawall, my back to the Mediterranean, and looked at the hushed city. In comparison to two months before, all was calm.

Most especially, me.

Of course, I had been excited just to get there, but when the competition actually started, everything kicked into a higher gear. Mostly because of the history of the festival. Because so many movies that meant something to me had played there.

In 1946, when the festival resumed after the war, *Notorious* was among the pictures present. As were *Gaslight* and *The Lost Weekend*. The next year: *Dumbo*.

In '51, there were *Miracle in Milan* and *Miss Julie* and *All About Eve* and *The Browning Version*. The year after that, Brando won Best Actor for *Viva Zapata*. In '54, America sent *Marty*, *Bad Day at Black Rock*, and *East of Eden*. In '58, Paul Newman won Best Actor for *The Long Hot Summer*.

1960 was my favorite:

Ben Hur	*The Source*
Home from the Hill	*Ballad of a Soldier*
Sons and Lovers	*L'Avventura*
Never on Sunday	*La Dolce Vita*
The Young One	

Henry Miller was the American on the jury that year, and don't you wish old Henry was still kicking up a fuss so we could gather round and find out what *that* jury discussion was like? That's also my Cooperstown Hall of Fame of directors— Bergman, Buñuel, Wyler, Fellini.

In thirty years, would people be asking the same thing about 1988? I had more than a rooting interest in a "yes" answer.

I got off the seawall and continued my July stroll. Then, with the pirate ship looking in the darkness as if it might actually set sail, Atlantic City suddenly filled my mind—

—because stretched across a beachfront building was a banner with these words: *MISS PLAGE OF 1998*, "*plage*" being the soft French word for beach. So in Cannes, as all across America, the pretties were sleeping with their fingers crossed. In Cannes, they were likely wondering would they become the next Deneuve, would they be able to stop being shop girls or students and find a world aching to embrace them?

And I felt sure the thousands of Miss America contestants were already fantasizing as they practiced what they hoped were their talents, and that, for at least a few of them, their plastic-surgery scars would heal sufficiently so as to be invisible come September.

As I stood in Cannes and saw the beauty-contest sign, the two events were somehow joined. In a skewered way, they were both about changing your life.

It was even quieter now. Restaurants that in May had formally attired couples waiting until (truly) two in the morning to get a seat now were nearly empty. Or, some of them, closed for vacation.

All glamour gone.

All sense of danger gone.

The Riviera napping wasn't really the Riviera.

ZELDA FITZGERALD: "Now all the gay, decorative people have left, taking with them the sense of carnival and impending disaster. . . ."

Asleep on a bench, a wine bottle still in his hands, a young student snored with happiness. He was wearing sandals. And jeans. And a T-shirt that read as follows:

SAME SHIT
DIFFERENT DAY

PART I

DIFFERENT

DAYS

ON THE SECOND OF MARCH of 1988, I called my good wife of twenty-seven years and said, "Ilene, you're not going to believe this either, but they've just asked me to be a judge at the Cannes Film Festival."

Her reaction was pretty much like mine—she wasn't sure if she was more pleased than surprised or surprised than pleased. "I'll bet you're already thinking either it's a joke or they must be pretty desperate to ask you."

After twenty-seven years, you get to know someone pretty well. "In which order?"

"I'm really proud," she told me, and she was. "When is it?"

"Two weeks in the middle of May, I think."

"You know what we might do?—we might go a little early and spend a couple of days in Italy first."

I guess I grunted.

Meaningfully.

Because right away she got it: "Oh, Bill, you didn't accept."

"Well, you know."

"Yes; yes, I do. Not new news."

Here's the thing you've got to understand about me: I tend to more or less resist change. I love surprises in books, hate them in life. If I were walking the streets of New York and ran into my oldest and dearest friend, Ed Neisser, who lives in Chicago, I would not, repeat *not*, be glad to see him. If I'd been warned he was coming to town, different story.

This weirdness of mine almost stopped me from ever getting into the picture business in the first place. Back in 1964, the movie *Masquerade* needed a doctoring job. Cliff Robertson had replaced Rex Harrison in the lead, and suggested that I be the one to "Americanize" the dialogue.

Probably the above makes sense to you, it's a simple enough sentence, but packed in there is how I got into the screen trade in the first place: by mistake.

I wrote a novel in 1964 called *No Way to Treat a Lady*. I wrote it very quickly and—I don't know why, probably because I thought it was going to be too short—I had a lot of chapters, with each new chapter starting at the top of a fresh page.

It was, no question, a weird-looking Heffalump of a novel: 160 pages, 53 chapters.

That style was going to change my life.

Cliff Robertson, a splendid American actor, was going through something of a career crisis: although he was well known and respected, his movie work was not on a par with his TV stuff. He'd been the lead on the tube in, among others, *The Hustler* and *Days of Wine and Roses*. But when they became movies, he wasn't around. He had recently done a TV drama, based on a glorious short story by Daniel Keyes, called *Flowers for Algernon*. This time, to be sure he wouldn't get cut out of the film, he himself optioned the movie rights and was looking for a writer to craft a screenplay. I'd written four novels and was finishing *Boys and Girls Together*, but I had never, at this point, *seen* a screenplay.

Robertson, out of some bizarre blue, calls and asks if we could meet. Bewildered, I, of course, say yes, so we do and he tells me what I've just told you. And then he says would I read the story, and if I like it, would I try and make a screenplay out of it. I'm sitting there flattered and totally confused—why is he asking *me?*

Then, in passing, he explains. He'd got hold of my "treat-ment" of *No Way to Treat a Lady*, and that made him pick me. I was still, of course, flattered—but it wasn't any goddamn screen treatment, it was a novel with a lot of chapters.

So Robertson's mistake started me off. But he wasn't done with me. Because when he suggested me for the "American-izing" job on *Masquerade*, he hadn't read a word of my *Flowers for Algernon* screenplay. (I finished it after *Masquerade*, sent it to Robertson, who wasted no time in firing me—an un-doubtedly adroit move—the flick was retitled *Charly*, and won him the Academy Award for Best Actor.)

At any rate, I met with the English producer of *Masquerade*, Michael Relph, in his suite at the New York Hilton. (We were, at one point, chatting away, when the living-room door, for no reason whatsoever and all by itself, decided to lock. When Relph and I realized we were trapped, it was no huge problem to have someone come from the bowels of the building and rescue us. Still, I have often thought that door locking on its own symbolized something about being a screenwriter; I've just never been able to figure out quite what.)

After we talked about the script a while, Relph, who I think was my first Englishman, said, "One never knows, of course, but I think this may work out quite well."

"Thank you; I'll do my best."

"We'll have to work quickly."

"I'm good on deadlines." (True—in twenty-five years of movie work, I've never been late. I do crazy things to make that happen sometimes—once I called and said I'd be late and asked for a week's extension, got it, then went into sleepless overdrive and turned the screenplay in by the original date. The work may stink, but it arrives.)

"We're into preproduction, so there simply is no time; now I assume your passport's well in order and—"

"—*Passport?* I don't have a passport, why would anyone need a passport?"

"To rewrite, obviously. With us. In London."

He'd been so bright up to this point. "Go to *London?* Go

to *Europe* just to do a little writing? *Leave the country?*" (As I'm sitting there perspiring, it might be noted that I am, at the moment, going on thirty-three, and am the only one I know who has never left the Continental Forty-Eight.)

"Try and understand," Relph says, "we need you right there with us. We're rather under the gun, you see. If you won't be with us writing right there at the studio, it's pointless for us to hire you."

I'm mopping away with my hankie now. "Look—Mr. Relph—here's the deal—I promise you—really, I mean this— I'll airmail you a bunch of pages every day. So there's no reason for me to go all the way over there."

"Think about it. We'd love to have you. But not in America." He stood. "Call me in an hour."

The living-room door (which had been unlocked by this time) was open. I left and slogged away.

Heading for my office. (Not strictly true. What I was doing in those days was writing in someone else's apartment. I'd been looking for an office and found an ad for a guy who lived nearby who was looking for a roommate. A deal was struck: I'd use his place from nine to six while he was at his insurance job. By the time he was done, I'd have scooted home. It actually worked. I don't know what would have happened if he'd ever got sick, but he didn't and I wrote a book and a half in a year and a half and was never once late in my rent payments.)

At the "office," I sat at my desk (he allowed me to bring in a desk) and called Ilene. We had spent hours the night before talking about the prospective meeting. Even though I'd never seen a screenplay until a few days earlier, I was convinced I could handle the assignment. "I'm at my pit," I said.

"And, and?"

"Ho-hum, they want me."

She was terribly pleased, not remotely surprised. "When?"

"I think kind of now. They're in pre-something; production, I think it was."

"Now? In May, that's so great—I hear London's supposed to be beautiful in May."

I guess I grunted.

Meaningfully, even then. "Oh, Bill, you didn't accept."

"Well, you know."

"I don't guess I do."

"Ilene, they're weird people—they're insisting I write in London. That's crazy."

"Did he say he'd pay your way over?"

"Oh sure. First class and everything. You and Jenny." (Jenny, our eldest, had just entered what was then called the "terrible two's.")

"Did he say where we might live?"

"Some kind of hotel suite somewhere. He said it's a fine hotel, and he was sure you'd like it. He wasn't positive, but he thought they had baby-sitters and everything."

"Let me just see if I have this: *they'll* give us a free trip to Europe, where neither of us have ever been, to do work that you said last night was kind of easy?"

"Yup, yup."

"And they'd pay you as well?"

"Oh absolutely. More than I've ever made on a novel." (My novels had all stiffed at this point.)

"I think you're absolutely right to turn it down."

Pause. "You do?"

"No question. I mean, a lot of money in a beautiful place for doing easy work—who would accept a rotten deal like that?"

"What you're really saying is, I may be making a mistake?"

"You don't think this wee resistance-to-change thing of yours is involved, by any chance?"

"Ilene, it is not at all involved, these are insane people."

"They sound just horrible."

"You think I should consider it, even with the travel, is that it?"

"Well, dear heart, since it has nine guh-zillion things in its favor and nothing going against it, I might *consider* considering it pretty hard."

It's very important as you go through life to have someone

around who can tell you you're an asshole without hurting your feelings. I hung up, called Relph, took the doctoring job.

And off we went a few days later, fresh passports in hand, young and sassy, into the Old World. . . .

I also (obviously) accepted the Cannes offer. The next day, I was talking with Rob Reiner on the phone and told him about it.

"Great," he said. "Are you excited?"

"Since for years my two greatest ambitions in life have been to be a judge at the Cannes Film Festival and a judge at the Miss America contest, I guess I would have to say yes."

A long pause. Then, from Rob: "I am now on a personal crusade to get you accepted as a judge at the Miss America contest."

He was not messing around. Shortly thereafter, he wrote a letter to the pageant not only suggesting that I was Good, True and Beautiful, but also explaining how helpful I had been in selecting an actress to play the title role in *The Princess Bride*— Rob had directed the movie, I wrote the novel and screenplay, and the lead lady had to be astonishing to look upon. Robin Wright played the part, and was, I thought, wonderful. But truthfully, she is so gorgeous, it wasn't really hard selecting her. It would have been harder not to.

Mark Pollack, the astonishingly effective vice president of Act III Communications, which had produced *Princess Bride*, got into the war room with Rob and coordinated the attack.

In early April, the pageant clutched me to its bosom.
Glory.

We are talking about two totally different happenings on two different continents that are, in their own way, joined at the hip. You might argue that they are the quintessential European and American pop-culture events. (I promise in this book never to use the word "quintessential" again.)

A few words of explanation might not hurt, however. Starting with Cannes.

What is it?

Pretty much what the name implies. A festival of films that occurs for two weeks in the middle of May. In Cannes.

On the French Riviera.

Important to note that. Probably, no slur on the Great State of Alaska meant, but if the identical films were shown in downtown Nome, for two weeks in the middle of May, there might be some seats available; at least for the morning shows.

Not that many years ago, an impoverished town in the Alps was looking for a way to boost tourism. Someone suggested, natch, a film festival—

—in the winter.

Well, no one turns this festival down. Not films that are invited to be shown, or movie people who are invited to judge. You look at movies in the morning, ski all afternoon. Better than a sharp stick in the eye. The festival has totally transformed the town. It has boomed because people have heard of it because of the resultant publicity. In fact, it is so successful that the city fathers are trying to dump the festival that made the town into a money machine—too many rooms are given away when the movies are rolling.

That's, as I'm sure someone must have noted previously, show biz.

So what Cannes is, then, is two dozen movies in the main competition, give or take, from all around the world. (Sixteen countries represented in '88.) And these chosen films compete for awards, just as the Oscars do.

The jury selects the award-winners.

That, if you will (and much more in detail later), takes care of the "art part" of Cannes.

There is also, believe it, plenty of commerce running parallel.

Approximately six *hundred* movies are shown out of competition. Every bookable movie theater in town is rented out during the festival. Let's say I've made *The Bill Goldman Story*, the thrilling sex-packed saga of a nerd from the Middle West who, for his sins, is forced to become a screenwriter and take meetings all his life.

Let's say it cost me $3 million (a nonunion epic). Well, I want to make some of my money back. Ideally, I'd like to make all of my money back, and even—gasp—turn a profit. (Profit was once described to me by a famous producer as this: "It's like the horizon; it always recedes as you get closer.")

The first thing I do is standard business practice: I spend money to make money. I accomplish this by taking out ads in the daily trade papers that flourish during the festival. I might spend a hundred thousand or so.

Then I rent whatever theater I can that's available. Just about every venue is booked solid with other people trying to hawk their flicks, but maybe I'll get one theater for showings at three and five in the afternoon on two consecutive days.

My trap is baited. I'm praying for distributors to come. In my heart, I am going pitty-pat that the yokel from Argentina will be seduced by *The Bill Goldman Story*. Or maybe that sucker from Thailand will actually smile.

The amount of advance I'm liable to get on the deal depends entirely on two things: the distributor's enthusiasm and where he's from. A five-*thousand*-dollar advance from Iceland is not unheard of. Nor is a five-*million* advance from Japan (action stuff, mostly—Schwarzenegger or Stallone).

Now this is not a Ponzi scheme. People do actually make money. The guy from Argentina might give me fifty thousand for all rights and we'll split the profits. (Any remote chance of my seeing profits disappears directly in relation to geography. The Philippines are a long way from my office—I'm not going to see any profit from there. *E.T.* is probably still in the red in the Philippines.)

My success obviously depends on whether or not I make enough in advances to cover my costs. My Argentinian guy has total rights—theatrical, TV, cassettes, etc. He might make a bundle in Argentina for his fifty.

He also might not. Let's say he picked, for example, the aforementioned *Pirates*. If he stiffs with my movie, when I come back with my sequel next year, he might, underline *might*, do business with me again. But if he gets burned a couple of years running, it's over. It's over for our relationship, and probably over for my making any money out of Argentina.

That is not, in itself, a big deal, but it is at least a nudge toward calamity—because if there are enough ''Argentinas,'' I will not have enough to make my next film.

Important aside: No matter how much shit you may have heard or read, movies are finally only about one thing: THE NEXT JOB.

If you will just remember that, you will know a lot about why you see what you see up there. Everyone in the business—I mean giant star actor, star director, studio head, all the way down to screenwriter—is ultimately obsessed with that and only that. The next job.

Why?

Easy answer. Because we all know one undodgeable truth: no matter how beautiful or muscular we are, no matter how great our skill with camera placement or narrative structure, there will come a day for each and every one of us when the phone will stop ringing.

Probably you think that is putting it a bit melodramatically. It isn't. Let's take one of the golden boys (and deservedly so) of our era: Woody Allen. You like Woody Allen? I like Woody Allen. *Everybody* likes Woody Allen. Well, one of his recent serious films opened at a sought-after big city theater. And on that very first day, with all the standard advertising and hype, it grossed something like six hundred dollars.

A little arithmetic now: it was a six-hundred-seat house, and it had six shows that day—thirty-six-*hundred* seats were ready for fannies.

Tickets were six bucks each.

Divide that: we're talking *one hundred people* who came opening day.

So *three thousand, five hundred seats* were empty.

It gets worse: seventy-five people more than likely came to the eight o'clock show.

So twenty-five people got to divide up those other three thousand seats.

This, remember, was for a major release by one of the most famous award-winning people on the planet.

And no one gave a shit.

Think he slept well that night?

Think the guy who had to call him on Saturday with the Friday grosses was looking forward to the call? "Well, Woodman, we didn't exactly swamp 'em, but my God, I wish I could have bottled the audience reaction at the noon show—those five people, I'm telling you, better than the Second Coming."

Woody Allen is still working. But D. W. Griffith was alive and unemployable for years before he died. Same with Orson Welles.

The phone goes silent on us all. . . .

There is a third part of Cannes that must be mentioned. (The first two being the official competition and the marketplace.) And that's the social aspect.

All of the companies that have pictures up for sale (and that can afford it) give parties. These range from cocktail shindigs in hotel suites to dances on the private beaches of the major hotels. You walk along the Croisette, the curved street that rings the sea, and it's dark, and you hear music. Then, at the edge of the walk, you look down and there are couples dancing and, ho-hum, caviar and champagne. To get to the beach, you have to take the private hotel staircase, and there's always someone standing there with a list—so you have to use some ingenuity to crash.

But oddly, I noticed, few did. There would be groups clustered on the walk above, staring down, young people mostly, I'm sure aching, and I remember thinking those parties would last maybe five minutes before being overrun Back Here.

The best-reviewed party (yes, that happens there) was thrown by Trans World Entertainment for *Full Moon in Blue Water*, a Gene Hackman/Teri Garr movie. It was given several miles out of town at the Château La Napoule, rented for the occasion. Several hundred were in attendance, and estimates for the cost of the event go as high as $150,000.

Two unusual points to be made:

1. The company had already sold the movie around the world, so the purpose of the party was not to seduce distributors. Why spend the money? Because Trans World had been making kind of schlock movies and it wanted to announce to their peers that it was still around, only different. In other words, the theme of the party might well have been, "Hey, look—we're not just making Ninja pictures anymore."

2. Trans World did such a splendid job in pre-selling the movie that it was millions of dollars in profit *before* it played in American theaters. Which put the Trans World people in a terrible bind. If they spent a ton advertising the movie, they would be spending their own profit. So they did what any sound businessperson would have done. They spent a middling amount only. They decided, basically, to take their money and run, which means, if you stop and think about it, that the movie was *too* successful for them to bother to let American audiences see it (and, thus, too successful to possibly make even more money in American movie theaters). If you're the filmmaker, it's probably better *not* to stop and think about it.

Obviously, at a party like the one at La Napoule, there is a reasonable amount of sexual energy in the area, but a lot of the socializing at Cannes ain't about sex. Remember that the marketplace is a twenty-four-hour hustle, it's business way over pleasure, and the following interchange between a handsome studio figure and a female independent executive I think illustrates this point.

Verbatim:

ATTRACTIVE INDEPENDENT
What are you doing tonight?

HANDSOME STUDIO FIGURE
(thinking she's really *very*
attractive)
When tonight?

ATTRACTIVE INDEPENDENT
(moving a step toward him)
Say one-thirty.

HANDSOME STUDIO FIGURE
(very Bogart)
What did you have in mind?

ATTRACTIVE INDEPENDENT
Seeing my movie, it starts
then.

HANDSOME STUDIO FIGURE
(stunned)
At one-thirty in the morning?

ATTRACTIVE INDEPENDENT
But the party doesn't start
until it's over.

Not an unusual occurrence during Festival Fortnight.

What Kind of Movies Show in Competition?

Not as artsy-fartsy as you think.

Clearly, *Police Academy* is an unlikely entrant. And you don't expect to find many Bela Lugosi *hommages*. But the crucial prize at Cannes, the Golden Palm, does not always go to flicks that are lacking in entertainment value. Since 1970, for example, the following American movies have won the *Palme d'Or du Festival International du Film*:

> *M*A*S*H*
> *Taxi Driver*
> *Apocalypse Now*
> *All That Jazz*

Not a snooze in the carload. But it's also clear that these are not your ho-hum standard-brand Service Comedy/Urban Drama/War Epic/Musicals.

It has been written that essentially there are only three kinds of movies:

1. Movies that were meant to be good and are.
2. Movies that were meant to be good and aren't.
3. Movies that were never meant to be any good.

The majority of movies, sadness sadness, fall into the last category. At Cannes, every picture in competition is in either of the other two. Some may stink. But they sure didn't start out that way. They were all, in the hearts and minds of those present at the creation, intended to be in the *Citizen Kane* Derby.

Hundreds of movies each year apply for the competition. About two dozen are selected. Since most of the movies that are picked never get to the States, it's not going to illuminate a lot if I talk about 1987's entries (1988's will be dealt with eventually). But what I am going to do now is talk about the four biggest box-office hits in America in '87. Because most of you will have seen them, or at least know something about them. This is all my conjecture now. I didn't speak to anyone dealing with the festival on this. But if I'm off, I'm probably not far off. In no particular order, the gold mines:

1. BEVERLY HILLS COP II

No imaginable way Cannes takes this. Not necessarily because it's a sequel. (I'm sure they would have been thrilled to have *Godfather II*.) And not because of all the sequels of the last ten years—and boy is this saying a lot—only *Rocky II* came as close to being an absolute carbon copy of the original.

But truth to tell, it kind of stank. Eddie Murphy is an amazing talent—I can't think of any other giant star ever who was as versatile as he is young (actually I can, Mickey Rooney) with his kind of lunatic following.

But here's the thing. When you sat there and watched it, you were aware of this: nobody much cared. It was a Cash Register picture, its only intent to coin money.

Which it did. The men who made it may have been hookers, but they were brainy ones. No complaint about the box office.

Just the (ugh) quality.

And the intent.

The intent of Cannes is somehow, just a little, to make movie audiences aware that flicks can both, please God, teach *and* delight. I don't think the honchos who rode shotgun on this baby gave much of a shit about either.

2. THREE MEN AND A BABY

No imaginable way Cannes takes this either.

All kinds of reasons, one of them, I'm pretty sure, patriotic. Probably some of you have heard of *Trois hommes et un couffin*; doesn't matter a lot. That was a recent French hit that, when it came to our shores, was called *Three Men and a Cradle*.

Anyway, what the folks at Disney did was buy the rights to the French flick and do a remake. So I think the powers at the festival might have been stoned nightly by the throng if they had allowed an American rip-off of a French original into the competition.

More than that though. This was not another Cash Register job. If anything, it's one of the biggest surprise hits of the eighties. Afterward, it's easy to say, "Oh a lock—look at that cast and that subject." But the cast, except for Steve Guttenberg, had been in nothing but disappointments or disasters on the Silver Screen. Danson and Selleck are *huge* TV stars. But the luster hadn't transferred.

Till this baby.

The quality here was certainly more in evidence than in *Cop*

II. (Another aside: people who work on movies almost never refer to the thing by its name if it's more than one word. *Butch Cassidy and the Sundance Kid* was always called *"Butch."* *The Great Waldo Pepper*—go rent it, it's better than you think—permanently *"Waldo."* I don't know what the Selznick employees called *Gone With the Wind*. [*"Gone"* seems unlikely.] I have no idea what the Murphy people called their opus either. [*"Beverly II"*?])

"Slick" was a good word for *"Baby."* "Skillful," too. Lovely comedy performers doing lovely comedy work. It had a lot going for it. Audiences liked it. And should have.

It demanded nothing.

No law says you have to.

But here what you had was a lot of professional people doing professional work.

What you didn't have was weight.

Cannes flicks don't have to be "important." But in the end, they want to be about at least a little something.

Not the case here.

3. FATAL ATTRACTION

Tough call.

Moviemaking doesn't get more Major League than this. (Too many *m*'s.) Michael Douglas won his Oscar for *Wall Street*, and I thought deserved it. I also thought he was even better here. Douglas is a wonderful actor who we can see blossom before us nowadays. But I never thought he had the kind of sexuality he showed here. And Glenn Close just scared the shit out of me. Spooky.

I saw the movie late, and the house wasn't full. Mattered not a whit. The audience *screamed*. Or just sat there like church mice. I haven't felt that kind of group behavior in this kind of movie since the first *Jaws*.

So? Isn't that enough?

As I said, tough call. But I think not.

Because because?

Okay. The producers of this movie were involved with the playwright Bernard Slade (*Same Time Next Year*, etc., etc.) at the time this movie was gearing up. Slade was writing or developing something for them. And during these months, Slade had a play running in the West End of London (their Broadway). A mystery.

Care to guess the name of his play?

Riiiiight. *Fatal Attraction.*

Point being?

Being this—it's indicative of why the movie, for all its sorcery, wouldn't be taken.

Another indication: In '71, Clint Eastwood directed his first movie, *Play Misty for Me.*

So?

Same plot.

The problem with *Fatal Attraction* as a Cannes film had nothing to do with its execution. But it simply wasn't original. A splendid rehash was what it was. Same old ingredients.

Not enough.

4. GOOD MORNING, VIETNAM

Toughest call.

Another beautifully crafted film. With a home-run performance by Robin Williams. (Not just the funny stuff. Best thing he's ever done. I hope, as a moviegoer, he does a dozen parts over the next years that are better. Right now, I just don't see how it's possible.)

But Cannes is not noted for raucous farce/comedies. (Not one of the movies in competition this year was much funnier than Maria Ouspenskaya.)

So that's why Cannes would turn it down?

Don't think so.

I think the festival would have grabbed it and been delighted to do so.

But *not*, please follow me, if the movie had been entitled *Good Morning, Chicago.*

Could have been. A down-on-its-luck Chicago station decides to bring in this weirdo disc jockey. And he tears the place up, is sensationally funny, totally disrespectful of authority, becomes a cult figure, ruffles the bosses, almost gets hurt on a trip into a Chicago slum, and eventually is eased out of his job: too hard to handle.

It would have worked as a movie. Would have worked as a commercial entity too.

But it wouldn't have been about much of anything.

That terrible war gave a core to the madness of Williams's work and a weight to the enterprise. We're not talking about *The Battleship Potemkin* here, but you knew, when you walked out of *Vietnam*, that it was different in heart and mind from *Caddyshack II.*

Different in soul too.

And that very present soul is why Cannes *would* have proudly shown the picture in competition.

At least say I.

So now I hope we're at least a bit more settled in our footing when it comes to Cannes. Hopefully, more light will be forthcoming. Now to the Miss America contest.

What Is It?

What is now called the Miss America Pageant began in Atlantic City in 1921. Pageant history would have us think that it lasted until undone by the Depression, whereas in truth, it clunked to a halt in 1927 through a combination of mismanagement and not much interest. In '33, it came up for air again, then nothing the next year.

In 1935 it began its unbroken string, which, if not going strong, or at least as strongly as it once did, is still going. And in those early days, it truly *was* what people think it still is, only they couldn't be more wrong: a beauty contest. What the judges had to deal with, back then, wasn't easy. Here is the official point system for an early year:

Construction of Head:	15 points
Eyes:	10 "
Hair:	5 "
Nose:	5 "
Mouth:	5 "
Facial Expression:	10 "
Torso:	10 "
Legs:	10 "
Arms:	10 "
Hands:	10 "
Grace of Bearing:	10 "

All that was supposed to add up to a hundred, and I don't know about you, but me, I cannot look at this list without wanting to giggle. *Fifteen points for head construction?* What language is that in? Eyes are worth the same as *hands?* Legs and arms are equal? Can't you hear those long-ago judges conferring?

FIRST JUDGE
I'm sorry, by me it's got to be
Miss Jersey, best biceps I've
measured in years.

SECOND JUDGE
But did you notice her pinky?
Shapeless.

THIRD JUDGE
(the most lecherous)
Did you catch the ass on Miss
Delaware? There's your
winner.

> FIRST JUDGE
> (consulting his
> scoring sheet)
> Ass isn't on here.

> THIRD JUDGE
> But "torso" is. You can't have
> a torso without an ass.

> FIRST JUDGE
> Big deal—the whole torso's
> only ten, ass can't be worth
> more than two, two and a half
> on the outside.

> THIRD JUDGE
> (appalled)
> An ass is only worth half a
> mouth? Something's wrong
> somewhere. . . .

And on into the night.

As the years passed, the pageant grew less arcane, more famous. In the fifties, it added television and Bert Parks, and for a while, it was as popular as anything the tube brought us.

Lately, it's been drifting. Lots of reasons: feminism, a proliferation of clone contests, a sense that there was something nineteenth-century about the endeavor, problems getting *anyone*, let alone a judge, to spend a week in Atlantic City.

It was still the dream of thousands of young women all across the country (but mainly in small towns). It was still a famous name.

But the TV ratings were down, getting dangerously so. And so this year, the pageant made some moves to try to reclaim the high ground.

But when a piece of pop culture gets in trouble, it's not easy to recapture the past. Ask the folks who gave us *The Saturday Evening Post* or *Collier's*, I'm sure they'll be happy to agree. . . .

IT WAS SATURDAY, MAY 7, and I wanted to look pretty.

Because Lexie was getting married. Lexie Masterson, daughter of Pete and Carlin, our best New York friends for twenty-five-plus years, had decided on a formal wedding. She was the first of her generation among our friends to do such a thing, and for all kinds of reasons (usually I dress *très* informally) I wanted this once to get it right.

I take precautions. The wedding was set for six in the evening, and practically upon awakening I had gone hunting for my tuxedo. I must wear it easily twice a decade, so I wasn't sure if I'd find it right away, but I did. And put it on. The jacket.

Poifect.

Now, the trousers.

They really hurt. The top just dug into my love handles. But if I sucked in my gut and pretended I enjoyed suffering, I could make it through the festivities.

Now for my tuxedo shirt. The one with the cuff links and the place where you put the three studs.

Nailed it first shot, put it on.

A tad tight in the neck, but it gave me, actually, a sort of pleasant ruddy look.

I contemplated wearing an ordinary white shirt.

Death.

One didn't. Not when one wanted to look splendid. Not when Lexie was getting married and all our friends would be there. I needed to be natty.

Black shoes shined. Dark socks at the ready.

Studs and cuff links in their tidy little greenish box that was in the top right-hand drawer of my dresser where I always put them.

Only the problem of the tie remained. I cannot tie the damn things. (I am not notably dexterous—it was actually the first grade before I could tie my shoes with anything resembling consistency.) I didn't trust a clip-on. So I'd purchased a bow tie that worked sort of like a belt. I practiced doing it until I was as confident as Greg Louganis doing a swan dive.

Sartorial problems solved, I had a busy rest of the day, because the next morning, Sunday, was departure time for Cannes. The first meeting of the jury wasn't until Tuesday, but a couple of days' layover in London would help with jet lag.

Besides, we had a flat there unseen in twenty months.

So I did some careful packing for the morrow; Cannes would likely be a lot warmer than London. I didn't want to lug a lot of excess around Europe.

I was terribly excited.

And amazingly nervous. You have to know me to realize what something like that means, because when I'm at my most calm, I'm jumpy.

It was ridiculously hot for early May. The city seemed to have skipped spring entirely. Some of the air conditioners in the apartment worked; more than a few were struggling.

As midafternoon approached, tensions increased. Ilene was pretty sure what to wear. So was Susanna, our twenty-three-year-old. But it was so ridiculously humid, there was a change of costume discussed, then attempted. Jenny, now twenty-six, was coming down from her place to join in playing dress-up.

Confident in my attire, I was amazed anew at the shit women have to put up with to look proper. I had an old teacher who when he died in the mid-sixties was still proudly wearing a blue blazer he'd bought at Brooks Brothers before we entered World War I. It had leather patches on the elbows, sure, but the style was the style.

Half past four now. Now, a quarter to five. I had to be ready to leave in a little less than an hour. The church wasn't far away.

I put on my underwear.

My dark socks.

Inhaled mightily as I gloved my way into my trousers.

My tuxedo shirt went on in Astairish fashion.

Opened my top right-hand dresser drawer, felt a moment of panic—

—couldn't quite locate the greenish box where my cuff links and studs reside.

It was silly how nervous I was.

A deep breath. Pull the drawer all the way out.

There it is.

The green box, in the deepest corner of the drawer.

I reach for it, open it—

—cuff links, no studs.

A wee moment of hysteria.

I banish it. Take the drawer in its entirety out of the dresser, go through it with care.

Eye patches. (I was shortly to have eye surgery.)

Knee braces. (I am given to swollen knees.)

Back girdle. (Don't ask.)

Nary a stud.

Well now.

A few queries. None of my ladies have stolen them. None of them had seen them. None of them even admitted to caring about them. (Krupke, we got troubles of our own.)

What to do?

The ordinary white shirt?

Not a bit of it.

I strip, redress in slacks and a T-shirt, then out into the steaming afternoon on a stud hunt.

The clock was ticking.

No.

No.

No.

These were the replies from the first three stores I entered. They were also in agreement about something else—I should give a try to Ralph Lauren's. Polo. Seventy-second and Madison, just around the corner from my home.

I have a thing against the place. No logic behind it. But I have only had one good television idea in my life. Right next to Lauren on Madison, contiguous if you will, is the St. James Episcopal Church, which is lovely and old and does a lot for the needy.

Every day, the boat people of the city come to the steps of the church, sit quietly, some of them smoking, some just staring silently, waiting for their noontime meal. They never bother you, never hit you up for money or butts. They just eventually overflow the steps, fill the sidewalks, waiting for their sustenance.

If you stand in front of the church, on Seventy-first and Madison, and look uptown, you see these two divergent worlds, mingling. Rich women going into and out of the store, rich men too; poor men waiting to be called to dine; poor women too.

And the worlds move through each other like some contemporary time warp—

—nobody, of course, getting what he truly wants.

I mentioned this to a friend who works on the tube, and a crew was dispatched to check it out. I'm told that the footage eventually made ABC News.

The Lauren reservoir is velvety and tasteful—but I'm emotionally now and forever one of the boat people, waiting, staring, on the steps.

Now, with less time and more humidity, I entered Polo, made a few inquiries as to where men's accessories might be, followed the answers, reached a lovely salesman.

"I'd like some tuxedo studs."

"We don't sell tuxedo studs."

"I was told you did."

"We do."

"You just said you didn't."

"No, what I said was we don't sell studs."

Feeling not in a perfect mood for Abbott and Costello, I headed him off at the pass by asking, "What *do* you sell?"

"Sets."

I didn't have to feign ignorance.

"Sets. *Sets.* Studs *and* matching cuff links."

"I don't need cuff links."

He was really very nice, said he understood my situation, suggested I try Brooks Brothers or Paul Stuart—

—thirty blocks downtown in the heat and the traffic, not to mention I didn't have the time plus they'd be closed before I got there.

"Maybe I could just see one of your sets," I said.

He showed me. The only set they had. As lovely as you'd expect of Lauren. Tiny little elegant studs, larger, still elegant cuff links.

Should I wear a crummy white shirt?

Dumb to hate Ralph Lauren. Especially when he's got what you want.

"Deal," I said.

"Don't you want to ask how much they are?"

"I'm gonna take 'em anyway, but if it makes you happy, how much?"

He told me.

You could have bought any number of middle European compacts for the price he quoted.

Should I wear the crummy white shirt? Should I, for Lexie's formal wedding, be insecure and sloblike?

Hating myself, as Irwin Shaw would say (and there are those who would add "and not for the first time"), I bought the frigging "set," raced home. Time was getting constricting.

Quick shower, dry off, wacky with nerves now, on with the socks, on with the trousers, on with the shirt, on with the cuff links, on with the studs, turn, grab the tie—

—and a stud falls out.

I look at it. Reach down for it, pick it up.

—and another stud falls out.

I am now approaching madness. Could even I have put the studs in wrong?

No.

Could the guy at Lauren's have been a joker, sold me trick studs?

Stop thinking that way.

I take off the shirt.

Replace the studs.

Put the shirt back on.

Reach for the tie—

—and as I'm reaching, the goddamn studs fall out again.

Rod Serling would have written an hour *Twilight Zone* about this.

It couldn't be fucking happening.

One last try.

Off with the shirt.

On with the studs.

Reach for the tie—

—you guessed it—pop, pop. I'm Wimpy with his buttons leaving.

I sit down for a moment, trying to figure what I'm doing wrong. The truth? And I didn't find it out until after I got back from Cannes weeks later and went back to return the "set" to Lauren's.

Another lovely salesperson.

"I'd like to return this set I bought from you because the studs—"

—he interrupts, "Fall out, don't they?"

"How did you—?"

"Well, we've had a bit of trouble with those studs, they

don't fit most shirts." Beat. "They fit *our* shirts perfectly. You could buy our shirts, if you'd like—that way you could keep the studs."

He was a nice-seeming fellow, so I didn't kill him.

But while I am there, I suddenly remember the worst movie meeting of my life: a producer had flown me to London for a lunch. We were to woo an English gentleman who owned a property we needed to commence a movie. The entire exercise was to convince him we wouldn't "Hollywood it up."

Anyway, during the lunch it turned out the guy didn't own the property, someone else did, so the producer wouldn't get to do the movie. Which made him so distraught he didn't complain about the turbot he had ordered, which, through some amazing gaffe, had come on his plate *raw*. Untouched by heat of any kind. And this was not a sushi place, folks.

Later I had this image of the cooks in the kitchen peeking out saying to each other, "Chap on table nineteen's got the raw turbot today, pay attention now, let's watch the look on his face when he tries to bite into it."

My memory is of course triggered by the notion of Ralph Lauren salesmen all across the land starting to chortle as they sell their tuxedo "sets," knowing the customers are going to shortly go mad trying to make them fit, betting with each other as to how long it will take before, beaten and confused, they return.

I ended up wearing the plain old crummy ordinary white shirt.

Some friends picked me up and drove to the wedding, and I told them my adventures while they assured me that no one would know, people would not point to my shirt and begin guffawing; more important, they wondered, would the church be air-conditioned?

It wasn't.

But except for that, the wedding went off perfectly. I sat with my friends on one aisle seat. Across the aisle, Ilene sat with my daughters.

If you're thinking that our seating arrangement was the least bit odd, you're right, of course, but there's something you don't know, and it's this—we were, suddenly, if anything can be sudden after twenty-seven years, getting divorced.

Early the next morning I awoke, fifty-six and alone, passport in hand, and set sail like Columbus into uncharted waters.

MY GALLEON WAS THE Good Shippe Concorde (Cannes paid transportation). Concorde is, of course, immorally expensive and remarkably uncomfortable.

But it takes away the jet-lag problem. Worth a detour.

Two notes about the trip:

1. The front sixteen seats, four times four, were occupied by a group of Orientals traveling together. How do I know they were together? Because they were all dead asleep. Totally zonked. Heads lolling in unison. When you looked in their direction, you might have been eyeing sixteen corpses. Not a budge from takeoff to touchdown. Then, after a bit of shaking, they trooped off in a weary clump.

2. My chief memory of the journey was of a tall, handsome, very well dressed gentleman, midforties. It was Harrison Ford, and what impressed me was when he went to his knees and changed his baby's diaper. I remember when I did that, and it was always a decent bet that one of my daughters would get stuck by a pin. Ford could not have been more expert.

It was probably half past seven when I reached the flat. Cloudy. Serious threat of rain.

Mattered not a bit. I was, in some strange way, home.

Those of you who have read this far know that I came to England only after considerable kicking and screaming. I arrived that quarter-century ago May late at night, and I remember dropping my luggage, immediately going out for a cab ride. The driver impressed me tremendously, but that was because I didn't know that London cab drivers are better at their job than any other group of people are at any other occupation in the world. I asked for a Cook's tour and he tooled along, showed me the river, Big Ben, Parliament, and a bit later we're passing this large, lighted place and he says, "And that's, of course, the Palace," and after a beat I said, "What palace?" and he said, "Why, Buckingham," and I said, "It's *here?*—You mean it's right here in town?—*stop the car.*" I'd always thought that it was way out in the country somewhere, surrounded by miles of countryside. I remember staring at it that night, feeling somehow welcomed, and the next morning, very early, I remember walking around my Knightsbridge hotel, tracking the tiny, insane streets thinking, I must live here someday.

Never quite managed it. I spent four summers there doing movie work, and in the early seventies I proposed to my three ladies that we move there.

Turd in a punch bowl.

No interest a-tall from the trio, and they had a valid point. They had lives and friends back in New York. I just wanted to move on a whim.

But I liked the me in London so. That person was more at ease with his surroundings than his Manhattan counterpart. The stomach churning, so constant in the States, was less. The always living on eggshells, the constant fear of falling, of making some dreadful miniscule mistake—that fear was always in retreat in England.

And so, a few years ago, we bought the flat. Two small bedrooms, a make-do kitchen, a glorious living room overlooking a square. As fine a room as any I've been familiar with. The logic behind the purchase was that we'd *use* the place, I'd write there, we'd find, maybe, peace.

Didn't work out.

No telling why. We'd hoped to take long weekends, just spur-of-it-all *go*, no big deal, travel bag under the seat with a skeletal wardrobe awaiting.

Now, as the clouds advanced on the city, as I got out of the cab in front of the house, it had been twenty months since I had visited my second-floor flat. (First floor, the English call it.)

A terrible waste.

Inexcusable, really.

Which doesn't mean I wasn't excited as I unlocked the front door of the building.

I walked up the one flight in the darkness, got out my keys, thinking how, since my life was clearly going to change, I had to find ways to include my flat into those changes. I envisioned the place inside—the lovely living room, the fireplace, even the television set, since their pictures are almost movie quality compared to ours. I knew what I was going to do inside: pour a welcoming Finlandia, light the fire (it was gas), sip, take a shower, change, then grab a cab for Scott's, the elegant fish restaurant on Mount Street that was open on Sunday. A pleasant meal, a half bottle of Beaujolais, crème brulée, then home, maybe a relaxing bath to get me in the mood for zonking, then—

—"Oh—oh dear—"

The voice was coming from behind me in the darkness; from up and behind me, actually, from the stairs.

Then a flashlight beam hit my hand as I was trying to insert the key in the darkness.

I turned.

Glanced up the stairs.

An older man was standing there. "It's Mr. Goldman, isn't it?"

"Yes." I'd never seen him before.

"Oh—oh dear," he said again.

I waited.

"I was so afraid it might be you." He took the flashlight

from his right hand, put it in his left. "My name is Bingham. We live—my wife and I, that is—two flights above you."

I held out my hand and we shook.

"This is really just dreadful," he went on, gently.

"What's wrong, Mr. Bingham?"

He gestured around in the darkness. "Did you try the switch down by the front door?"

"I did." There's a switch, as he said, just inside the front door. It lights up the stairwell for quite a long time, in theory giving you time to get to your floor without stumbling. But more often than not, the light's burned out. "It's not working again."

"It's a bit more than the bulb, I'm afraid. That's not working, I mean."

"What else?"

"You see, Mr. Goldman, there was a storm last night, quite a severe storm, in point of fact, thunder, rain, lightning, menacing in its way, but actually, as my wife pointed out, in its own way, also beautiful, that is, if you weren't caught out in it—" His voice was lovely to listen to. Or would have been ordinarily. But I wanted him to drop the shoe.

"Mr. Bingham," I said, "what else isn't working?"

"Everything isn't. I put that rather badly, didn't I? Perhaps I should have said that nothing is." He paused. "Put it badly again, wot?"

Ordinarily, I love it when the English say "wot." Now, I wasn't as enthused as ordinarily.

"I know you don't get here often," he said. "That's why it's such a shame you've chosen today to appear. I think you might come up to our flat a moment—we've an extra flashlight we'd better lend you." He headed up, putting his beam on the steps behind him for me to follow.

"Are you sure I'll need it?"

He stopped. "Mr. Goldman—there's nothing. No light. No heat. No water. No electricity. Nothing at all. I've spent the whole of the day peering out the window waiting for the electricity board men to come and fix it. I called them and they promised to appear—that was this morning. The reason I have to peer out the window is because the bells out front don't work, so if he came and pushed, there'd be no one to hear. That's how I happened to see you when your cab stopped. My wife has spelled me looking out the window. Actually, it's been a rather dreary way to spend the Sunday. But there it is."

When we reached his flat, his sweet wife insisted I take their other flashlight. I took it gratefully, promised to return it once everything was working again, went back to my place, unlocked it, went in.

Nothing, as Mr. Bingham promised, worked.

I bumped into walls for a bit, getting familiar with the layout after so long, lay on the floor and did my back stretches in the dark, got out of my grungy airplane clothes, dressed with the aid of my flashlight, and went to Scott's.

The maitre d' looked at me, I thought, somewhat strangely, but then I'd been more than a little paranoid of late. It was only when we passed a mirror as he escorted me to a table by the kitchen that I realized his look: I was wearing a blue shirt and what I'd thought was a dark blue tie. It was, alas, quite brown. As were my shoes. Throw in the blue suit, and Beau Brummell had nothing to feel worried about. Not only did the two colors clash, the shades of blue and brown didn't do a whole lot for each other.

At least my fly wasn't open.

I had the lovely meal I promised myself, and it only cost me $125.

Staggering. But I hadn't been there since the dollar had gone all wimpy against the pound. (The next day I didn't buy some underwear in Harrod's, since the price, when converted, came to thirty-six smackeroos.)

In the darkness back at the flat, there was a note from Mr. Bingham—the electricity board man had come. But only for a moment. He lacked the proper tools to have a good look. But he'd sworn to return in the morning.

I went inside, undressed. Eleven-thirty. I was exhausted. One of the wonderful things about Concorde. Within five minutes, I was out.

And slept magnificently.

Until just before three in the morning, when I came wide awake and knew there would be no more rest that night. A steady rain had begun, which meant I was trapped inside in the darkness. Couldn't walk, couldn't read, couldn't do a goddamned thing but stare the night away and try to block out the past.

Hard cheese.

The only good thing about it all was that in the darkness I didn't have to see myself. I was alone.

No need for the cursed sunglasses.

One thing that ought to be kept in mind is, throughout the whole of Cannes I was never without these large, very, very dark sunglasses, with extra side pieces going around the sides. I hated them, needed them, or felt I did.

Briefly, in 1971 I caught an odd pneumonia that attacked my right eye. For a year, I had double vision. Then, for a decade, all was normal again. Then, a few years back, the condition returned. I could look to the left and all was well. When I looked to the right, I saw double and my eyes crossed.

It did wonders for my self-esteem.

I was always sitting in such a way as to not feel like Quasimodo, and turning myself so I'd appear to be all right. In the months of "turning myself," I managed to exacerbate an arthritic condition in my neck.

I was told and told that surgery was no use, I'd have to live with it.

I lived with it.

But I began wearing these goddamn sunglasses. They hung around my neck all my waking hours. When I was alone, no problem. But the minute anyone else came around, on they went. Someone said to me he didn't know who I resembled more during this time, Ray Charles or an Italian film producer.

Then, in the months just preceding, the eye got worse. I could almost feel the muscle sag, the eye wander. I sought out surgeons, found one who said he might be able to help.

Surgery was set for after Cannes. But during this time, with my eye pressure a constant, with vague headaches constant, the neck pain too, the sunglasses were almost always on.

A very gray dawn. Too dark to read in the place. A drizzle dying outside. When it went, so did I, out for a morning stroll. When I returned, Mr. Bingham was standing on the front steps, chatting with a thin, very edgy fellow who quickly got into a small truck and churned away. It was drizzling again by now, dark, getting darker.

"That was the electricity board chap," Mr. Bingham said. "It seems that in order to fix the house, he's going to have to turn off the electricity in the entire area."

"He did seem upset," I said.

"Oh, that's not what's upsetting him," Mr. Bingham explained. "When he saw the box, he said, 'Let me out of here!,' and I said, 'What's the matter?,' and he said, 'This entire area could blow up at any minute.' "

After twenty months away from my flat, I decided to spend the night in the Dorchester Hotel.

I spent most of the day (I was leaving for Cannes in the morning) going to familiar spots, saw a few acquaintances. One, when told of my marital situation, asked how things were, and I said the truth: really quite friendly. The wedding forty-eight hours earlier had been the first time we'd been out together since we'd gone public with our decision, which, I suppose as much as anything, contributed to my paranoia and the madness with the shirt studs. "I think it's going to be fine. Not easy; but fine."

My friend draped an arm around me. "You actually believe that?"

"Of course."

He smiled. "This isn't meant to upset you, because I like you, Bill, and I would never try and upset a friend, but it's going to be awful, it's going to be so awful you can't believe it, you'll be wishing it was only a nightmare before you're through, it's the worst experience of your adult life, I promise you, I know, I'm your friend, I've been through it twice and ended up with nothing, just ashes, Bill, you'll be wishing for death before it's done."

He went on and on, smiling, and all I could think of was what would he have said if he'd been trying to upset me? . . .

Steak Wars

That night I had a wonderful dinner at a restaurant I've been eating at for a quarter of a century, only I can't tell you its name.

British food and British taste in food have improved amazingly in the past ten years. (Sort of like Los Angeles.) But if you're an American and you every so often crave a steak, you can't go by their restaurant guides. Because they just don't understand about beef. There was one place and one only you set your compass for, the Guinea, a small grill on Bruton Place just off Berkeley Square. In front was a pub. You walked through it.

And there the maitre d' met you with a pencil and paper and took your order. Behind him was what they had that night. Always the freshest and the best available. Melon, asparagus, artichokes, berries. Standing behind the maitre d' was the chef, grill alongside.

And between these two men were these glorious piles of Scottish beef that you could have cut to whatever thickness you wanted.

Not a place for fancy sauces.

But you couldn't buy better basics.

The British guides never much took to the Guinea. "Too American." And Americans did flock there. The place was always packed. But knowledgeable Brits went too: it was simply the best steak house in town.

Then, a few years back, came the cataclysm.

For reasons no one will ever ascertain, a split happened in the ranks. A splinter group formed. And moved away.

Across town?

No.

Across the street?

Nyet.

Right next door. The two restaurants touch. In fact, the main room of one of them looks like it was once the second room of the other.

There is now the original grill, the Guinea; and there is also its clone, the Guinea Grill.

Both with maitre d's that greet you at the door. Both with the same glorious produce. Both with the same piles of Scottish beef.

And both, now, with doormen.

No one has any idea, at least the first time he goes, which restaurant he's booked into. "We're looking for the Guinea on Bruton Street," he says.

"WE ARE THE GUINEA ON BRUTON STREET," cry both doormen at the same time.

And then they pull and tug at the potential customers, now so totally confused. "We booked," they say.

"OF COURSE YOU DID," cry the doormen, neither relinquishing his grasp.

Understand, these are not cheap places. But one of the glories of English street life now is to stand on quiet little Bruton Place and watch the Steak Wars fought continually between the doormen. Sometimes people who have booked in one can't find the rest of their party who are next door. Constantly, diners with napkins come hurrying out of the one, run the gauntlet to the other.

Sometimes, when no customers are in sight, it's enjoyable to chat up the doormen. (Rob Reiner, I think, began this.) He'd go over to one and say something like, "Now you're the original place, right?"

And whichever doorman he addressed would say, "OF COURSE WE ARE."

Which would bring the other one tearing over. (Understand, the doormen are scrabbling for customers always standing within five yards of each other.) "HE LIES, HE IS THE ORIGINAL NOTHING. WE ARE THE ORIGINAL."

"IF YOU ARE ORIGINAL, WHY ARE YOU EMPTY?"

And then you just stand there and watch them shout at each other.

On my way in this night, I stopped, asked one of Rob's better questions: "Who's doing better business tonight?"

"WE ARE."

"HE LIES. *WE* ARE."

"HE LIES. WE ARE ORIGINAL *AND* WE ARE BUSIER."

"YOU ARE THIEVES."

"THIEVES? YOU DARE TO CALL US THIEVES?" He grabs my arm. "YOU SEE? HE HAS NO QUALITY."

Now, the other one is on me. "I WOULD NEVER TELL YOU WHERE TO EAT. YOU ARE GROWN *MAN*. YOU CAN USE YOUR OWN JUDGMENT. BUT DON'T EAT THERE."

I ate in one or the other. I either had my steak grilled at the Guinea or the Guinea Grill. From a trencherman's point of view, it doesn't really matter: they are both the best steak houses in London. I left the doormen yelling at each other.

Inside, of course, it was much more civilized. The table next to mine was taken up with an attractive British couple in their late thirties. I sat quietly, studying the wine list.

He dug out a piece of ripe melon with his spoon. "I wanted to love you," he said.

She squeezed some lemon onto her perfect smoked salmon. "That's such a load of shit," she said.

Then they both silently went on with their meal. . . .

4. THE VISION

I LEFT THE DORCHESTER Tuesday morning in more than enough time to catch the plane for France. I do that. Leave in more than enough time. I always pretend I might get a flat tire and have enough leeway so that even if the catastrophe occurred (it hasn't yet) I would still catch my plane.

I am, in other words, a careful flyer.

Especially internationally. I can't begin to estimate how many times I feel for my passport, touching my inside jacket pocket from the outside for the reassuring pressure of cardboard. I also look at my passport more than once. The passport was all I needed.

I was positive of that because the travel book I had been using to prepare myself for the Riviera said so. (The book, for the curious, is *The American Express Pocket Guide to the South of France*. New & Revised. Second edition, 1987.) (Edited, for those who crave all info, by Christopher McIntosh.) The first paragraph of the Basic Information chapter reads as follows:

BEFORE YOU GO:
Documents required.
A valid national passport is all Americans need.
No visas are required, and no health or vaccination certificates are required for entry into France.

When I travel, prissy as it may seem to you, I need to know that kind of thing. I went to Africa once (best trip ever, A+), and was edgy until I'd got through customs that I'd be detained or turned back because I didn't have the right shots or whatever.

So as my cab pulled away from the hotel, I was aware that even a mediocre marathon runner could have left half an hour later and still made the plane. But then, I wasn't visiting, however briefly, just any airport. No, no. Heathrow is different from them all.

Decades ago, when I first encountered the place, I actually thought it didn't like me. Because no matter what airline I traveled, regardless of the day or night time of my arrival, I was always getting off the plane at the gate that was absolutely farthest from passport control. The walk, especially when you do it with young children, is remarkably unpleasant and time-consuming. It was during this period that I attributed a brain to the place and thought Heathrow was out for my ass.

It was only years later that I realized the magical truth: *every* passenger who tippy-toes from his plane into the airport is also getting off at the gate that is farthest from passport control. I don't know the secret, because logically, of course, it isn't possible. Someone *has* to have a convenient exit.

Except no man or woman alive can make such a claim. You might think that since I now know that we all suffer equally, my hatred for Heathrow would have been brought under control. Alas, no. Because with the modern era of flight upon us, Heathrow has become increasingly diabolical. For example— the Heathrow people movers. You all know what a people mover is: a horizontal escalator. They're wonderful. A sense of uplift is universal when you first see one up ahead.

Heathrow has people movers.

Spanking tidy, they are.

For good reason: no one has ever ridden on them. They never ever work. Silent taunts is what they are. (Personally, I'm convinced they're built without motors.)

Enough. Let it be said I am wary when at the place. I expect pitfalls. Little did I know, as they say, that a very special young woman was about to enter my life. One who, no matter how long my allotted span (why does that sound dirty?), I knew would always be lingering, blond and perfect, in the remainder of my brain. . . .

The most beautiful woman I have ever seen is British, Jacqueline Bisset from Weybridge. She is still, of course, stunning at forty-two. But twenty years ago, she'd just been brought over from London, and I was working on the Fox lot during preproduction for *Butch Cassidy and the Sundance Kid*.

I, of course, remember exactly the moment. It was lunch, I was walking up the steps to the Fox commissary chatting with a friend. Bisset was leaving the place, coming toward us. I was talking on, flicked my eyes toward her, did the standard double take, stared now in her direction—

—and fell *up* the stairs of the commissary.

I met her briefly the next day—someone suggested her for the role that Katherine Ross played so well—and what we talked about was could she lose her accent. And I still remember what it was like being close to a fellow human who was different, being, through I suppose genes and exercise, possessed of a genuinely eerie physical beauty.

But Bisset is in show biz, and the girl who worked for Air France at the check-in counter was a civilian, by far the most stunning-looking I had ever seen.

Light blond hair down to the shoulders. Unusually pale blue eyes. Her skin from my distance (I was fourth in line) seemed just about perfect. (Later, when our bodies were close, that supposition turned out to be true.) She was seated, so of course I could not tell then about her body. (Later, within less than an hour, actually, I would know that her body was as fine as her skin.)

We are talking here, in case you've been snoozing, about a Vision. Capital V.

And I wondered, watching her, how she dealt with the public, because even remotely attractive girls get hit on all the time. This one I was curious about. So I, as surreptitiously as I could, studied her, and found her secret.

Remoteness.

She was as efficient with the people she was checking in as any machine. She did not make eye contact. She did her job as distantly and quickly as it was possible to do it. That was how she got through the day.

To tell the absolute unvarnished (as they say) truth, I was a little sorry she didn't goof up some, so I could see her a little longer. I know it's sexist and all that to talk up girl-watching as an Olympic sport, but God it's fun. I wrote a character in an early novel of mine, *Soldier in the Rain*, who graded women for a hobby. He would give them either "A, B, C, D, F, or incomplete." Incomplete was his biggest category; he was a very hard grader.

At any rate, my time with her was going to be brief, because she was whipping through her chores, I was no longer fourth, now third, soon to be second—

—then I caught a break.

Heathrow, it must be admitted, smiled on me: a voice came over the loudspeaker begging our forgiveness and understanding but explaining that the luggage conveyor belts had become jammed and no more check-ins would be processed until the overload was cleared, which should take, the voice swore, less than ten minutes.

Groans from the Air France–area passengers.

Me, I was happy as a (as they say) clam. (Who are "they"? I'd like to know. The ones who are always saying things. Me, I wish they'd come up with better phrases. Do you realize how "they" must bore each other spitless with the dopey things they're always spouting at each other?)

I don't even think she was aware I was clocking her. I do it, I like to think, with some degree of dignity. And as I said, she didn't make eye contact. She just sat behind the counter, looking sort of half down, until the conveyor belts were conveying again. Then she finished off the guy two ahead of me.

I was now third. The guy in front of me was in the wrong line.

My turn.

I handed her my passport and ticket, put my luggage where she could tag it. She was, close up, just amazing to look upon. I glanced at her left hand.

Amazing to look upon and single.

As, we all know, was I.

Not that it would do me any good, I realized as I stood there waiting to be short-shrifted. When I was young, I could never summon up the guts to begin conversations with stunners. And I was sure no longer young. Probably close to thirty years older than the Vision. She was under thirty by considerable. Might even have been twenty-five. But there was a wisdom in her great face that made me know she was decades away from adolescence.

It was then that the first in a series of unexpected wonders began: as I stood there, however brief the instant, her eyes flicked up at mine.

Why had she done that? She hadn't done that for anybody else. No glances, no attention paid, not even half-smiles—

—she was now, it should be noted, half-smiling at me.

Now, another eye flick.

Then, so studiously, she was back looking at my passport, fingers idly flicking from page to page. Now, she was glancing at my ticket.

And now, she was looking dead at me.

And I was looking at her.

I like to think I didn't blush or look away. But there was a lot of heat in the area. Sudden and surprising.

She was looking at my passport picture now, and the half-smile was back. (I don't know why, but I have a looney tunes passport picture. I'm not suggesting we should all go see Scavullo for our tiny black-and-white, but mine is bizarre. I'm unshaven, hair totally unkempt. What I look like is a revolutionary early in the day.)

It was then that I realized something about my passport was of more than a little interest to her.

It could only be—and this was very hard to admit, but there was no other possible solution—my name.

She knew who I was.

This doesn't happen often. But when it does, it's always for one reason: *The Princess Bride.* I have been a professional writer for a third of a century, published close to a couple of dozen books and screenplays.

And have gotten more letters on *Princess Bride* than on anything else.

More letters on *Princess Bride* than on *every*thing else.

Put together.

To put a mathematical edge to this, I would guess that of every ten pieces of correspondence I've been sent over the decades, at least nine have been about *Princess Bride.*

It's my one cult book. And people who like it like it a lot. (Nice aside here: I like it too. It's not just my favorite book of mine. Since I don't much care for my writing, it's the only book of mine I can look at without embarrassment.)

The movie had recently opened in London, had been well enough received critically, was doing okay with the public.

Did she know me from the movie or the book? I wondered.

Greedy, greedy, I hoped it was from both.

Our eye play was heating up now. The half-smile was constant, as was her constant looking away to my ticket, my passport.

I was thinking lunatic thoughts.

But that shouldn't be unusual—my God, a marriage comes clattering to an end after twenty-seven years, you're entitled to a little madness.

And perhaps I realized at that startling moment that if the movie business is about the next job, then the business of being single is about this: the next woman.

Had the phone stopped ringing for me already? No, that would be too unfair. I wasn't dead, for chrissakes. Didn't there have to be at least someone out of all the billions of us who might glance in my direction? Yes; of course yes. And this one, this as yet mysterious beauty, would it be so terrible if we gave each other a few laughs, a bit of tenderness, maybe even, please God, pleasure?

Could I be looking at her now?

It was ridiculous, I told myself, helplessly standing there. I was twice her age. We wouldn't have shared references. She wouldn't know about Irwin Shaw and *Gunga Din*, I wouldn't know about "Wham." *The New York Times* recently referred to Cole Porter as something like "one of America's better pre-rock composers." I wanted to choke the asshole critic, by the by. Well, she wouldn't know who Porter was. Probably she hummed Andrew Lloyd Webber.

We were not a perfect pair.

And even if she was interested in me—and no question about it, she *was* interested in me—I had to get to France. The jury was having its first meeting late in the afternoon, and I had to be there for it. *Had* to. I knew that all jury members had to actually see all movies or they wouldn't be allowed to vote. What I didn't know was if all jury members had to be present at all meetings. Did they? I'd given my word. I had to get to the Riviera.

Even if she wanted me to stay.

Madness.

"Even if she wanted me to stay." Who was I kidding? Why would she want that?

Maybe *Princess Bride* was her favorite book.

Couldn't hurt.

Or—

—or—

—maybe she wanted to come with me.

Unlikely, sure, but what if she had some vacation time coming up and she loved the book and thought I was Special for having written it and is it so terrible, vacationing on the beach at Cannes?

Of course, I could always return to England the instant the festival ended and I was released from active duty.

You get the picture by now: I am staring at this not just beautiful but beautiful-with-soul young woman, who is smiling and staring at me in such an unusual way, far from her normal manner, the clicking machine. I'm having major-league fantasies, fantasies that I haven't really allowed myself to have in many, many years.

Should I say something?

Not in me.

She might laugh.

No, if there was to be intercourse of a social nature, she would have to incept it.

I glanced away.

It was noisy in the check-in area, and I wasn't looking when it happened—

—but that was the moment she spoke to me. It was the moment my fantasies turned real.

"We can go to France," she said.

I turned, looked into that superb face, the oh-so-pale blue eyes.

It was, in point of fact, possible. Obviously, not on the same plane—mine was leaving shortly and she hadn't expected me to come careening into her life so she'd have to finish work and then go to her flat (or home, if she still lived with her folks) and pack and get back to wonderful old Heathrow (such gifts it had suddenly brought me, and I realized why it had tormented me so long: to see if I was Worthy).

But by early that evening, certainly no later than late that evening, we could be entwined on my bed in the Majestic Hotel; later, so satisfied, we'd walk along the beach.

Hand in hand.

But what kind of a girl does that kind of brazen thing? Not many do it to me. Or at least they sure haven't during this reincarnation.

AIDS.

What about that? If she wants to hit the sack with me before introduction, who else has been there? Can you ask someone that? On your first, you should pardon the antediluvian expression, date?

How do you do that? I've been out of circulation for the last few millennia? Wouldn't she get ticked? There we are, alone at the Majestic Hotel, Mediterranean moonlight streaming in, and I say, "Who have you . . . um . . . been with lately? . . ."

Got to put a damper on things.

Got to.

But this was not your everyday ho-hum opportunity. I had recently been involved with something I never, ever dreamed I'd be involved in: my wife had left me.

What if this creature, this on-the-outside-at-least perfect *thing* had an interior to match? What if, don't laugh, what I was looking at was my one best shot at, roll of drums, please, Happiness?

She wanted to go to France with me.

She'd said that.

Hadn't she??!!!

The truth was this: half.

What she'd said was this: "You can't go to France."

Now, she said it again.

"You can't go to France."

I just stared at her.

The wonderful smile. "I'm terribly sorry, but there it is."

"There *what* is?" I managed, entering into a new reality I never dreamed existed but a few seconds prior.

Her eyes flicked at me, at my passport, as she deftly turned the pages, at me, at the pages. Her voice was lilting, her English accent sweet: "You have no visa, you see."

"I don't need a visa."

"Ah, but you do."

"Not to go to France."

"I'm really terribly sorry." She started to look past me to the couple standing behind.

By now I had the book out, my trusty *American Express Pocket Guide to the South of France*. I turned to page seven, handed it over. "No visa is required," I quoted.

She handed it back, unimpressed. "Perhaps it's an old book."

I flashed the cover. "New and revised. Eighty-seven."

"I can't help you, I'm really terribly sorry. Americans aren't allowed into France without a visa, it's against the law."

"I *have* to get there. Today. I'm a judge at the Cannes Festival. We meet late this afternoon."

I would like to say here that after this encounter I realized I'd overrated her complexion, that her teeth were yellow, that her figure, when she stood, made you feel pity and fear.

Alas, none of these. She was still my Vision, only now I was an impediment. She sighed, stood, beckoned for me to try to keep up as she lockstepped me behind the check-in counter to where there were a number of cubicles and offices. She stopped at a room that was, for the moment, empty. "I'll leave you here," she said.

"This isn't going to take long is it? My plane and all."

"Ah well, I can't say on that, Mr. Goldman."

Why wasn't she in show business? I looked at her and wondered what nutball path had taken her to Heathrow. The world was waiting for this one—

—now, she looked at me sadly one final time—

—and shook her head. Then I was alone.

What did that mean? That she sensed what might have been between us? Was she shaking her head over that loss? Or was it this: that I was doomed?

Surely a silly thought, but less so when her superior immediately entered. You've heard of the Beast of Belsen? Of Nurse Ratched? The woman who exploded into the empty room now would have considered them softhearted. One glance at this Beast of Air France who was scowling at me, and I knew I was in very deep trouble.

· · ·

I'd only had trouble once before while traveling, in '85, when I was on my way from London to Edinburgh. I was going under the seat, a quick overnight trip, and I had really nothing much with me, just a toilet-article kit, a change of clothes, and a pair of those black two-pound soft weights with Velcro closers that you wrap around your wrists or ankles for exercise purposes.

My bag went through the X-ray machine. The black weights showed. An airline lady on the far end asked me to open my bag.

Not a problem.

She wondered what the black weights were.

"They're black weights," I explained. "You put them around your wrists or ankles when you exercise. The Velcro fastens them tight. They're very popular in America."

I was about to discover they weren't what you might call household items in the UK.

The airline lady signaled for a guard.

They huddled.

He nodded, came over to me, picked up the black weights. "What might these be?" he asked.

"They're black weights," I explained. "You put them around your wrists and ankles when you exercise. The Velcro fastens them tight. They're very popular in America."

He picked up one, shook it. The sand or whatever it is inside that provides the weight went *whoosh, whoosh.*

The guard signaled for a second guard.

Now, *they* huddled.

The second guard nodded, picked up the black weights, took me by the arm, and suddenly I was in a room close by the X-ray-machine area, and in a second, *three* guys came in.

All four huddle.

They break, shake the weights, listen, nod. "American product, you said," from the second guard.

I nodded.

He examined them. "Why don't you show us where it says that." He handed me one of the weights.

There was no manufacturer's mark.

They all studied me. No smiles in the county.

"Perhaps you might explain," one of them said.

"Explain?" I have been, in my time, more debonair. "These are just everyday ordinary weights. You put them around your wrists and ankles when you exercise. The Velcro fastens them tight. They're, I promise you, *enormously* popular in America, they're on sale practically everywhere, you must have this kind of thing here."

"We have nothing of that nature here." This from another. And they are really studying me now.

"Well, come on, what else do you think they could be?"

They thought they were bombs.

I realized this as yet another man entered, carrying a large tray of test tubes, liquids, razors, knives. In the next ten minutes, they questioned me, shook my weights, prodded them, were about to cut them open with a razor when something I might have said made them stop and release me. In the end, though none of them apologized for the inconvenience, one of them almost smiled.

Now, visaless in the bowels of Heathrow with the Beast of Air France staring at me, I realized there would be no smiles from this one. She was leathery, sharp-featured, French. Angry at my intrusion.

"This was a very stupid, avoidable thing—you should have asked someone or gotten a book, so you'd know about the visa."

"Please look at this." I pulled out my goddamn copy of *The American Express Pocket Guide to the South of France*, edited by Christopher McIntosh, who was very lucky he was not in the immediate area. "See? No visa is required."

Was she ever unimpressed.

"You'll have to go back to London. The American embassy."

"I have to be on the plane." It was leaving in half an hour.

A smirk. "Not today, I'm afraid."

"But I'm on the jury of the festival."

"In three days, you'll be able to leave England."

"At Cannes. We have our first meeting this afternoon."

"So you're on the jury."

I nodded.

"Who else is?"

Total blank. (I'd been told a couple of people, but their names skidded from memory.)

Now, clearly, on top of everything else—an idiot traveler, a Pest (the American species, the most detestable from the French point of view)—she also realized this: I was a liar.

"Well, who do you know in Cannes?"

Total blank.

In just a few minutes now, the plane is gone, and the next one, assuming I could somehow get on it, didn't arrive until after the first jury meeting.

She's controlling her anger, stomps out her cigarette, lights another. "Really now—you must know *someone* in Cannes."

"Gilles Jacob!" I manage, loudly, Jacob being the creative head of the festival, the one who selects the films to be shown in competition. I'd met him for dinner a month or so before, in New York.

She wasn't impressed with my memory feat. "Again? And there's no need to shout."

"Gilles Jacob. He runs the festival. Get in touch with him, he'll vouch for me."

"Where?"

Hadn't a clue. I was staying at the Majestic Hotel, and I remembered that he wasn't. The only other place I knew in Cannes was the Carlton. "Carlton Hotel."

"You're sure?"

I wasn't sure of much just then, except that if I ever met Christopher McIntosh, he had zero chance of survival. "Absolutely."

She hesitates, one hand on the phone. Another cigarette hits the floor, a fresh one goes between her lips. Deep breath. Glance at me. I could tell how much she wanted there to be no Gilles Jacob at the Carlton Hotel. Probably she wouldn't have minded if the Carlton had gone poof. She inhales. Dials.

Waits. Jabber-jabber in French with the hotel operator. Waits again.

Ring.

Ring.

Another glance at me.

Then scowl—Gilles answers.

He's there!

I'm home and dry.

I stand there, Frenchless, listening anyway, as the battle rages. Jabber-jabber-jabber from her. Muffled reply from Jacob. Jabber-jabber.

Muffle-muffle.

Yet another cigarette goes bombs away.

She's rat-a-tat-tatting at him, holding my visaless passport. His replies are brief.

And unsatisfying.

She's shaking her head now, sharply.

I'm just transfixed, stomach knotting.

One final burst.

Then she slams down the receiver.

Then she hands me a piece of paper.

"Sign."

I sign. "What is it?"

"Air France is now absolved of all responsibility."

It was then that I realized it was over and I'd won—no point of absolving me unless I was on my way. "I'm glad it all worked out. It really was essential for me to be in Cannes this afternoon and—"

"*Cannes?*" she cuts in. "Who said anything about Cannes, you are not going to Cannes, you're going to Nice, nearby, except you're not even going to Nice, you're going to the customs men at the airport in Nice."

"The customs men?"

"Of course. They will handle you. It's what we always do when this happens. We just send you to the customs men in Nice."

"And they'll handle things for Cannes?"

"Oh no—they'll send you right back here to England. It's what they always do. You have no visa. You can't get into France with no visa. You should have known that. Hurry up, bring your things or you'll miss the plane."

I pursued her toward the boarding area. "They *always* send people back?"

"Certainly—you'll be in England again by the end of the day."

I was the last one on.

She didn't say good-bye.

Seat belt fastened, off we took.

And only three days earlier, I'd thought tuxedo studs were a problem. . . .

WHEN I WAS VERY YOUNG, growing up outside Chicago, I stole something. From the dime store. A pencil eraser. All the big kids I knew—the nine-year-olds—were into heists of a similar nature, and for the standard childhood reason of belonging, I cased the dime store.

My memory is it had red bricks on the outside and was on Central Avenue. A big store for a small town, but I was not impressed by its size: I had traveled by then, had seen Marshall Field's on Chicago's State Street. (One of my happiest childhood memories was riding the escalators in Field's. I'd never seen them before, and I still recall the blind joy of carefully getting on one, riding it up to the second floor, two to three, and so on to the very top of the edifice, pausing only to circle around, then the whirring trip down. I don't suppose I ever did that all day. But I wanted to.)

I entered the Woolworth's unsure as to what to grab. It wasn't a store I used much, preferring Larson's Stationery, much closer and they were nice to me. (It was there, I think in 1941, that I found my first copy of *Variety*. They never got it before at Larson's, and I don't think they ever did again. But *I* was there the same day *it* was, and I was an arithmetic whiz then, and the numbers—"box office" was a phrase I wouldn't know till decades later—fascinated me. I've always believed that had I not met that magazine that strange day, my entire life, insofar as it pertains to the entertainment business, would have been not even close to the same. I can truly see the me of then standing by the magazines, turning the pages by the window. It was afternoon . . . hot, before air-conditioning.)

I wandered along the Woolworth aisles, and as I did, I was, of course, scared just shitless. I had never stolen anything before (nor have I since, and I'm not sure if that's good or bad), but I was given some cold comfort by this: no one paid me any mind. I was just a kid in short pants and tennis shoes and a T-shirt.

Why I decided on the pencil eraser I have no idea; probably because it was so small. I circled the counter, glanced around—still ignored.

I was halfway into the not-enormous store. I went to the next aisle, giving my conscience one final sounding: did I dare? Was I of sufficiently stern stuff? If I (inconceivably) got caught, would it make the papers? The headlines? Would my parents die of the ensuing shame?

I believe I had told my peers I was going to commit the robbery, or I would have fled.

The fingernail-sized eraser was suddenly in my pocket and I turned, started out of the store—

—which was now, horribly big, far bigger than Field's ever was.

And everyone, every single person in the store *knew*.

Billy Goldman had a hot pencil eraser in his right pants pocket!

Everyone watched me.

Would not stop.

Would—not—

By the time I reached the safety of Central, I was a much older man.

Everyone watched me in Nice now.

We were bused from the plane to the customs area.

All the passengers knew.

The driver of the bus clocked me in his rearview mirror. He knew.

I had no fucking visa.

At the age of fifty-six, I was going to be collared by the French cops, manhandled, put in a room alone, then shoved onto a plane back for Heathrow. The Air France Beast had said it: "They'll send you back to England. It's what they always do."

What kind of a public-relations thing was that to say? Making me sign that paper as if I were a Middle Eastern terrorist?

My fiber was returning.

Let them look at me, the bastards.

The bus belched us into the customs area—the standard zoo. I was hoping for a bilingual passport inspector who might understand my plight, let me zip through.

I got Erich Von Stroheim.

(Two minor points: 1. It's strange, but in moments of crisis, people begin reminding me of movie stars. 2. Why should I hope for a bilingual guard when I'm so linguistically impoverished myself?)

He grabbed my passport into his cage, went smack to the page where the visa wasn't, said something to me I didn't come close to understanding but the thrust of it was this: "Don't move your ass."

He shut his cage, stepped outside, signaled for a guard; they clustered. Then he went back into his cage while the guard led me along with one hand, held my passport with the other. (The guard, for those interested, was Dan Duryea. Not a heavyweight, but dangerous all the same, though I thought if I could have spoken to him, he might have been good for a bribe.)

Do you remember the story "The Man Without a Country"? The main character was very much with me as we marched along. I had somehow sure knowledge that when I got back to England, the Air France bitch would have loaded the dice against me and now *they* wouldn't let me out of *their* customs area, and so I would live for God's allotted days, shuttling from one European country to another, customs area to customs area, a Jewish leper, sleeping in baggage areas, eating who knew what, a twentieth-century untouchable.

Then the sun decided to shine on me.

Spencer Tracy at last put in an appearance.

The guard led me into the boss's office, they conferred but briefly before the boss gestured for the guard to leave. We were then alone, and he looked at me for the first time—

—it really was Tracy. (Jean Gabin, if you're French.) Not a tall man, but powerful. With the most wonderful, rough-hewn face, understanding, bright. He looked at the passport and said it: "Yes?"

I was so happy to have found salvation, I began, I hoped, not to babble but to be cogent and helpful about the ridiculous situation. "Look," I said, "my name is William Goldman, I'm not a terrorist or anything, I'm just an American who bought the wrong book, I'm supposed to be in Cannes right now, I'm on the festival jury, everything okay so far?"

He nodded. "Okay."

"So what happened," I said, "was this: I get to Heathrow when this silly goddamn mistake is discovered and the Air France woman wanted me to go back to London and get a proper visa but I can't do that, because, as I just told you, I'm on the festival jury at Cannes and we're about to have our first crucial meeting so she made me sign this paper absolving them and she stuck me on the plane telling me I'd get sent back there and I don't speak any French and until now, it's been kind of a sticky wicket as our British cousins like to say on occasion." I smiled at him.

Hopefully.

The most wonderful warm, understanding smile in return.

"So what we have to do," I said, "is end this charade and get me to Cannes, okay?"

"Okay."

The relief. If I'd been chatty before, now I let it all out, thanking him, explaining that I'd be at the Majestic Hotel if he needed me, that I didn't know how to go about getting me a visa, but if he wanted to keep my passport, by all means, I wasn't going to leave the country, since the festival lasted the fortnight.

I said this, I said that.

I gestured, I smiled.

I said this again, I said that one more time.

I was just so damn grateful that it was over.

About two minutes later, I realized it wasn't over, because that was how long it took me to realize "okay" and "yes" were his only English. I'd been talking to a *mur* (French for "wall").

I don't know why he didn't stop me, but he didn't.

I don't know what he thought I said, and I doubt I ever will.

But eventually he muttered, "*Je ne parle pas Anglais*," and left me alone in the room.

You had to laugh, you just did. I did anyway. I was sitting by myself in the room, howling, when Spencer came back with Angela Lansbury. I don't know what they thought I thought was funny, but it didn't matter much once Angela said, "Mr. Goldman? Mr. Jacob of the festival has been on the phone, and we're giving you a temporary visa. He said they'd handle the rest in Cannes."

"Cannes?" I said.

"Yes," she said, in the most beautifully French-accented English. "They're waiting for you just outside the customs area. You're free to go."

I went. And just outside the customs area were a woman festival worker and a driver by his car. I got in.

"You've had some trouble, yes?" she said.

"Never laid a glove on me," I answered.

And with that, we drove off into the heart of the Riviera.

Let the games begin. . . .

PART 2

THE CANNES

FILM FESTIVAL

OR

INCOGNITO

(WITH MOTORCYCLES)

THE GREAT THING ABOUT THE gorilla was not her cute yellow skirt, all short and frilly, or the way she flounced along the sidewalk clutching her handler. What made it special was that no one was paying much attention.

This was Tuesday, the tenth of May, and the day before the official opening. The town was not yet exploding; those in the vicinity were not tourists—it would take more than a performer in a gorilla suit to excite them.

I meandered the five-minute walk from the Majestic to the Carlton, where the first jury meeting was to begin, after several delays, at six. These two famous hotels battle for pride of place during the festival. Old, white, and gingerbread in feel, they overlook the beach and the sea. Until recently, the Carlton was the clear winner, since the theater where the official entries were shown was next to that hotel.

But since the Palais had been built a few years back, with the resulting shift of where films were shown, the Majestic had been running stride for stride, since the Palais was located across the street from it. There were even those who felt, with some sadness, that more deals were now made on the Majestic terrace than on the more fabled Carlton's.

The above is stuff I didn't know at the time, and if I had, it would have been of less than no consequence. Because I was genuinely excited. I was to meet my fellow members having absolutely no idea who they might be.

We assembled in the suite of Pierre Viot, overlooking the sea. Viot is president of the festival, works for it three months a year. I suspect he is in charge of the financial end of things. I shook hands, introduced myself; he was very pleasant and we got through the preliminary exchange, but I was already aware just how the fact that I was so linguistically limited was going to be a factor in what was to follow.

I said hello to Gilles Jacob, who had got me out of the clutches of the Beast of Air France. Jacob, a slender man with a sensitive face, is the seminal figure of Cannes, and has been so for a decade. Forget his job title: he picks the films.

But not like some emperor sitting on a throne while the riches of the continent are brought to him for a quick thumbs up or down. Jacob *moves*. He lives in Paris, and after each festival, exhausted, he goes home and for three months tends to see but one movie a day—old films, if possible, classics. To make him remember what the Grail looks like.

After this respite, he begins to see movies that might show at Cannes. Many are not finished—if they were, let's say in September, it would cost a lot of money in interest to keep the film on the shelf until the ensuing May. He begins to travel by fall, coming to America usually twice a year if not more, going around Europe while assistants hit more distant shores. In the months before he makes his final selection, he's seeing three movies each day—maybe not every frame of all three, but he sits *a lot* until he makes his picks. He's very bright, quiet, and can even be funny in English, a language he's not altogether comfortable with. He's a man, when you think about it, with an unusual occupation: he spends his lifetime sniffing out, hopefully, masterpieces. Usually, of course, they're not to be found.

Ahh, but sometimes.

And those moments are, I suspect, what keeps him both young and going.

The third crucial figure was a stylish woman, Christianne

Guespin, who is in charge of the jury. If there are questions, problems, needs, she is the one to turn to. She is also the person in charge of seeing that all jury members sign in for all films.

Also present were a couple of translators.

And then us.

At the end of the meeting, I still had no idea who the hell they were, because the program I was given that listed brief biographies was written in French. Eventually, of course, I found out. And in the weeks to come, we were to argue and harangue one another for hours on end.

And they were all, all, terrific.

I would love to have all kinds of juicy stuff to report. Alas. They were knowledgeable. Serious but not somber. Critical but not cruel. Funny when the need arose.

An A+ bunch.

Before I introduce them, a brief word about my movie career. I've been at it a quarter of a century. I've won two Edgars for best mystery-movie screenplay, two Oscars for best screenplay, and the Laurel Award, given annually, for lifetime achievement in writing for the screen.

The point is, I was average for the group.

All of them had been, one time or another, one place or another, honored. We came from nine countries, with seven different movie-job titles (billing alphabetical):

ACTORS: *Nastassja Kinski*: Daughter of a renowned and difficult star, she became internationally famous in 1980 with the release of *Tess*, when she was still in her teens. She is totally fluent in four languages, and we immediately elected her as vice president of the jury. There has been a sexuality connected with her that I don't think has helped her career all that much. When she speaks English, if you close your eyes, the voice you hear is that of Audrey Hepburn. I think if Kinski played that kind of part, she would have that kind of success.

Elena Sofonova: A famous actress in Russia, unknown here. (I asked her how she felt about walking the streets like the rest of us; she smiled and her face glowed.) She was about to win the Italian Oscar for best female performance for her work opposite Mastroianni in *Dark Eyes*. If Kinski is a young Hepburn, Sofonova is Anouk Aimée twenty years ago.

CINEMATOGRAPHER: *Robby Müller*: Dutch, born in Curaçao. One of the major international cameramen. Few American movies. *Paris, Texas; To Live and Die in L.A.* Never satisfied with the beauty of a shot. Always demands more.

COMPOSER: *Philippe Sarde*: Bright, funny; a leading French award-winning musician.

CRITIC: *David Robinson*: Shy about his erudition. A Cambridge man, he has been film critic for *The Times* (London) for over a decade. Has also directed. Has also written perhaps the best books on Keaton and Chaplin. His first time on the jury, hardly his first experience with the festival. He has been coming for thirty-three years, and always tries to see five movies a day. At a minimum.

DIRECTORS: *Claude Berri*: Also a leading French producer. Most recent films to show in the States were *Jean de Florette* and *Manon of the Spring*. The best doodler of the group. Soon to do his first American film. Almost angry about the low state of French movies today.

George Miller: Known in Hollywood as "the Doctor George Miller" because there are two Australian directors with the same name. (The other one did *The Man from Snowy River*.) Began as a physician. Very low key, very funny, obviously decent. Five films, five hits. (The three *Mad Max* movies, the only good episode of *Twilight Zone, The Witches of Eastwick*.)

Ettore Scola: President of the jury. Italian. Once a brilliant screenwriter—*The Easy Life*. Now does directing as well. Most recent movie in America: *The Family*. Did a terrific job herding us into shape.

Looks like what you imagine the secretary of state of a European country should look like. Heavy smoker. (And not the only one in the room.)

PRODUCER: *Hector Olivera*: Argentinian. Also a director. Passionate about going by the rules. The third worst in terms of languages. Far surpassed in incompetence by George Miller and . . .

WRITER: *Moi.*

We sat around the table, and as the meeting began, the language "thing" (or, more precisely, *my* language "thing") became quickly apparent. Cannes is in France, it's a French festival, guess what the language is? I am (as is Miller) totally at the mercy of the translator. How it operates is, whoever is speaking speaks away, and the translator whispers what's being said. You're always a little behind, but it sort of works as a system—unless you've got a shy translator who doesn't want to speak while someone else is speaking, which Miller and I had on more than one occasion. He and I often flanked a flustered linguist, leaning in, our heads on each of her shoulders.

The peak of the translating madness was always when Elena Sofonova spoke. She is fluent in French, but when she gets passionate or wants to make a difficult point, she would go into Russian. She had her own translator, also named Elena, and when Sofonova would speak in Russian, everyone at the table would lean forward silently, all of us looking, I'm sure, wise as hell, none of us understanding zip. Then she would pause, and the second Elena would speak French, and as she did this, the English translators would go into their act. Kind of a ripple effect.

As the meeting got under way, we were given our set of rules. (Understand that throughout all these meetings, I was particularly colorful, since not only did I have on my shades, I also wore my handy dandy bifocals underneath them.)

In the ensuing ninety minutes, during which Viot spoke and Jacob spoke, we learned a lot. In no particular order:

1. The whole thing is dead serious. We would vote on the

films that were shown in competition. Twenty-some. We had to see all the films in order to be allowed to vote. So if we missed one, whatever the circumstance or reason, out. We had to sign in when we went, so they had proof of our attendance.

2. We were, in essence, gagged. We could not talk about the movies to anyone except other jury members, and then only when the jury met. (Scola decided we ought to meet to talk approximately every six flicks, and it worked out well.)

3. We should not, if at all possible, do interviews. The giving of the awards in two weeks' time would be televised internationally, and just like the Oscars, they wanted, demanded, the whole thing be dealt with privately.

4. There were several awards to be given, but the main ones I felt would be actor, actress, director, critic's prize (second place), and the grand prize, the *Palme d'Or* for best feature. (There were also awards for shorts, etc., that we had to see, but they did not capture my interest as much as the main awards.)

5. On the final day, we would be picked up early at our hotels. We would be taken someplace secret. We were to wear comfortable clothes for the hours of decision making. We should also bring our formal wear, as we would not be allowed out of each other's sight until after the announcements had been made live on the television show. So wherever this mystery rendezvous was, once we got inside, we couldn't leave. (We didn't know then that the place would be gated, the gate locked, the place patrolled by police and guard dogs. When I say they were serious about the voting, I'm serious.)

6. If we could decide on the best performers early, that would be a help, since they might then be alerted to fly to the festival on prize-giving day to accept their honors; if they weren't in America or Asia, that is.

7. The festival would pay our air travel, first class. Also for a companion, be she/he wife/mistress, husband, mother, etc. They would also pay our hotel bills. They would also pay for two meals per day if said meals were eaten in our hotels. Extras—wine, liquor, laundry, outside meals—came out of our own pockets.

8. Most important: *how free were we to vote?* The Oscars
are famous for sweeps. Rarely does the Best Picture award-
winner only win the Best Picture award. Last year, I don't
know of any screenwriter who didn't want to regurgitate when
The Last Emperor, which had an egregiously horrendous (I
didn't like it much) screenplay, won the Oscar. But the picture
won everything it was up for.

Cannes is famous for precisely the reverse. Rarely does a
picture win more than one award. And there are constant
rumors: the jury was not allowed to give more than one award
per picture.

True?

Jacob handled it head-on. Cannes was an international festival. No question they would prefer it if the awards were
spread around.

Prefer it a lot.

But . . . and here he paused.

What we all wanted when we went to the movies, wanted
more than anything else, was to be moved, to be thrilled, to
be given memories by a masterpiece. Masterpieces were, alas,
rare. But if we saw one, if we felt one of the experiences we
were about to have qualified, well, we must honor that movie.
And give it what we felt it deserved.

In other words, we were free.

I went back to the Majestic exhilarated. The sidewalks were
far more crowded than the street as eight o'clock approached,
so I chose the easier path.

I'd decided something during the meeting. Today, I think
it's impossible to see a movie as a movie. With the average
Hollywood opus now over $16 million (and that's sickeningly
true), the studios now hype every picture with millions of
dollars more, trying, logically, to frame their product in the
public's mind, to cut it away from the herd. So it's ads and
interviews and more interviews and bigger ads as opening date
approaches, and no matter how you try to mute yourself from
it, it's damn near impossible.

So what I decided was this: to know absolutely nothing about

the movies I would see. Not their names or nations or who
was in them. I would look at them as virginally as I could.

And I would also try to see them in the morning.

That reads like madness, I'm sure. But at Cannes, there are,
in general, two movies shown officially per day. And each
movie is shown three times: morning, afternoon, night. The
evening showings are formal. No blue suits, please. Tuxes
only. And since (a) I hate wearing a tux and (b) my pants were
too tight, I figured why put myself through the torment? (And
with a few exceptions, I didn't.)

Which left the mornings and the afternoons. I thought I'd
give a whack to hitting the 8:30 A.M. screening and then the
eleven o'clock follow-up. That way, if it worked out and I could
stay awake, I would be relieved from active duty to follow
other intellectual pursuits—

—by which I mean, of course, food.

Most beautiful places have rotten restaurants. The logic
being that you'll come for the view, why bother getting a decent
chef?

Not the case on the French Riviera.

I was having calorie-filled fantasies as I hurried along in the
street when I was hit by the car. "Hit" is too strong a word,
I suppose. But it was more than a nudge. His fender and my
kneecap definitely made contact. And I was scared. "Watch
where you're goddamn driving!" I yelled at him.

The Frenchman opened his car door, stood with one foot on
the street. "What?"

"I said learn how to drive!"

"Hey, schmuck," he said, his French accent thick, his slang
perfect, "I wasn't driving on the sidewalk, *you were walking
in the street.*"

His logic was, alas, irrefutable. Triumphantly, he got back
into his car, and we gave each other the finger. I limped back
to the sidewalk, cursing my bad eye because I can't see when
things come at me from my right, and I hated my goddamn
sunglasses and I felt like a freak—

—only I wasn't a freak, not now, I was a *judge*. At Cannes. A Figure of Importance. One to be Revered.

I limped ahead, as kinglike as I could manage, conscious of one word and one word only: "fart."

Someone behind me said that word. Then again: "Fart. The loudest fart of all time."

I didn't turn.

From behind me, the voice went on, "You know what I'm talking about, don't you?"

The horrible thing is, I did.

During rehearsals of *Butch Cassidy and the Sundance Kid*, Paul Newman and director George Roy Hill got into a running two-week argument over the placement of a scene in the screenplay. Those weeks we were seated at a small table— Newman, Hill, Redford, Katherine Ross, and myself—in the middle of a huge empty soundstage. Think of a basketball court with a curved roof on it, and that's kind of it. *Way* across this soundstage, by the door, a lone figure, a "gofer," sat. One day, he let go with this whopper of a fart. It was an amazing feat, not just the noise but the duration. We are talking *Guinness Book of Records* stuff.

It should be noted that the guy was asleep all the while. Sitting there snoozing while this remarkable natural sound quieted Newman and Hill. There was no way they could argue after the fart. I wrote this up in some detail in an earlier book of mine, *Adventures in the Screen Trade*.

"Loved that fart," this voice from behind me said.

I turned and saw a strange guy holding out his hand to me. He introduced himself—I didn't catch his name, but he worked for some studio in some capacity or other. "Great fart," he said, pumping my hand, moving on.

I reached the Majestic, and by then I realized it was going to be hard to consider myself a revered Figure of Importance when at least one member of my profession would now and forever remember me only as a recorder of bodily functions.

THE FESTIVAL OFFICIALLY OPENED with the showing of *The Big Blue*, a French flick, supposedly the most expensive in the history of that country's film industry. We, the judges, were to be introduced to the throngs from the stage prior to the start of the movie at seven-thirty. In all our splendor, meaning I had to do battle with my tuxedo pants. We also had a rehearsal for the ceremony and were to meet at a press conference held by Scola, the jury president, during the afternoon. Until then, we were released from active duty.

Breakfast

Since this was the start of things, the Majestic had not yet gone crazy. (People tend to come to Cannes, a lot of them anyway, when they have a particular picture showing. They screen, they schmooze, they sell, they get the hell out. Not counting the press and all the other media, few stay the entire two weeks.) Which is probably why the dining room where the breakfast buffet was set out was empty.

There was me.

And there were these two movie sellers, one American, one British. They took the table next to me and even the baseball stats in *USA Today* could not keep me from overhearing, since they talked in a normal tone and the sound boomed. They bullshat each other for a time—"When I call studio heads, they answer—" and then got down to this exchange:

> AMERICAN BULLSHITTER
> (stuffing down his
> eggs and coffee)
> We're a different kind of com-
> pany, this one I'm
> representing.

> BRITISH COUNTERPART
> (yes, they do drink
> tea)
> Different? How different?

> AMERICAN BULLSHITTER
> Well, we're into three-to-five-
> million-dollar pictures, action-
> oriented.

> BRITISH COUNTERPART
> I fail to see how that makes
> you different.

> AMERICAN BULLSHITTER
> (dropping his voice
> slightly)
> We wouldn't mind if one of
> our pictures, every year or so,
> had some intelligence attached
> to it.

> BRITISH COUNTERPART
> (impressed)
> That makes you different
> from everyone.

The only other item of note, at least to me, was that the Tony nominations were in the paper and they made me terribly sad. Not because I agreed or disagreed, but because I'd seen so few of them: one of the four plays (the wonderful Mamet) and two of the musicals (the Sondheim and the Lloyd Webber). And why did that make me sad?

Because I used to see *everything*.

I've been going, constantly, since I was ten. I wrote my master's thesis on the comedy of manners. I spent a year and a half of my life writing a nonfiction book about Broadway. There was a time when I knew as much about the theater as anyone who wasn't involved in it professionally, as arrogant as that sounds.

As I sat there spooning down my French yogurt (the best, believe it), I realized it wasn't just the theater. I used to see every movie too. One of the reasons I came to New York from Chicago was because of Forty-second Street. In those days (early fifties we're talking about), the slime content was considerably less, and there were, at least I think there were, seventeen movie houses with double features that changed constantly. One of them was an art house. One showed just westerns. I was there a lot. Between Forty-deuce and the Thalia, I got the bulk of my movie education.

Now, you have to drag me.

And then I remembered a not-that-long-ago lunch in New York with a bunch of Random House editors (all of them gone now, some fired, one of them, Judy-Lynn del Rey, the most brilliant and wondrously likable woman I ever met in publishing, dead). Editors read an incredible amount of stuff compared to human beings, and I remember saying, sadly, that the crucial part of my serious reading had been done before I turned twenty-five.

There was a pause.

Then they all nodded. "Same here." "Same here."

I finished the yogurt, wondering what the hell I was doing with my life. Three of my early passions are still my passions, and they're just outside my window—

—but I don't take advantage.

You don't live in Manhattan for the fucking climate. The theater is there, the bookstores are there, there are dozens of movie theaters within a ten-minute cab ride of my home, five within a five-minute *walk* from my office.

And I don't go.

Why? I still want to. At least in the abstract. Hell, I'm still me. But somewhere I got trapped into going to my office too much and watching too many sports on the tube and drinking too much to knock myself out for sleep.

Some shitty trifecta.

If I still read everything and saw everything, would Ilene have stuck around? Did I bore her into departure?

Sweet thought, that one.

Still, why *don't* I go?

Maybe I don't go because I've been. I know too much about how the magic tricks work. Once I got something out of damn near anything. Now, I see the artist palming the card, and you know what?—

—it's painful. It actually hurts seeing a rotten play or movie, reading a rotten book. Or even mediocre stuff. Even stuff that's damn near decent.

I want to be thrilled now. Surprised too. "Amaze me," I want to say to the movie. "Show me what I haven't seen. And don't let me catch you palming the card."

What better place for magic than Cannes? . . .

The Morning

I took what Harry Truman called a "constitutional." It was a gray day. (As were the days that followed.) The Croisette— the main street that curves along the Mediterranean, palm- lined, famous, justly so, was sort of quiet. I left it, went to Rue d'Antibes, which parallels it a block inland, home of fancy shops.

The French drive differently from those of other nations. Maybe it's their laws, but they consider the sidewalk fair game. I was stopped at one point as one guy simply drove up over the curb, parked, got out, and went about his business.

Nobody seemed the least distressed or surprised.

I decided to buy all the stuff I could on the festival. I found a large bookstore (a French one—I found an English one later) and went inside, looked around. Zip. Which surprised me. Finally, I stopped a clerk.

> ME
> Excuse me, but do you speak
> English?

> HIM
> (imperiously)
> Of course.

> ME
> Well, I'm looking for any-
> thing you might have on the
> Cannes Film Festival.

> HIM
> On the what?

> ME
> (a bit taken aback)
> On the festival. The Cannes
> festival.

> HIM
> (louder)
> *The what?*

> ME
> (it's Abbott and Costello
> land suddenly)
> You know—
> (gesturing frantically)
> Movies.

> HIM
> Ah, the Cannes Film Festival.

ME
Yes.

HIM
Books on the festival.

ME
(we're now into Pinter)
Yes.

HIM
In French or in English?

ME
Either, but I'd prefer English.

HIM
There aren't any.

ME
None in English?

HIM
None in either language.

ME
Then why did you ask me
which language I preferred?

He made no reply, simply scowled and turned away. (Obviously, he'd been trained at Gucci.) I should mention that all this took place right next to a large French book, mainly photos on the Cannes Film Festival, which I bought.

Then I returned to the Majestic to lie down.

My Back

I lie down a lot.

One August afternoon, it was 1962, I was walking home through Central Park after seeing the dentist when I began crying out with each step. I went to the ground, I guess eventually crawled my way to a cab. Ilene lowered me into a very hot tub, and I lay there hoping the pain would go away.

It did but it didn't. The pain, sure; the fear of the pain is with me as I suppose it's with everybody who has disc problems (mine's L 3) because, at least for a man, it's the most goddamn unglamorous ailment, the reverse of the Heidelberg dueling scar. I mean, when your back's out, you just lie there and you crawl to pee, fun things like that.

Anyway, one of the things you do when you have a bad back is you rest it when you can. Some things are bad for it— riding in a car over bumpy roads can be the worst. Sitting anywhere on soft chairs can present problems.

Like in a movie theater.

Since it was essential to see all the flicks, I guess my most irritating fear at the festival was that my back was going to go on me.

So I rested after my walk—my knee, from the collision with the car, was only a little swollen; probably it was dumb to walk as long as I did—and looked at the French book on Cannes. Obviously, the text eluded me.

Not the pictures though.

God, they looked so young, the dead ones. Chevalier and Sartre and Hitchcock, Picasso and Dorothy Dandridge, Gabin, Ingrid and Grace, Truffaut, Welles (almost only plump) and dear Natalie Wood and the local boy who I think would have challenged Olivier as actor of the century, Gerard Philippe, and Cary Grant, sixty looking forty, Welles again, edging toward gargantuan.

I was reading Kazan's autobiography and Ingmar Bergman's also, two of my three favorite directors of all time (George Stevens is the third of my magical trio), and they were so talented, but all it brought them was torment, ashes, and I wondered about the dead faces. Did any one of them enjoy their gifts from God?

Everybody knows that writers are miserable—the link between novelists and alcoholics is constantly talked of. But we're weird. We're antisocial, and if you've seen us on the tube, you know that, except for Gore Vidal, we're not a whole lot of fun. You expect the unhappiness.

But stars?

Gorgeous golden creatures?

Unhappy?

Impossible.

How can you be unhappy if you look like Rock Hudson? How can you be miserable if you're as talented as Barrymore? Or Brando? Or Welles?

And yet they are. Not all of them. Maybe only 99 percent.

The first famous face I ever came in contact with belonged to Judy Holliday, backstage during her triumph with *Born Yesterday*.

A treasure she was.

Brilliant.

And talented. And adored. And a suicide.

I don't pretend to know why stars are so bleak. (Not *actors*, necessarily, and not necessarily *English* stars either.) But there is a horrible deal American stars strike: we give them everything. And then we give them *everything*. In other words, when you become not just Bud Brando but "Marlon"—first name only is quite sufficient—there are no limits put on you. You can have whatever you want.

And no human can deal with that much freedom of choice. . . .

Lunch

I was to eat at La Mère Besson at least once a day for every day of the fortnight. Probably that was stupid. Certainly it was unadventurous.

If I had it to do over again, I'd do it over again.

We are not talking about one of the great restaurants of the world. What it is, is one of the good ones.

(I was to say to Scola later that day that I'd had a wonderful lunch and he said where and I told him and he smiled and said, "La Mère Besson, of course." Then he paused. Then he said, "Even more better at dinner.")

Just your plain ordinary home-cooking bistro. Bistros are, in any country, my favorite eating places. If I have to get all dressed up and insulted, the food better damn well be exceptional.

Margaret Martin works the front, while her husband, Yves, cooks. She takes all orders in a seemingly endless parade of languages. Ordinarily, the place is open six days a week, closed Sundays.

During the festival, they go mad.

It's seven days a week, and they get to the restaurant, say, by nine, getting ready for the lunch trade. They are packed for that meal, maybe two seatings per table. They close at four or thereabouts, take as much of a deep breath as they can, because at dinner they really get busy. (I have seen forty people in tuxedos waiting patiently on the street to get tables. This was, let me add, at one o'clock in the morning.) They just go and go during dinner, eventually locking up by four. Then home for a quick nap until Margaret gets up at seven to get their two children off to school. Then, by nine, back to the restaurant.

Amazingly, she's always polite, efficient, smiling, charming in many languages.

I had the pâté to start. They bring you two wonderful slabs along with the French bread. And a tray with three jars: olives, cornichon, and their own special mushrooms in olive oil.

Goes down easy.

I had their *plat du jour*: called veal brisket. Sort of nirvana-ish. This, with a bottle of Badoit, and a half-bottle of a light local red.

Better than a sharp stick in the eye.

As I was sitting there, the novel happened.

A French couple came in. She was midforties, sleek, not pretty but well turned out. He was the same age, ordinary, slender. They chatted happily with each other, their French perfect.

I had seen them earlier, they had not seen me. I was kneeling in a corner of the English bookshop when they entered briefly, asked for something or other, were told it wasn't in stock, left.

They'd been speaking perfect American then.

Now, in the restaurant, as I walked by them on my way to the loo, they were talking very softly to each other.

Their British accents working to perfection.

By the time I was back to my table, I knew I had some part of a novel. Because maybe the main character was a young waiter at the restaurant who is trying to improve his English, which is why he's in the bookshop and he gets involved—

—no-no, he doesn't get involved, *Scylla* does, Scylla being the brother in *Marathon Man* (Roy Scheider in the movie), brought back surgically refaced in the sequel, *Brothers*.

It's a Scylla novel and it's told in the first person—

—because he realizes that what they are is spies and God knows what their real language is but they're so damn skillful—

—and since he's on the Riviera because there's the possibility of a job—

—they must be here for the same reason—

—except he has an advantage because he knows what they look like and no one knows what he looks like—

—only now she senses something and she tells the slender man not to look at him for a while—

—so Scylla looks away but he's got them in a reflection or something so he can clock how long it will be before the guy makes his glance and one minute means really good and two means expert and three means international class—

—and five minutes later the guy risks a glance at him—

—so now Scylla knows that either he is eventually going to ally himself with this couple or he will have to remainder them—

—unless they get him first—

—unless there are others there, other spies all after the same job—

And sitting there in La Mère Besson, I knew the title of the book or Part I of the book would be this: *The Audition*. I liked the title okay but liked the notion more: a bunch of the world's best agents all in a glamorous, crowded spot, all of them up for the same job—

—all of them knowing not what it was but that to gather them all in one spot it had to be Important.

I ordered another coffee, tried to figure what the job might be. Nancy Reagan's astrology was in the news, so maybe that was it: maybe our people wanted to remainder the astrologer. Or force her to give incorrect information.

Or maybe an agency was just out to remainder the First Lady because maybe someone from the other side had already got to the astrologer, or maybe—

—maybe—

I never got the maybe. I paid my bill, left, walked slowly along the streets, wondering if any other connectives would occur. They didn't.

This kind of experience happens all the time, and I assume it does to other writers too. I have drawers full of notes back in my office. Sometimes when I'm trying to find something else, I glance at them. "Novel idea," it will say Or "movie notion." And more often than not, it's just gibberish. I have no idea a-tall what I must have been thinking.

Two reasons I went into detail here: 1. Story, or the lack of it, or the lack of telling it skillfully, properly, was to become of increasing import to us all as the festival went on. 2. I only remembered this detail because, for the first time, I was using a tiny tape recorder to remember things, figuring I would never be able to stir up memories accurately of all those movies without some verbal jab. These tapes became the absolute core of this book, which, by the end of the festival, I felt I wanted to write.

Which was why I got so frazzled and panicked the last night in Cannes when the tapes disappeared. . . .

The Press Conference

On my way to rehearsal, I saw my first movie star in the Majestic: Rosanna Arquette, looking very small and terribly tired. (I didn't know then that she was the female lead in that evening's *The Big Blue*.)

By the pool, on the cloudy afternoon, a deeply tanned woman looked at me. Noted me, more precisely. As I walked by, her eyes flicked like a reptile's tongue after an insect. She was wearing a bikini. Her body was slender. Her hair was in Bo Derek cornstalks.

She was at least eighty-something years old.

And her eyes flicked at everybody.

And she was always there, clouds or sunshine, by the pool. Clocking men.

I tabbed her as a symbol. Of something having to do with show business. A game, horny symbol. Older than Garbo . . .

The press conference was held in a large room in the Palais. (The Palais, by the by, which is where the main features were shown, is of recent vintage. It was originally hammered for an undeniable bunkerlike resemblance, but now it isn't a butt for jokes anymore, and besides, the festival is a tad sensitive on the subject.) It is just huge. Many-floored, many-theatered, it has offices, a nightclub, a casino—I got lost in it constantly and having spent my (laugh) military service at the Pentagon, I figure they're a draw when it comes to square footage.

Press conferences are interesting for me in only one way: how in the name of Christ were they ever invented? They don't dispense information or provide pleasure. I sat with Robby Müller, the cinematographer, who recalled he was once asked, at a press conference, "What does light do for you?," to which he replied, "It makes things visible."

This press conference was for Scola, as head of the jury. There were several hundred reporters, fifteen or twenty TV camera crews. Scola was, as he always is, charming.

At least he looked charming, because I sat there from 3:40 until 4:20, when a stampede began for the door, understanding not a word, since it was entirely conducted in French and Italian. But I was told later, they asked him some fun questions like "Why don't you ever win prizes?" and "Why aren't you held in higher esteem, considering how old you are?" (I resented that last question when I heard about it, since we're the same age.)

The jury gathered during the conference, and after it was over, we were herded from that room to a hallway to another hallway to another room where we were to wait for rehearsal to start for our evening's introduction to the audience.

It was while we were in the first hallway that the photographers attacked Kinski. Twenty, thirty, forty of them, flashing their lights in her face, not giving her room to walk, to move—

—what I was thinking of immediately was the premiere of *Butch Cassidy and the Sundance Kid*. George Hill, the director, had gone to Yale and had given that university the premiere for charity. Latish September.

The Hills and the Newmans drove up to the theater in one car.

The Redfords and the Goldmans right behind.

What we didn't know was that (a) classes weren't in full swing, so there were a lot of Yalies with nothing to do and (b) security had broken down.

There were suddenly dozens of faces pressed against our car, which soon began to rock.

NEWMAN: "I tend to keep moving. You have to keep moving when you're on the streets. I always try to look like I'm late for an appointment. Once, I remember, a young girl came after me and caught up with me and looked at me and then she said this: 'Stuck up.' But it's a problem. As long as they didn't expect you and you're free, it's not much of a problem. But if they know you've got to be someplace at a certain time, you're just trapped."

We were trapped outside the theater in New Haven. The car couldn't move. Ilene and I managed to get out of the car and were pretty much lost in the crowd so that we made it to the theater unscathed. Then, a good while after, the Redfords made it. (My memory is his lip was bleeding.) He said, "People kept grabbing at me and yelling, 'Who is it? Who is he?' "

Then (again memory) I swear Miss Woodward appeared swinging her purse as a last line of defense. Ruffled and rightfully ticked. Her husband, since he is still driving race cars, must have made it too, but I can't summon up quite how.

It's not so much having their faces known that drives stars bonkers, it's the intrusions that follow hard upon. I don't have sympathy for them—they chose their profession and knew what might lie ahead—but it is, truly, not a lot of fun.

I have, in my life, been recognized twice by total strangers. Most recently I was on my way to the dentist with a toothache, it was early morning, my mood was less than yummy.

Now this young woman was walking alongside me, looking at me. Then she said the famous phrase that drives performers mad: "I know who you are." With that she skipped on ahead of me, walking backward as she got out a camera and started taking pictures, all the while explaining that she worked on occasion for *Women's Wear Daily* and wondering what I was doing in New York. (People assume that, except for Woody Allen, everyone in movies lives in Hollywood. Once, decades past, there was a certain truth to that. But now, with pictures shooting all over the world, it doesn't pertain. Anyway, you're always explaining that you live in Manhattan, that you've lived here for *centuries* and, meanwhile, you can see your questioner's eyes start to glaze. *Now*, if people ask what I'm doing in town, I might answer that I wanted to see some theater.)

Anyway, again, with aching jaw and this photographer moving really very adroitly backward, I felt this sudden burst of anger—she-had-no-right. Hemingway, sure, but he took the fame franchise with him. There hasn't been a truly famous writer since he died. At a Knicks game last year, Norman

Mailer was introduced to the crowd and half a dozen people around me said, "Who?" and one guy went so far as to ask, "Who did he play for?"

The first time I was I-know-who-you-are'd was back in the middle seventies. I was eating with my family and another family at a largish luncheonette near Lake Powell. Suddenly this terribly excited figure appeared, running up to me.

> HIM
> I know who you are.

> ME
> (stunned)
> Huh?

> HIM
> (pointing)
> You—I know who you are.
> You're Robert Redford.

> ME
> (just as amazed as
> you would have been)
> I'm not.

> HIM
> Yes, you are.

> ME
> I'm really not.

> HIM
> (he's not buying)
> You're just saying that.

> ME
> (passionately)
> I swear to you—I'm not.

> HIM
> (a pause; he studies me)
> You're sure?

                        ME
        Really.

                        HIM
        (one last long look,
        then, turning—)
        Aw.

                        ME
        (calling after him—
        I feel guilty)
        Sorry.

                        HIM
        (back turned)
        Not your fault.

I was, I assure you, the only guilty person at the table because
the rest were falling about with laughter, as the English say.
Because Lake Powell is in Utah, and this was the summer I
was there for *All the President's Men* rewrites and the other
family was the Redford clan, and he was sitting at the other
end of the table watching it all, not unamused. . . .

In the Palais hallway now, I watched them going after Kinski.
(They were worse at dinner late that evening. I was seated on
one side of her, her husband on the other, and three feet away,
on the far side of the table, were endless photographers clicking
away. What was so fascinating about Nastassja Kinski trying
to eat I had no idea, but she got through it with really remarkable grace.)

I liked that she was in Cannes. Because she was a last-minute
replacement for Isabella Rossellini, who had finked out, and
Kinski, knowing she was sloppy seconds, might have easily
told them to take a very long hike.

Memory: I helped write the Oscar show one year. And yes,
it has to be kind of awful. Because most people won't rehearse,
and all the awards, contractually, must be shown, and it may
well be the only show about movies done for television on a

legitimate stage (at least it was my year), which meant the union situation was out of a Marx Brothers epic.

Anyway, this was the year Charlton Heston got a flat on the freeway and didn't get there in time.

I was standing on the side of the theater when the producer came hurrying to Clint Eastwood, who was in the audience, and explained the absence and asked would Eastwood replace Heston. Eastwood, as big a star then as now, didn't even hesitate. "Anything to help," he said, so they got him up onstage to read the introductory remarks that Heston had been expected to deliver.

What he didn't know, what no one really knew, was that the remarks were loaded with Moses jokes. Moses did this and said that, all of which made sense for Heston. *Only* for Heston. But Eastwood never flinched, just went on gutsily. I watched from the wings as Heston appeared, mightily upset. (Understand this about Heston: in his entire career, all of it, every movie, every play, he might have been late a total of thirty *seconds.* Now, just before a nationally televised show, his tire blows and no one will give him a lift in time.)

Introductions

The jury convened, formally attired, in Gilles Jacob's office in the Palais prior to our being introduced to the audience. Rehearsal that afternoon had been okay. If properly led by the hand, I felt convinced I wouldn't embarrass the family name.

Earlier, I had been taking a bath back at the hotel when the phone began to ring.

And it didn't stop.

Ring.

Ring.

Now we've all had this, and we know if we'd got active when it started, we could have made it, but now, too late.

Ring.

Ring.

Now, it was really too late.

Ring and I'm dripping my way from the bathroom to the phone, which I picked up to hear this desperate voice saying, "Mr. Goldman? Mr. Goldman, please. You can save me. I'm from an Iron Curtain country and I've written this screenplay and if you'll read it and recommend it and get it made it would change my existence, so please, do that for me, change my life, just read it, that's all I'm asking, is that so much to ask?"

All I could think of was the old terrible joke about the Polish starlet who screwed the screenwriter. I tried explaining to him that I couldn't get anything made, his movies or mine. I tried to be gentle.

But I couldn't change anybody's life, much less his. Much less my own.

There are still a few lost souls who actually think that screenwriters have some authority. If only it were so. We have none. (I'm talking here about screenwriters, not hyphenates—i.e., people with two jobs, writer-directors, writer-producers.)

There are lots of reasons. We're not, most of us, so terrifically talented. And we're so easy to fire—at least half of the people in positions of authority in Hollywood know the alphabet. You don't fire composers often; editors are safe too. But it's not unusual, despite what you see on the credits, to have two or three or *eight* writers write on one film script.

As well as being inept and disposable, we're also, truly, disliked. Why? Because you can't make a movie without us. If it's going to be a decent flick, it better have a decent screenplay; directors know this, and it drives them *maaaaaad*.

Sometimes we're asked to do things. Once I was asked to take care of Dustin Hoffman, who was in town with some friends and nothing to do for an afternoon. The producer called me and said, "Dusty's here, be nice to him."

I'm always nice to Dustin Hoffman—he can fire me.

Anyway, I invited him and his cohorts to the hotel I was staying at, and we all sat around the pool. A standard L.A. afternoon—the sun was finally burning through the clouds.

And Hoffman—a brilliant actor and a very intelligent man—was bored.

So one of his friends scampered up to the high diving board and jumped off.

His clothes were on, understand.

Dustin laughed and laughed.

The jumper was a talented playwright, a man I admired. I felt so sad when he jumped off the board and got thrown out of the pool—

—nothing's worth that kind of laughter.

Recently, I had a meeting with a producer and a star. The director of the project was locked in a death struggle with the star over creative control (guess who won?), and gave *me* the joy of handling things.

The producer was producing his first movie—he had been the star's business manager until very recently, when the star had promoted him. Which meant the star couldn't say anything against his producer without totally deballing him.

We meet.

A first draft.

We're—if we go like lightning—a *year* away from shooting. The three of us are going through the script while they give me their notes for changes. We were in a time bind—planes had to be caught, etc.

I'm not going to name names or be specific here, for legal reasons. Just let me say this in all truth: what follows is infinitely more intelligent than what actually transpired.

The script opens with the usual setting-the-scene crap, which in this case was Wall Street, with the hero coming out of the subway going to work.

> JOE SMITH comes out of the subway. He's an attractive man moving in on forty. He wears gray pants and a blue blazer, with a matching blue shirt and yellow tie.

There is nothing conceivable to get interested in on the first page, so I turn to page 2.

> NEW PRODUCER
> Good point.

It was not a good point. It was a moron point. I could not believe this conversation was happening. The movie might never start, and if it did, it might not start on Wall Street, and if it did, it might not begin in the morning, and if it did—
—infinite numbers of ifs.

It was madness talking on like this. If the new producer had been a friend of mine, I would have said, "Hey, get your head out of your ass, it doesn't matter what I write here, it's a first draft, what we want is for the studio to say yes to the project, and they're not going to be influenced by *the fucking color of his neckwear!*"

We get to page 6 when he says—

> NEW PRODUCER
> It's the blazer—

> ME
> (I'm quicker now)
> —there's something that bothers you about a blue blazer?

> NEW PRODUCER
> He's going to work on Wall Street, he should be wearing a suit.

> STAR
> I hate wearing suits—

> NEW PRODUCER
> (so fast)
> —I don't mean a suit suit, nothing stuffy at all—

>   ME
>   —you want him in a casual
>   suit?

>   NEW PRODUCER
>   Let's think about it a minute,
>   it could be important—

We didn't think about it for a minute—we thought about it for *hours*. I wanted to scream so loud; I wanted to choke the asshole—

But I was so sweet. I took notes. I grunted and nodded. I smiled when it was conceivably possible.

You see, this guy would never have dared behave like that in front of a studio executive or the director.

But I couldn't harm him.

I was the screenwriter.

So it goes. . . .

When it came time to be introduced to the people, we trooped out of Jacob's office to where an elevator was being held for us, a formally dressed young man running the show. We squeezed in, the bunch of us. What followed was one of those moments you had to be there for, but there we are, sardined, and there's this kid whose only mission in life is to push a button and take us to the right floor—

—well, he took us to the wrong floor.

Ooops.

Finally, he got it right—there were only five floors, how much could he screw up?

We were, when our names were called, gently pushed onto the vast stage of the Palais theater. It seats twenty-four hundred. Comfortably. And is, though I didn't know it yet, by far the finest movie house I've ever seen. The color, the sound, screen size—it's all perfect there.

We stood, together with some young French stars of tomorrow, looking out at the packed mass of formally dressed folks, spotlights crossing, staring at the size of the place, the reddish seats, the whole deal.

It may be a bunker outside; but inside, they sure got it right. I stood there and it was remarkable, the length of the journey from the Alcyon Theater in Highland Park, Illinois. . . .

In 1960, there was a run-through of *The Sound of Music* before it went on the road. It was an amazingly touted show, Mary Martin back with Rodgers and Hammerstein, and the lobby was a crusher. Then the doors opened and we all pell-melled our way toward seats, and someone hipped me, I lost balance and landed in a seat, a good one, so I was pleased.

Then I realized I was in a *very* good seat, because all the faces around me were famous faces. And I remember fanta-sizing (truly) that this gigantic finger was going to appear from the ceiling of the theater, and this huge finger was going to point down at me, and these words would be intoned: *"You—Goldman*—you don't belong there."

Now, on the stage at Cannes, I didn't finger-fantasize. I felt I belonged.

I hope that's what they call progress.

The Big Blue

Although it officially opened the festival, the movie was not "in" the official competition. (Three movies were shown out of competition—*The Milagro Beanfield War* halfway through, and *Willow*, which closed up shop.) To put it another way: I did not have to judge *The Big Blue*.

The problem was, I *did* have to sit through it.

Sheer embarrassment. Agony.

It's about—no, I'm not going to detail what it's about, be-cause there's no reason for your brains to be burdened with such minutiae, and besides, the jerks and clowns who made the thing never goddamn decided what it was about.

But it showed something that was to haunt much of the

festival: the look of the movie was wonderful. (I think two thirds of the movies shown would have been Oscar nominations for Best Cinematography a decade back.)

And the storytelling sucked.

Two examples:

1. It opens twenty years or so before the main part of the flick, on some bucolic Mediterranean rocky island. A bunch of poor kids are running along. Then one of them peels off and by himself heads down toward the water.

Now when he gets to the edge and the sea is below him, he reaches into a rocky area and pulls out his flippers and jumps in and feeds the fishies.

Obviously, the flippers are his most prized belongings.

And he leaves them unattended by a rock where anyone can steal them? What happens as you sit there is you stop paying attention to the movie and your mind goes tripping. Why does he leave them? Does he want them stolen? Did the director not want him carrying them around his shoulders when he came running into view with the other kids? Why didn't he?

What's going on here?

Obviously, the minute your mind is preoccupied with such stuff and nonsense, the movie's out the window, down the tubes, gone.

2. The movie has to do with deep-sea diving tournaments— world championships. (And you thought the Super Bowl was a breathlessly looked-forward-to event.) Well, in this turkey, you weren't sure for half of the picture whether the object of the tournament was to go deepest underwater or hold your breath longest underwater. (I told you, you didn't want to know what it was about.)

The sad thing about the movie was it showed how skillful we—Americans—are in making big dopey action pictures. Because this was France's attempt at making a Big International Blockbuster. I wish we were more skillful at making anything else besides big dopey action pictures. (I guess we are: dumb dopey comedies.)

Rosanna Arquette gives, by the way, the most irritating

female performance these eyes have seen since Grace Kelly almost destroyed *High Noon*. I felt, of course, uncomfortable for her—she was in the audience. (I later learned that one of the unusual things about Cannes is that at each of the evening performances, the crucial people are present. At least as many of them as the studio can afford. And they sit in the center of the main floor, and after their movie ends, spotlights hit them as the lights come up and all the twenty-four-hundred formally dressed people rise and applaud. If the applause is sincere, it must be a wonderful moment.) I also felt strange about Arquette being that bad; she's not your normal talent, but she's a talent nonetheless. Odd . . .

What isn't odd is this: why are stars in bad movies?

I think few things drive those of us in the business more up the nearest pole than the asshole print or tube interviewer who will ask a star this kind of question:

> IDIOT INTERVIEWER
> Well, your new movie is a lot
> better than *Junkyard Nazis*.
> I've often wondered what
> prompted you to take that
> part.

> STAR
> Oh, the same reason I always
> pick—the character. There
> were a lot of things about the
> character of the incinerator
> cleaner in *Junkyard Nazis* that
> appealed to me.

Forget the lightning bolt that is headed down toward the star's cranium—stars generally take parts for money, and if they're big stars who don't need the money, they take parts because they are worried about what? Class?—right, *the next job*.

Here is the truth: *he didn't fucking know*.

Look at it logically—why would anyone pick a part in a

turd? When a movie is gearing up, people have hopes, but that's all. Dede Allen, the great editor, once said, "Every movie has a soft underbelly." When you're preparing, you hope to hide it. Sometimes you get away with it. Most often you don't, and the movie stiffs.

I'm a huge fan of Steven Spielberg's talent. I think he does a lot of things better than anybody, maybe better than anybody ever. And he never had a better time than in the years 1975–82. Here's what he did:

> 1975: *Jaws*
> 1977: *Close Encounters of the Third Kind*
> 1981: *Raiders of the Lost Ark*
> 1982: *E.T. The Extra-Terrestrial*

Amazing. Because those weren't just phenomenal hits, they were wondrously received by the critics. Oscar nominations up the kazoo. I am not comparing this to a seven-year-period in the career of Bergman—they work different sides of the street. I'm not comparing this to a period at the peak of Billy Wilder's wondrous career either. (From 1958 to 1960 he directed *Witness for the Prosecution, Some Like It Hot*, and *The Apartment*.)

But in the area where Spielberg works—the kind of comic-book superadventure—for me, no one compares. Now, if you'll check those movies listed, you'll see a gap in the middle. Want to know what filled that gap?

> 1979: *1941*

You probably don't remember that one too well, and I'm sure Spielberg hopes you continue with your happy amnesia. It was a very expensive picture, an action comedy with an enormous cast headed by Dan Aykroyd and John Belushi, and it was not just bad, it was one of the worst movies in the history of the world ever made by a director in his prime. (All directors whiff—often at the end of their careers.)

But this was smack in the middle of his wonder four. How did it happen? Do you think Spielberg sat up nights and decided it might be fun to make a stinker? Do you think he wanted to cast away the cloak of invincibility that was gathering around him?

> SPIELBERG
> (to the head of the
> 1941 studio)
> Hey, I gave you guys *Jaws*
> and I'm going to give you
> *E.T.* in three years, so if you
> don't mind, I'd like to piss
> away thirty mil on this
> turkey.

> STUDIO HEAD
> Great, fabulous news, wait till
> I tell the board of directors.

I'm sure if you talked to him before and during shooting, he thought it was going to be the most unusual and maybe most interesting movie of his career.

He didn't fucking know.

Spielberg's frequent cohort, George Lucas, is the most successful producer of the era—the Star Wars trilogy, the Indiana Jones trilogy—

—he also produced *Howard the Duck*, which makes *1941* seem like Ernst Lubitsch.

He didn't fucking know.

Commit the phrase to memory, so the next time you're watching the tube and some star is asked about some stiff and talks about how "interesting" the character was, you can shout it out loud:

"He didn't fucking know. . . ."

Casting

One last point that might be mentioned here is this: isn't it strange that Arquette, very American, was in a French underwater epic?

My guess? They didn't want her—you never get whom you want when you make a movie.

But they wanted somebody.

Somebody American.

We're the biggest market in the world, this was meant to be an international extravaganza. A Yankee was a requisite. You want a familiar name to make it seem less foreign.

This kind of international casting reached a kind of glorious high point for me in 1972 with the release of an action pic called *Red Sun*. The producers had Charles Bronson for us, Alain Delon for the Europeans, and Toshiro Mifune for the Japanese. In spite of that, it did some business.

Casting is as important to the success of a film as any aspect. Do it right, you've got a chance, do it wrong, you're dead in the water; it's as cut-and-dried as that. We all know how Albert Finney turned down *Lawrence of Arabia*, how George Raft turned down both *The Maltese Falcon* and *Casablanca*, thereby making Mr. Bogart an international star.

Personally, I love casting stories. These are two that happened in films I was involved with.

1. *Butch Cassidy and the Sundance Kid*

Briefly, I researched it off and on for eight years, wrote it over Christmas vacation the year I taught at Princeton, 1966–67. It was turned down by just about everybody, although Paul Newman, who did my first American screenplay, *Harper*, liked it enough to say he wouldn't mind seeing it again if I did a rewrite.

I did a rewrite—a tiny one—and for no logical reason, almost every studio wanted it. Fox got it.

And Newman was set to play the lead.

Not, by the way, the part he eventually played, but rather

the Redford part, the Sundance Kid. (The title originally began with the Kid—it changed when Newman changed roles—and I know it's crazy, but I liked the original title better.)

Somehow, Steve McQueen got hold of it. (I don't know the truth, but I was told that someone actually stole the script off an agent's desk and got it to him.)

He wanted to play Butch Cassidy.

Talk 'bout lightning in a bottle. John Wayne was around, but he was getting a bit old. Clint Eastwood was around, but he maybe wasn't quite what he became.

So it wouldn't have been wrong in saying that the script was going to be acted by the two most popular movie stars in the world.

Their agents meet. *Pro forma.* Not only are the two parts meant to be equal, Newman and McQueen are both pros, they knew each other from the Actor's Studio in New York.

Salary? Profit participation?

Piffle. The same for each.

Travel expenses and trailer size and per diem?

Get away, boy, you bother me—both the same.

It's a done deal.

It's not set, it's set-set.

Oh. Only one last minor thing—

—who gets first billing?

Newman's people have a sensational answer: Paul was on the project first, Paul, if you will, discovered the thing, Paul should have first billing, that's fair.

McQueen's people didn't think so. McQueen's recent flicks had done better than Newman's, especially in the foreign market. McQueen should get first billing, that's fair.

Now, there comes a period of intense logical discussion, followed by a period of intense illogical discussion, then a bit of screaming, a cooling-off period, then back to combat. (This took two days, let it be noted.)

Idea: Newman gets first billing in all print ads, McQueen gets first billing on the film itself.

Unacceptable.

Idea: McQueen gets first billing on print, Newman's name is higher on the page.

Unacceptable.

Idea: Newman gets first billing in America, McQueen in the rest of the world.

Unacceptable.

Idea: McQueen gets first billing on odd-numbered days, McQueen gets first billing on even-numbered days.

Unacceptable.

Idea: their names are crossed:

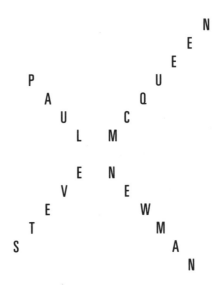

Forget it.

At the end of the first day, an acquaintance whispered to me of what was going on: "If this deal doesn't make, it's because of their agents' egos."

It *didn't* make, and that was the reason. Neither company that represented the stars dared to go to its talent and say, "We got everything except first billing, but you don't mind that, do you?"

Stars do mind it. They leave agencies over little things like that.

Would have made an interesting movie—I don't mean McQueen and Newman as Butch and Sundance. I mean the fighting that went on in the room.

2. *The Princess Bride*

The title role, Buttercup, was just a bitch to cast. Because she has to be, for reasons of fancy and story, the most beautiful girl in the world.

Rob Reiner went crazy trying to get a girl. The problem was simple: the few that he liked enough as actresses weren't beautiful, and the few that were couldn't act.

Reiner is going, let it be said, crazy.

He's got to find this young incredible beauty. He's been in New York, L.A., London. Nothing.

Now, he's back in Los Angeles, and the phone rings. It is, to use their terminology, a "heavy" agent from one of the major agencies calling in. Rob takes the call. The rest is history.

> HEAVY AGENT
> Hey, Robbie.

> REINER
> Hi.

> HEAVY AGENT
> You still haven't got a
> Buttercup?

> REINER
> Have you got one?

> HEAVY AGENT
> I sure do.

> REINER
> Great. Who?

> HEAVY AGENT
> It's amazing casting.

> REINER
> I'm waiting, I'm waiting.

> HEAVY AGENT
> Whoopi Goldberg.

CUT TO:

REINER IN CLOSE UP. That sound you just heard is his
jaw hitting the floor. He is a very bright fellow and
words have never been his enemy, but now he has all
the vocabulary of a beached whale. He just sits there,
stunned.

CUT TO:

REINER'S OFFICE AS THE SILENCE GOES ON. And on.
Then—

> HEAVY AGENT
> What, is it the black thing?
> (Note—if I ever write another book about the business,
> *The Black Thing* has got to be the title.)

> REINER
> No—no—she's great and
> everything, except we were
> thinking of going a little
> younger.

> HEAVY AGENT
> (relentless)
> Have you heard her do her
> teenage Valley Girl routine?
> Hilarious.

Anyway, the guy won't let Rob off the phone. On and on the
conversation goes. Finally, cordially, it ends, but Reiner is done
for the day.

I told another heavy agent that story—but he didn't laugh,
didn't smile. He just shook his head and said the following:
"Those phone calls are hard. . . ."

Of All He Surveys

It was after one-thirty before I tried getting to sleep. The first
movie in competition was less than seven hours away.

Still, no way I could close my eyes.

Because after we were introduced from the stage to the full, formally attired theater, we didn't just walk to our seats. We could have. We could have gone down from the stage to the aisle and found our way. Or we could have walked outside the theater but stayed inside the building and got around that way.

Cannes has its traditions.

We left the stage and were taken along a corridor outside to a protected area. Cars were waiting. Festival cars and drivers. We got in.

And they drove us around the theater. All the traffic has been sawhorsed off, so they move right along. Until they get to the front of the building.

Where the staircase is.

The staircase is very wide, railed, red carpeted—

—and surrounded by thousands of fans. More than five thousand certainly. Probably less than ten.

And there is processional music playing.

And someone is saying who you are as you approach the staircase. The music and the voice build.

You start to climb.

The cheering begins. Up a dozen steps. Then there's a wide area marking halfway. And it's there that you turn and the noise is crescendoing as you turn and face them, all those bright-eyed faces, staring up at you.

PAUL NEWMAN: "Last year I had *Glass Menagerie* in competition. I didn't know about the staircase then. But they drove us up and we got out of the cars and the sound started and when I got halfway up and turned and looked out I thought, 'Oh, I get it, I'm an emperor now, I can deal with that.' "

To hell with him. He had his year, this was mine. I was the emperor now. I waved to the thousands. Across the street, there were apartment buildings, and people stood on their terraces waving at me—

—at *me*, folks.

Did they know how wonderful I was?
Must have.
Did they realize my sensitivity?
Why else would they be cheering?
Had they been waiting all those hours just for this moment?
Absolutely.
Just for me?
Positively.
Did I disappoint them?
Impossible.
Have I ever disappointed anybody? . . .

I HAD NOT REALIZED THAT 2,399 other people were going to the movies with me at half past eight on Thursday morning. Reporters all.

Tough house.

I don't know quite what I expected as I walked over, but it sure was nothing like the mob attending. You showed your credentials, and up the stairs you went, just like the night before, when the thousands were standing screaming for you.

Would you believe hundreds were standing there now? Every morning they would be in place. Looking for what or who (whom?) I couldn't tell you. I cannot speak with authority concerning the hours I zonked, but when I was awake, the area around the stairs was *never* empty. Babies, old folks, 'tweeners. Some of them begging for tickets, most of them just eyeing us.

Usually, the press sees a lot of movies at Cannes. Not perhaps as many as fellow jury member David Robinson with his five per day (although I did meet an Australian critic who saw six, hurrying from theater to theater, his timing immaculate). There are two press screenings for the official-entry films. The reporters and reviewers are dressed casually, and if you want to impress them, you better damn well be impressive.

The Abyss (not 1989's underwater epic starring Ed Harris), which opened the competition, had few admirers. (Fear not, I won't tell you what it was about. At least not in painful detail. Since most of the films that were in competition will never hit these shores, I cannot see why you must be burdened with information concerning them. The only ones I'll go into are either those that figured in the final voting or those that I think you might actually see or hear of.)

The Abyss, a Belgian film (actually, Belgian-French) concerns itself with the final troubles of an alchemist doctor in Flanders during the religious upheavals of the sixteenth century. (Eyelids getting heavy?)

It looked glorious, was technically fine, and boy was it not a lot of laughs. What it was, was an Ingmar Bergman film if Bergman had been born with no talent, just conviction.

Still, as I left the theater at 10:20 A.M., I felt both discombobulated and fine. The first because I can't remember the experience of leaving a flick at that early hour. The latter because there was something exhilarating about leaving a flick at that early hour. I didn't nap once. Half my day's work was done.

Twenty-some to go and I wasn't a virgin anymore. . . .

On Being a Successful Judge

I discovered the crucial attribute by the end of the second movie on the first day. (The jury would have its initial meeting five movies on, and I'll get to that in the next chapter. These are simply thoughts that took place in between.)

A keen mind is not the chief component, though I'm told it helps.

A solid history of cinema ain't it either.

Nor is a sense of story the most important.

Or the problems facing a director.

Not a strong visual or aural sense.

All of these are pluses, no question, but they pale when it comes to the big stuff.

The answer, and I'm sure there will be those that doubt (but no one on the '88 jury would)—the shining, unalloyed answer, O great unwashed, is this: more than anything, you need chewing gum.

Wads of the stuff.

This truth began to become evident after the jury session when we all met. Afterward we got to chatting about what really was on a lot of our minds: jet lag. Anybody who travels great distances to get to Cannes is aware of the problem. You're whipped, you sit down in that comfortable seat in that perfect theater, the lights go down, and the next thing, you're watching the end credits roll. There was a very genuine worry that we'd all zonk, at least in the early days, which wasn't being totally fair to the films in competition.

Then someone, I think it was George Miller, said he'd heard from someone, somewhere, once, that chewing gum kept you awake in the movies. Miller, the onetime medico, had no logic behind his news. He wasn't sure whether it was the requisite jaw action or the sudden sugar shot. But someone, somewhere, once, had told him.

Don't think my pockets weren't bulging as I plunged into *The Abyss* at 8:30 A.M. And don't think I wasn't besieged by fellow jurors. Eventually, most of us had our own private stashes.

And the crazy fact is this: the stuff works. I'd start to nod off, pull out my trusty packet of French whatever, fold a stick into my mouth, and my eyes stopped closing.

I put this into a scientific time capsule for the eventual answer. All I can say is, no juror at any movie I saw got any sack time. . . .

Whose Fault Is It, Anyway?

Back to poor dreadful Rosanna Arquette.

When a performer stinks up the joint, he or she tends to get blamed. Not always, but most of the time. It's fun for critics to potshot. But enjoyable as that may be for the working stiffs, it's not always fair. Because really rotten work can come from four sources:

1. the performer
2. the part
3. a combination of the above—
   i.e., miscasting
4. the director

Arquette can be terrific (*Desperately Seeking Susan*). She is, for me, a definite offbeat talent. And my guess here is—

you'll have to take my word for this, because probably you'll never see the movie, and if you do, it's been announced it's going to be radically cut for America—that she was the least to blame. It was a terrible role, so ineptly written that no one would be well cast in it. Simply unplayable. And the director, whose heart was clearly with the stunning underwater stuff, allowed unacceptable excesses.

I'm not asking sympathy for a star, understand. I would rather be committed to Bellevue than do that.

But there are reasons, good ones, why they're so crazy. . . .

Maybe you didn't know stars were crazy. (We've already established that they're miserable.) Well, ask anyone in the business. I know one top executive who has a wonderful habit—whenever the subject of performers' behavior comes up, he says nothing, just quietly raises his hand. There can be half a dozen people ranting about this guy's looniness or that lady's impossible demands, he still says nothing. Eventually, though, that hand gets attention, and people say, "Well, what is it?," and he always replies, "Remember, we're talking about actors."

A great bracing truth in those five words.

Well, why are they?

Impossible to answer, because they're not all nuts in the same ways.

Richard Burton, when he was I guess the most famous man in the world, was holed up in the Dorchester Hotel in London with Miss Taylor, and a friend of mine went to visit him. When I said "holed up," I should have said "trapped," because that, in actuality, was the case. He could go absolutely no-place—every exit was flooded with hysterical fans and media.

This particular evening, Burton is in a very sour mood, because Taylor, exhausted, has gone to sleep early. My friend wanted to take off but Burton insisted he stay—he was desperate for company.

But they couldn't go out to a pub or a restaurant, couldn't go to a movie or play or take a walk as the rest of us might—the hassling fans and the photographers made it impossible.

Burton becomes increasingly morose until my friend gets him sidetracked to the subject of his early acting days, and Burton begins to get at least a bit jollier. He was, from all accounts, great company when sober, an all but compulsive reader, a startling wit. (Mike Nichols said one of the great lines once when he was asked how many really intelligent actors he knew. Nichols thought for a long moment before he answered: "One and a half—Anthony Perkins is smart, and Richard Burton is something.")

But eventually, his stories begin to slow, and depression returns. Perhaps he knew even then what his obits would be in England—the gist was this: RICHARD BURTON DEAD—A DISAPPOINTMENT.

Now, in his suite, Burton lights up. *"The dogs,"* he cries. "We'll go see the dogs."

Translation: during their peak years, they didn't travel alone much—their entourage was bigger than some army battalions. Miss Taylor, a longtime animal lover, had dogs she adored—

—but England has very strict laws on animal entrance. I think it's six months in seclusion before they're allowed into the country.

The Burtons came up with a solution—they hired a yacht with a captain and, I suppose, crew, and kept the boat anchored in the Thames, where it was perfectly legal to visit them. So Burton, more than a bit tipsy but genuinely excited, arranges for the limo and how to get to it without getting mobbed and how to get through the mob without getting injured—

—then he phones the ship.

No answer.

He phones again.

Same.

The captain of the ship, whose only job is to look after the dogs, has chosen this time to slip into London and visit friends. Burton erupts—"I'm paying a fucking fortune for that fucking yacht and those fucking dogs, and blahblahblah!" Then he huddles up to his bottle and drinks and drinks.

My friend was able to leave once Burton was blotto.

One of the things that drives stars crazy, then, is this: fame.

But again, in weird ways. During the height of the *Cleopatra* madness, when it seemed like half the press of the Western world was camped outside of her Rome hotel, Elizabeth Taylor, the most famous female star, I suspect, in the history of sound, suddenly snapped. She couldn't take the hounding.

So she and a friend got up at dawn. She put on a wig and they took the service elevator and spent the entire day free, roaming the streets and the Borghese Gardens like any tourist. No one bothered her, and you know what?—

—she *hated* it.

And never did it again.

Bob Dylan story. I know a Rock Impresario who had some clients playing Vegas and Dylan called him up and said he'd like to see what it was like playing a showroom in Vegas, could it be arranged so he might slip in and out and no one would be aware.

The rock guy set it up.

He was waiting early by the showroom entrance when, across the lobby, there was this amazing commotion—

—the gamblers had spotted Dylan.

Well, they had and they hadn't.

What they had spotted was this weird-looking guy wearing guess what?—

—*a foot-high turban.*

So they gawked—that kind of *chapeau* draws stares even from gamblers on a hot streak—and then their eyes traveled down to the face and guess what?—there was secretive Bob Dylan slipping into the hotel in a way that no one would notice.

Let me coin a phrase: fame is a two-edged sword.

But the craziness of stars is there before the fame hits. Mostly, they are people not content with the hand they were dealt, which is why they choose to role-play for a profession.

But you have to throw in this: most stars are frauds and they know it.

They are not great actors and they know it. (Except Brando, who was great, probably knew it, and despised the occupation.)

They are not great beauties and they know it. (Except Paul Newman, who is handsomer than thee or me. And I'm told the same was true of Cary Grant.)

Plus this: it's shitty work.

Not the money, not the power, that's all neat. But have you ever been on a movie set?

Death.

It's all mechanical stuff. Done in quick snippets. Sure, there's craft involved in sustaining a character over a four-month shoot—but most stars only play themselves, so even that isn't so hard.

Ask anyone—movie acting is the snooze of all the world.

So it's shitty and it's phony and the fame doesn't last. No wonder they're crazy. Maybe the real wonder is that they're not crazier than they are.

I think, for most of them, when stardom hits, they really each believe they'll be able to handle it. (Like cocaine addicts, if you will.)

But fame can't be handled. It can disappear, sure—Meryl Streep has only to gain fifty pounds and the parts will stop coming. Stallone lets his body sag and turns into Pee Wee Herman, he'll save a ton on his bodyguard bills.

The shocker for them when fame happens is this: it's *there*. And it won't go away when you want it to. You can't order it around. You can't give it terms. You can't have it when you want it and banish it when you don't.

You can't make requests: "I'd like an hour of fame please." As far as fame is concerned, there ain't no free lunch. . . .

Tears, Idle Tears

I mentioned that moment at the end of every single movie when the whole audience, so beautifully attired, rises and cheers the talent. There have been some interesting reactions to that.

Sally Field is the most talked about, at least of late. When *Norma Rae* showed in '79 (she was to win the prize here for best actress, which I think can be argued to have been the turnaround of her career) there was just an explosion for her.

Now, those of us addicted to the Oscars know that Field, a wonderful actress, can get the tear ducts going pretty good. And so she did this night at Cannes. At least, so legend has it.

She cried.

And cried.

The cheers ripped the house apart.

She could not stop crying.

Truly.

The outpouring went on and on for her. Justly—it was a marvelous piece of work.

She stood there in the spotlight.

Weeping.

Who wouldn't have wept?

I would have.

You would have.

What Field did that we might not have done was this: she didn't stop.

Not then.

Not later that evening.

Not late that night.

Not the next morning. (At least so the story goes.)

Eventually, she did, of course, but by then a theory had begun as to *just what hit her.*

Of course, it might have been the relief of sensing she wouldn't have to Gidget her way through life.

That's not the theory, though.

The theory is that what unhinged her was this: the sound. *It was live.*

In the "golden era" of pictures, the thirties, forties, it was a rare performer who didn't get his grounding on the stage. Today, that's not so true. Yes, a lot of actors did: I saw Paul Newman several times on Broadway. Robert Redford was a brilliant young stage comedian. Meryl Streep can be magic when she treads the boards. Brando was the most electrifying

American actor I have ever seen or will see. Burt Reynolds, though I've never seen him, has done a lot of stage work. Pacino, De Niro, Hackman, Scott, Dudley Moore, Jane Fonda—they've all worked with varying degrees of success and effectiveness.

I don't think Eastwood has.

And I don't think Sally Field has either. At least, that's the Cannes theory. She's a child of the tube. She's worked a lot and she's a pro.

But you don't *hear* the reaction.

The love comes later—autographs, snapshots, gushing fans. But when you're *there*—when it hits you, that blast of blind emotion—well, it's not the same as a director saying, "Cut, print, thank you."

Quick ramble . . .

I've worked in both theater and films, and aside from the obvious reasons of money and fame, I don't know why anyone chooses to be a movie actor—*for a lifetime.*

Not that theater work is oodles of fun. Doing it eight times a week every week can stultify the soul. It's no pleasure being in a flop, sensing the audience's disappointment, occasionally hatred. Being in a rotten part in a hit isn't such a much either.

But at least you can improve.

You can deepen.

And when there is laughter, when there are tears, *you* did that. In this increasingly capsuled world, you moved another human being.

Not many of us get that chance.

And far fewer of us know when we do it.

Movie actors sure don't.

It is cold, technical labor. You're given a snippet to accomplish. You learn your few lines, hit your crucial marks, say what you've got to say. Over and over, maybe ten times, maybe fifty.

I truly think if the pay were the same, no one would choose to work in movies or the tube instead of where the people are alive. And it's that real life, so they conjecture, that rocked Sally Field.

I hope it's true. Anyway, something sure did.

The Market

Every hotel lobby and many hotel suites were taken up with the marketing of films. But the center of it was the massive basement of the Palais. People from all over the world were trying to sell movies, mostly schlock, to other people from all over.

Have you ever been to a business convention? That's what this is. I've described earlier how to sell *The Bill Goldman Story*. In the Palais basement, there were hundreds of booths and endless aisles—mostly named after film directors. People hustling and trying to make deals. (There is one guy who reportedly sells cassettes by the *pound*.) All genres are available, from porn (down in presence from earlier years, so the pundits said) to sweet German cartoons. (A porn booth was contiguous with a German cartoon booth, if that's of any interest.)

Horror was big, but it seemed to me that action/adventure was the biggest genre of all. But for the same reason: they are mainly visual and move most easily from country to country, language to language. And you don't have to spend much on dubbing. It's because of this that an Arnold Schwarzenegger, though perhaps not as big domestically as some of the comedic graduates of *Saturday Night Live*, is a far more formidable figure on the international scene. Comedy doesn't translate.

There were over six hundred films available for showing at the market this year. I saw none of them. I guess the one I most wanted to see had some posters up in the basement of the Palais. It was an Australian muscleman film, and it starred some guy who was billed as "Mr. Western Suburbs of 1982." He was also "Third in Mr. Melbourne." I mean, that's the best they could say about their star?

Talk about truth in advertising. . . .

Buns and Such

At the end of *The Abyss*, the movie about the alchemist doctor
in Flanders during the sixteenth century that I didn't tell you
much about, the main character commits suicide by maybe
emasculating himself. The reason for my tentativeness being
I couldn't quite see. He has a knife in one hand and he brings
it down into that vicinity but his arm is between his privates
and the camera so all I could tell for sure was he wasn't a
happy camper and pretty soon he was gushing pretty good.

After the flick, I cornered the good doctor, Mr. Miller, and
as intellectual to intellectual, put the query thusly: "At the
end there, did he cut his schlong off or what?"

"What," Miller assured me. The man had severed some
artery in that area, thereby unleashing the torrent.

Actually, it mattered not to me, because I was tripping off
by then, the subject being naked men in non-porn films.

I'm agin it.

For all kinds of reasons: I don't much like, personally, looking at us unclad. We are not, for me, lovely, as our ladies so
often are. I also don't think it enhances the viewing experience
much, even when done for quote artistic close quote reasons.

It also screws up the story.

Because we stop paying attention.

Because we *know* they're not going to show it, so what we
do is watch to see how close they stop the shot. Do we see the
star naked from chin to navel? A centimeter below? A peek at
the hairline? Don't we all gag at the shot of the unmarried
couple arising afterward, her in the buff, him suddenly slipping
into his panties? I mean, *nowhere* in the world do men keep
their underwear as close by as in the movies.

Personally, I wish the "filmmakers" of this world would do
the honorable thing and get rid of the shots altogether. Get
us panting some other way.

I must, in closing, quote my daughter Jenny on the subject.
She had just seen *American Gigolo* starring Richard Gere. I

asked her how she liked it, and she kind of shrugged. Then she said: "It was full of sidal nudity. . . ."

The Only Game in Town

Each day the crowds and sense of excitement grow, with absolutely no correlation to the quality of the movies being shown. Or even of the stars putting in appearances.

Gilles Jacob, the main man of the festival, has said that in order for a film festival to truly work, it must command, it must be the crucial event in the area. Which is why the New York festival is and will always be kind of a pimple.

No question that nothing in Cannes matches the festival. There are over three *thousand* media people in attendance, over sixteen thousand receive accreditation. Last year it was estimated the festival brought in more than 300 million francs. And this is not a major city.

Yes, the Olympics are bigger. So is the World Cup. But those only happen every four years. Cannes is simply the biggest annual media event in the world.

Heading South

The third movie in competition was an Argentinian flick directed by Fernando Solanas, entitled *Le sud* (South). I mention his name the way I do and not "directed by someone named Fernando Solanas" because even though I hadn't heard of him, others had; "Oh yes, the Solanas picture," they'd say. It kept reminding me of *Butch Cassidy* for reasons that will not be clear from the official description of the movie:

> 1983, and the military dictatorship in Argentina ends. It is late in the night when Floreal finally gets out of prison. Five long years he has waited to rejoin his wife but the night will be long and their reunion forever postponed. The couple changed, just like the country which longs to find hope and freedom once again. A long journey through life and death, desire and fear: that is *Le sud*.

If you think that sounds like it's working the pretentious side of the street, bingo. The movie was full of dead people not being dead and time blending into time and phrases rich with meaning.

So why *Butch?* Well, do you remember a scene where they accidentally blow up a train car by putting in too much dynamite while what they're trying to do is blow up a safe? And the money flies through the air and everyone chases after it?

Well, in *South*, there are an *amazing* number of shots when newspapers blow along the streets. Or if not newspapers, then ripped-up posters. Blowing along, past the actors, the sets, every little thing.

I remember talking to George Hill, who directed *Butch*, and he told me what a bitch the explosion with the money had been to shoot. Because the money had to always be blowing in the same direction at the same speed. He went on about the problems of working with the wind machines and all the other paraphernalia needed to make it work.

That was mostly what I was thinking of during *South*. What was their wind-machine budget? They must have rented every one in Argentina. What if some other Argentinian wonder boy is shooting a film and *he* needs a wind machine? Does he fly one in from Brazil?

I'm serious—every damn time one of these wind-machine shots happened, there went my concentrating on the flick and I'd be thinking about this poor schnook on long distance, trying to get a Colombian wind machine because the one in Brazil was broken.

This is, of course, totally a personal judgment call, and a lot of people—almost all *auteur* critics, for example—would say I'm wrong. But I think direction that calls attention to itself stinks. I like the totality of the piece to unfold, and I love suspending disbelief. But when a director starts getting clever, shooting scenes through coffee-spoon reflections or in a corpse's ear, I have to stop the train.

I wish Mr. Solanas had gone south without me. . . .

The War at Home

After lunch at La Mère Besson (I ate alone: mushrooms Provençal, grilled chicken, great frites, half a bottle of local red), I went back to the Majestic and called New York.

We've put the apartment up for sale. Twelve people came tromping in, real estate folk, potential buyers. Here I'm watching Argentinian wind machines with Nastassja Kinski, and meanwhile, the family homestead is going under the gavel.

I left my hotel room—it was unsettling and, even though I knew it was due to happen, startling. I wandered a bit, thinking of the place and our fifteen years there, and as an ambulance went by, I remembered being with Ilene one morning and she'd just had major surgery. Suddenly, she hemorrhaged, blood fauceting from her and I called the doctor, got her into a cab, and we went east on Seventieth Street toward New York Hospital. She's fading in my arms and the blood won't stop—

—and now traffic congeals, we're crawling, and what the hell do you do or say at a time like that?

Just then, Jerome Robbins rode by on a bicycle.

I mentioned that to her and I think she said that probably he must live around here and I said something back to her, maybe that I'd recently seen Balanchine running for the bus, and we chitchatted our way until she got to the operating room just in time, and I wondered as I walked those crowded French streets how many memories of the apartment would I keep, how many would I be able to forget, and would I be bushwhacked forever, as I just had been, by the ambulance siren so many miles from home. . . .

Bill Goes Hollywood

Barry Norman is an English television figure specializing in show business. He's been nice to me in the past, and asked if I'd do a quick BBC interview on what I thought of Cannes.

We did it outside by the pool, and for the first time since

my arrival, during shooting, the sun started blazing. The stones by the pool reflected the brilliance.

I had begun the interview without my sunglasses. When the sun came out, we began again, and I tried and tried to do it as before. But I couldn't see. My eyes wouldn't stop tearing. Finally, I put on the goddamn glasses and did the interview. I hated doing it that way.

All I needed was a lot of gold chains, and I'd be just like the enemy. . . .

No Business Like . . .

The guy was walking up and down the red-carpeted steps of the Palais.

The crowd, perhaps a thousand, did not applaud.

The guy was wearing not a tuxedo but a skintight leopard costume.

The crowd was unimpressed.

The guy walked up and down the stairs again. If you can be a muscular anorexic, he was. Now, he went over to a table that was unused. Card-table height. He moved on top of the table. He had a whistle in his mouth. He moved toward the edge of the table, blew the whistle sharply. Again. Again.

Now, he moved to the very teetering edge of the table, prepared to jump.

The crowd was suddenly silent.

Another shrill whistle sound.

All eyes now on him.

He pauses.

And a woman cries out, *"Don't!"*

He heeds her, backs away.

The crowd does not relax. He's still on the tabletop, walking around it. He has their attention now. He begins moving faster across the tabletop.

Tension only builds.

Why? What's the big deal about a guy walking up and down a few steps, leaping off a card table to the pavement?

Only this: the guy is a supreme contortionist and he's doing all this on his hands, his legs tucked under his arms, his entire body no more than ten inches from table to head top. And if he jumps off, and you know he's going to eventually, there's a chance his head will naturally give a little and smash into the cement. Now, his scuttling speed increases as he crabs his way around the tabletop, people running to join the crowd, kids getting hoisted onto Daddy's shoulders, listening to the whistle that he always has locked between his clenched teeth.

Cannes is filled with sideshows. The promenade of the Croisette is almost never empty of would-be Dylans, failed sketchers, rock groups blaring away.

But they weren't the Magic Johnsons of their crafts. This guy on the tabletop was in a higher league, Magic's league. Probably he would have been a figure of note had he been in some other line of work—but my God, who wants to be a contortionist? And at his age. (Guess: late fifties.) Where is the pleasure in starving and stretching yourself into positions that must provide intense pain?

Suddenly, he launched himself with his fingertips, crashed to the pavement, and yes, his head did connect with the cement, but it was a light bounce, no blood. He whistled and whistled and scuttled to his cap, nodding toward it, indicating it was time for the crowd to pay up. No one moved for a while. Then a little girl dashed up, embarrassed, dropped some coins into the cap, darted back into the crowd.

That was it? The contortionist looked around, eyes bright with disappointment, and as he pinned us with his stare, I could only think of the old joke about the guy who worked for the circus whose job was shoveling elephant shit. Every day. Followed the elephants around, cleaning up after them. And one night, drunk in a bar, he talks to the drunk on the next stool, saying that he wasn't a kid anymore and what did he have to look forward to but more years of doing nothing with his life but shovel elephant shit, and the drunk said, "Why don't you quit?," and the circus guy just stared at him incredulously, saying, "Quit? And leave show business? . . ."

The Biggest Star

As the days in Cannes passed, I realized that in twenty-five years of screenwriting, I had worked with, obviously, a lot of American actors and their British counterparts. Not to mention Dutch actors, Swedish actors, and Germans.

But in all that time, only one Frenchman. *Monsieur* Rousimoff. Probably better known by his athletic tag, André the Giant. André played one of the four leads in *The Princess Bride*, Fezzik, the strongest man in the world.

The movie had an agonizing past. Written in 1973, it took fifteen years before it finally got filmed, thanks to Norman Lear and Rob Reiner. It almost started an amazing number of times. Once a studio actually *closed* just before it was to happen. Twice, studio heads got fired on weekends just before they were to make it a "go" project.

During those years I saw André on the tube and, several times when he worked Madison Square Garden, I was in attendance, mostly because I knew that if *Princess Bride* actually did ever become a reality, André had to have a shot at Fezzik.

Rob Reiner had no problem with meeting André for the part. In fact he *wanted* to meet André. The problem was that André was like Gertrude Stein's words about Oakland: there was no there there. Reiner would call the World Wrestling Federation, and they would always be nice, but André was always touring Japan or the like. Personal contact proved impossible.

So Reiner sent out a casting call for giants.

I was there for some of this, and giants are not as easy to find as you might think. Big guys would come in and read— huge guys—but they weren't giants. Fezzik is probably the only part Bubba Smith ever lost because he was too *small*.

We eventually saw some giants. One looked great, but he couldn't act the part. Then we found a giant who *could* act the part. He was terrific. He was also skinny, and it was hard believing a skinny giant was the strongest man in the world.

The hunt went on. Reiner was in Scotland scouting for the

"Cliffs of Insanity" when he got word: André was in Paris. Off Reiner and his partner Andy Scheinman went to Paris. The doorman at their hotel said, "A *man* is waiting for you in the bar."

Rob and Andy went into the bar and, indeed, André was there. And, of course, after the meeting, he got the part.

As to his size: he's like the Pentagon; no matter how big you think it's going to be it's always bigger. André's publicity has him at seven feet five inches and 550 pounds. The truth is, he doesn't know for sure how much he weighs. (This is not a fat man, remember.) He does know that a couple of years ago he got pneumonia and lost a hundred pounds in three weeks.

But the size isn't in the numbers. It's in his *presence.*

André is very still. In a room, he often will find a place large enough to accommodate him (chairs without arms, benches, etc.) and stay there without moving. I think he does this because he's never sure what reaction people will have to him. I've seen children meet him and go mad with glee and start to climb on him. Other children scream in fear and run away.

His hands may well be the most remarkable thing about him. A can of beer disappears. A catcher's mitt is what we're talking of now. Shaking hands with André is like dipping your hand into a well.

The movie was shot in London and in Sheffield, England, and André was by far the most popular person on the set. One night we were shooting some exterior castle scenes and it was miserably cold; André sat watching the scenes very happily. (He loved the experience because it was the first time in over twenty years he didn't have to go someplace the next morning—for all that time, he'd been wrestling over three hundred times a year.) At any rate, the crew was layered against the cold, but we were all still shivering except for André, who was bare chested, with a light towel over his shoulders. Many of us would wander over and ask if we could get him a shirt or a blanket. He would politely shake his head and say, "I'm fine, boss," boss being what he called everybody. It was silly—here we all were freezing and he was fine, and we were all fretting lest something go wrong with surely one of the strongest men anywhere.

He played gin gummy with his driver, named Freddy. André would keep score, dividing the page in half, putting an *F* on the top of one side, an *A* on the other. One night he played cards with our producer, Andy Scheinman. André wrote an *A* on the left half of the page, then he hesitated a moment thinking. Two *A*'s would never do.

After a pause he wrote *G* for his score.

He was a constant source of pleasure—and a constant surprise.

One day he asked us if we knew who Samuel Beckett was.

Being familiar with *Waiting for Godot*, we said we did. Then we asked why he asked.

It seemed that André was brought up in a tiny town, population maybe thirty. And one of the other thirty was Beckett himself. When André was young, sometimes when he walked to school, Beckett would stop and give him a lift.

Talk about your odd couple.

We wondered what in the world they chatted about before deciding that André probably pestered Beckett for his views on symbolism in modern European literature while Beckett was after André for his secret to getting out of a Hulk Hogan stranglehold. . . .

The last shot of *The Princess Bride* was to be of the four main characters on glorious white horses beckoning to the little kid who has been told their story to come join them for more adventures.

We had actors. We had horses. We also had problems. Chiefly this: André would kill the horse if he sat on it. But Reiner wanted the shot (it eventually didn't make the movie), so some of the technicians went to work. At the end of one particularly long shooting day they asked Reiner to look at what they'd come up with. It was heavily misting as he walked the length of the studio, and when he got there they threw open the door to the sound stage—

—there, through the mist, Reiner saw André, swinging on a harness thirty feet up in the air. (The notion was to lower him down onto the horse so the harness would carry his weight.)

It was the first day that year Beaujolais Nouveau was being sold, and André had a bottle of it (not his first) in one hand. He smiled down, waved his free catcher's mitt and said, "Hello, boss." Reiner smiled, waved back, and what Reiner remembers thinking as he stared through the mist was, "What *do* I do for a living?"

And when I remember André, as I often do, I like to place him back up there, beloved, swinging on the harness, the bottle of new red wine tiny in his great hand. . . .

Party Going

I got an invitation from Viot, the head of the festival, to have dinner at the Carlton, where he was staying. I didn't know how dressy it was, whether I needed a necktie or not, but I decided better safe than sorry. Resplendent in my blazer, blue shirt, gray slacks, and yellow knit tie, I wandered over. The only other time I'd had dinner with him was for the jury and guests, close to twenty of us. It was pleasant and casual, and I was looking forward to more of the same.

Dinner was in the same elegant room as before, but a few things had altered. This was not casual; it was a sit-down supper for seventy-five, it was formal, and not only was I the only yellow tie in shrieking distance, I knew nobody in the chandeliered room.

To be honest, I was a bit paranoid. Parties are never where I hang my hat, and I imagined a bunch of people were wondering what was that creature in the practically neon neckwear doing here. I couldn't wait to sit down. There were three long tables, each with name cards. Once I found my spot, I knew I'd feel infinitely less conspicuous. I wandered from corner to corner, sipping my Badoit until it became evident that cocktails were over, the meal about to begin. I zipped to the nearest table to find my spot. I was wearing, of course, my huge sunglasses over my reading glasses, but I took off the monsters while I located my anointed place.

Scurrying down the first side of the first table, I cursed slightly. No me.

Round I got to the second side of the first table. Others are looking for their names now, and since I am blind on my right side, I am soon literally bumping into people, which doesn't do much for my ever-green self-confidence.

No me.

I attack table two now. Both sides.

No me.

I am now totally overcome with the conviction that I will not be at the third and last table either. I get crazy at parties from time to time, but before I started my final search, I snuck out my invitation and looked at it.

I *had* been invited.

Breathing deeply that at least I'd got *that* right, I slow my pace as I begin the first side of the third table. All around me now, people are sitting.

No me.

As I begin the sixth and final side, *everyone* is sitting. And I'm, of course, convinced they're watching me, knowing that I must be in the wrong place. Which was, of course, nonsense. They could not have cared less. (But why was everyone staring at my tie?) Step by step, I traverse the final side. There are ten cards left. I know my name's not there. Seven places. I know my name's not there. Three places. Two.

Guess what, my name's not there.

Tempted as I was to feign the vapors and flee into the night, I did nothing. If you always think when you go to a dinner party that your name's not going to be there and then your name's not there, it's not paranoia anymore. Anyone can deal with madness—it's reality that's impossible.

I don't know what happened next, what shuffling was done, but I found myself seated, and no thumb came down from the ceiling telling me I didn't belong.

Patty Hearst was just across the table from me. (I realized that *The Patty Hearst Story*, directed by Paul Schrader, was playing the next day.) She hadn't seen the movie yet.

She was the shock of the festival. No performer got better press. She's a lovely young woman, one of those much prettier than she photographs. And poised. Genuinely charming. And you got the feeling there is no question on this earth she hasn't been asked.

And we'll never know what really happened to her.

Final Thought

The crowds were getting crazy now. Streets full, restaurants packed. People pouring in from all the continents we have. No more quiet moments at the Majestic breakfast buffet.

And yes, a lot of it is chintzy—

—but—

—if you love film; if you can't get enough flicks to quiet your addiction; if you want to bathe in the flickering lights; if the celluloid strips bring you hope and pleasure, Cannes, flanked by mountains, bordered by the sea, bathed from time to time in soft Mediterranean sun, surely is the last best place on earth. . . .

SCOLA HAD DONE HIS homework wonderfully well.

That was clear once the doors were shut in Viot's Carlton suite and the jury was alone with just Christianne to represent the festival, and the translators.

The purpose of the meeting (as those to follow) was to get a jump on what would be the hectic final day when the voting took place. If we had a sense of where we were, it would expedite the end process. So Scola took out his notes, read a short paragraph about the first movie, and then we went around the table talking in turn, always saying what we thought.

There was, I felt, a genuine and welcome seriousness about us—not that we weren't funny, because there was a lot of laughter. But we realized that we had, perhaps, a rare opportunity: we could change someone's life.

If, for example, the grand prize went to a new director or an unknown film, if some performer leaped from the pack to capture us, his or her existence would be, more than likely, permanently altered. I decided that had I had a film in competition, I would desire the best from the jury. Being on the jury, I decided to give my best back. So did we all.

The first meeting, we talked about six movies. (Understand this: they were all of them gorgeous to look at, serious, and skillfully made.) That wasn't enough, of course—we wanted someone to creep in and steal our hearts.

Two of the six I've talked about already. *The Abyss*, the Belgian snooze, and *South*, the Argentinian flick with all the papers blowing along the streets. Here are the other four, with their own brief descriptions of themselves. (I've used the English titles of the movies. Mainly for reasons of simplicity. The next one, for example, was called both *Araski Ga Oka* and *Onimaru*. I think, for our purposes, *Wuthering Heights* is a bit easier on the tongue.)

Wuthering Heights (Japanese)
In troubled times at the end of the Middle Ages in Japan, Onimaru, a vagabond boy, is adopted by the Yamabes, a family of priests destined since time immemorial to quell the anger of the Mountain of Fire. But Onimaru upsets established hierarchy and defies the ancient local rites. He falls in love with Kinu, the Yamabe daughter, who weds the heir to the rival family so as to escape fulfilling her destiny by becoming a priestess. Deeply scarred by his hopeless love, Onimaru becomes Lord of the Mountain to recover his beloved. But Kinu dies and Onimaru wallows in limitless cruelty, only equal in intensity to his unabating love for the late Kinu. It is Kinu's daughter who will put an end to the terror spread by the diabolical Onimaru.

Whatever its excesses, this was as pretty to look at as any recent film. It also had the weirdest moments with the lady translators and their high, expressionless nanny-type voices. (Think of an insanely prim Julie Andrews and you'll have it.)

At Cannes, they handled the language problems for the films in competition in the following manner: French movies had English subtitles. English movies had French subtitles. For everything else, you were supplied with headphones, the arm of your seat slid down revealing a place to plug the earphones in, and you flicked around until you found a language that enabled you to understand the movie.

Then you sit there and listen to these high-pitched translator ladies. (They weren't really there, it turned out—we were hearing a taped copy of the ladies. I had visions of these poor creatures up there all day slogging through one foreign tongue after another. There are no people in the translating booth. Just this wire going round and round. I don't know what happens if it breaks; I guess it wouldn't dare, not during the festival.)

Anyway, there's some good old-fashioned Japanese gore in this flick, and while it's going on, you hear this nanny in your ear saying, "Oh look, Onimaru in his anger has cut off the warrior's arm—see, the arm is flying through the air."

That's a rough translation, but you get the idea.

Pascali's Island (UK)
It is 1908, on a Greek island in the Aegean, under Turkish occupation. The Ottoman Empire is on the verge of collapse. Basil Pascali, for twenty years the loyal servant of the Sultan, watches over the comings and goings on the island—his private domain. With the arrival of the mysterious Englishman, Mr. Bowles, Pascali senses that their destinies are inescapably linked. Seduced by his charm, yet unable to trust him, he finds himself caught up in a web of intrigue. *Pascali's Island* is a story about the cruelty of beauty and indifference of fate.

Top cast—Ben Kingsley, Charles Dance, Helen Mirren—in a movie written and directed by the author of *Fatal Attraction*, James Dearden.

I never met him, but I was told that Dearden's father, Basil, was the director of *Masquerade*, the movie that got me into the business, back a quarter century. Proof of the old saying that there are really only seven people in the world, and four of us know each other. . . .

El Dorado (Spain)
El Dorado really existed for 16th-century Spaniards. They thought it was just waiting to be discovered across the Atlantic in America. Its most probable location was somewhere beyond the impenetrable Amazonian jungle. Greed for the gold of El Dorado was the reason behind the Spanish expedition of 1560 which inspired my film. *El Dorado* is the passionate story of a disastrous expedition. It is also the tale of Lope de Aguirre's fratricidal struggle for power and survival. It is a cruel, barbaric

story, sometimes more of a nightmare than a historical fact. Even today, Lope de Aguirre's own cry for freedom is utterly contemporary, its echoes still reaching across Latin America. More than anything else his actions reflect a desire to choose his own destiny, and to do this he had to rebel against the most powerful empire in the world.

This was a well-intended, heavy-handed epic that could have practically been shot in the studio. We were a long way here from Mr. Lean and *Lawrence of Arabia*. This was one of the movies the jury didn't talk about much. A few grunts and huffles, and then it was as if it had never existed. Now, the last of the first half-dozen and the only American film of the bunch:

Patty Hearst (U.S.)
The Patty Hearst kidnapping had an unreal quality. One would follow the case in the newspapers, watch it on TV, think about it, debate it, go to bed, dream about it—only to awake and discover what you had been dreaming about had actually occurred: the heiress had joined her captors, become a revolutionary, robbed a bank. And everywhere you went, people asked, "What do you think of Patty Hearst?"

In the two hours we discussed these flicks, a lot of truths were suddenly evident. I preferred *Patty Hearst* to the others. Not so my fellow jurors, who felt, to sum it up, that this subject demanded a great film, and this clearly wasn't a great film.

Why did I prefer *Patty Hearst?*
Because I felt comfortable with it.
And why, class, did Billy feel comfortable? All together—
—"because it was American."
Riiiight.
I understood the conventions, was at ease with the thing, not just the language but all of it. The Japanese film was a reach for me. My ignorance was right there on display. I didn't get the acting style, so I really wasn't sure about the performance level.

I've said how beautiful it was. Dead on. But I didn't know was that brilliant camera work or was that what the terrain looked like? Could any film-school freshman have achieved the same results?

There is a wonderful and famous fish restaurant in New York, Le Bernardin. You can take me there anytime you want, I promise to clean my plate. But am I sure how good it is?

Not really. When I tell you the Carnegie Deli is the best in Manhattan, I'm on pretty good ground. I've eaten at a ton of delis, I can compare. When I tell you that Peter Luger's across the Williamsburg Bridge is the best steak house in the history of the civilized world, you can argue (you'd be wrong, but you're entitled), but no matter how you rave about some Kobe place in downtown Kyoto, you won't shake me—I've eaten at steak places in most continents.

But Le Bernardin is the first and only fancy French fish house in my experience. I think it's in all ways splendid, but some Frenchie might tell me, "What? *Zat* you like? We have twenty better in Lille alone."

If he said that, I wouldn't know what to think.

And I didn't know what to think about the Japanese movie. I haven't seen many in the last decade. Sure, Kurosawa and a few others, but I'm simply ignorant of what I'm watching.

Which is the reason, folks, that Cannes is famous for not having sweeps, just as the Oscars are the reverse. Makes total sense. The Academy membership is essentially made up of the same kinds of people who live in the same burg and share the same taste. No wonder they *kvell* over *The Last Emperor*.

But here in the Carlton suite, we weren't homogenous: two women, eight men, specialists in seven different jobs, coming from nine different countries.

It's amazing we agreed on anything.

We did agree, though, on one thing this first meeting: none of the movies were prizewinners. At the end of the meeting, Scola said, "We must play a game—the festival ended today, we are the jury, who gets the prizes?"

Groans. Thrashing. "Do we have to vote?" "Yes." "Can we abstain?" "No." Much writhing in our seats—

—and then a shocker. *South* would have won. The pretentious one I kind of hated with all the papers blowing along.

I could not believe it.

Whyyy?

It was the most original. (True.) And in a situation such as ours, that mattered. (True.) It was personal. (True.) Serious. (Yawn, true.)

"We must hope for better films," Scola said as we packed up to go.

All heads nodded. And nodded again . . .

REDFORD JUST STANDING THERE.

And the first week of the festival climaxed. Sunday evening, 7:16. Perhaps ten thousand packed around the staircase. By far the biggest crowd. By far the earliest gathering crowd. And as you looked at them looking at him—the most glamorous film star of his time—there was almost a disbelief moving across them: *My God, is he really truly here?*

He sure was. Not happily, but he was there.

The Milagro Beanfield War, the movie he directed, was showing out of competition. There were those who said the releasing company, Universal, wanted it in competition, but he ruled otherwise. In any case, when it played for the press that morning, it had received by far the most enthusiastic reaction of any of the films preceding it, and even at the end I suspect would have won some prize or other.

The picture had failed badly in America. It cost an amazing amount of money for what it was—kind of a sweet Capra film for the eighties. And probably his appearance was because, as has been said, the movie business is about the next job, and the publicity of his being at Cannes would be a tremendous push to the European release of the film.

He was charming at his press conference earlier in the day, facing perhaps nine hundred reporters (the only similar gathering would be Eastwood, a week later). There were some complaints about the translations of the questions put to him. But none about his sometimes serious, sometimes witty answers.

And he was charming now as he stood halfway up the staircase, waving to the mob, smiling, graciously having the performers from the movie he'd brought along share the spotlight with him. And he would be charming as the numberless reporters followed him into the lobby of the Palais, snapping away. He would be charming all the way to his seat until the lights went down and the movie started. Then he would leave the theater, slip out of the building and the city, his obligation done and done skillfully.

If his film directing had been as skillful as his appearance, the movie would have been a worldwide success. Even as a failure, it marked a tremendous step forward for him, odd when you consider his only other movie, *Ordinary People*, done eight years earlier, had won him an Academy Award.

But that honor, earned as it certainly was, might easily have been considered a personal victory rather than an artistic one. *Ordinary People* triumphed over *Raging Bull*, which many critics consider the finest movie of the decade.

The Milagro Beanfield War takes place in an amazingly small town in New Mexico, where an ordinary guy named Joe decides to illegally irrigate his parched beanfield with water that's been earmarked for a major development. A clash follows with all the power on the side of the big guys, the land developers against the poor oppressed townspeople.

Guess who wins?

We are dealing here with fable, and if satire is what closes on Saturday, believe that fable is no walk in the park either. The fact is, fable just can't be made to work in this jaundiced era except in remarkable circumstances. Yet miraculously, Redford pulls it off.

The movie is more or less in two different worlds, the fable and real life. Once you've got the fable, the real-life chunk— the villains—is easy.

And Redford louses it up. He's got terrific actors—Christopher Walken, Richard Bradford, Melanie Griffith—playing the villains, but they've none of them got anything to cheer about. They're instructed to overplay, their characters become grotesquely cartoonish, and they fatally damage the rest of the film, the fable part—if the enemy is made of marshmallow, the soldiers can't have much of a victory. Why Redford was so wrong with the villainous land developers no one can say— he's a land developer himself, that may have altered his "take" on their attitudes. The fact is, he was "this close" to a glory.

And the fact that two thirds of the movie was so different, difficult, and wonderful makes several things evident: the eight years between films was a waste of major proportions. And should he desire, he doesn't have to act anymore—he is a director now, or could be if that's the way he wants to move; his talent is that impressive.

But it wasn't his talent that brought the ten thousand to the steps of the Palais this May evening. And it wasn't his beauty, though as he stood there waving in his tux and glasses, he looked better preserved than most of us on the planet.

Astaire had it.

Rogers didn't.

Grant had it.

Wayne didn't.

Garbo had it.

Gable too.

No TV star has it—except Selleck.

Stallone couldn't spell it.

Newman wishes it would go away.

Brando had it—three hundred pounds ago.

Dean didn't have it—till he died.

The subject, of course, is glamour, the greatest special effect in movies. Also the most difficult to achieve. Also, again, the most important.

Glamour is what elevates fandom.

Without glamour, movies are just, ugh, movies.

And everyone in the business knows this essential truth: *close up, glamour does not exist.* The dictionary throws a bunch of words at us in definition—charm, fascination, magic. Preceded by the phrase "often illusory."

My definition? Not so hotsy. But you know how all of us go through life with our noses pressed against the windowpane, trying to peek inside where all the good stuff's going on? Well, all those people inside, to us individually, are glamorous.

Without glamour, Cannes is just these strips of celluloid.

Which is kind of how it began, in '46. There was a certain stated loftiness of purpose. (Although there are those naysayers who claim that the entire reason for the existence of the festival is tourism. No one came to Cannes in May. The festival, if it succeeded, would bring gobs of money to the town when not much else was going on. In other words, "Hey, gang, let's put on a film festival.")

The Venice Film Festival was in existence first. (Cannes was going to be France's answer to Italy.) In '46, there were your normal glitches and stumbles, but after '51, the event became annual. But it was just this town in France with movies going on.

Then Simone Silva took off her scarf.

She had been married to a Mr. Silver, but a name change was no problem. Twenty-five and stacked, she'd done a few movies, bad-girl parts. Small ones. Not enough for one of her ambitions. "My bust measures an inch bigger than Jane Russell's . . . after all, how long can a bust last?"

Time not being on her side, she needed to speed things up a bit. The opportunity came in the spring of '54, at a picnic held in connection with the festival. Her picnic costume consisted of a grass skirt, the soon to be legendary scarf top. Robert Mitchum and his wife were also at the picnic. Surrounded by photographers. Spotting Simone, the paparazzi apparently implored her to rid herself of the scarf. Simone moved right next to the actor.

Where this took place isn't quite clear. The books say near a cliff. The pictures of Bob and Simone look mighty close to water level. Unimportant.

She doffed it.

There was a considerable scramble once the event occurred. Three cameramen fell into the Mediterranean, another broke an ankle, a fifth fractured an elbow.

Mitchum, ever the gent, put his arms around her, covering her breasts with his hands. Or did his best to. And if the calendar photo of La Monroe is the most famous pinup shot in America during this epoch, the Mitchum/Silva set runs it a pretty close second. She was gorgeous, he was not just a famous star, he was a dangerous one (jailed for marijuana).

My God, the world wondered, what's going on over there? What are all those beautiful people doing?

I want to do it too.

It's very safe to say that no actress did as much to lock in the fame of Cannes as Mrs. Silver. She and it got amazing amounts of publicity. It survived, she didn't, dying three years later, still in her twenties; of what, no one is quite sure.

The festival and the stars have been feeding on each other in ever-increasing need. This year, as well as Redford and Eastwood, the Cannes publicity listings indicated that Schwarzenegger was there, Chuck Norris too, Belmondo, Deneuve, De Niro, Gere, Kirk's son Michael, Hoskins, Von Sydow, Sting, Braga.

What they do is add to each other's reality.

And that's important, because you must know this about the life of a movie star: it's fake. By definition. (All acting is, that's why they call it "acting" and not "realing.") But stage actors don't generally get locked into the heroic mold.

Not *that* much bigger than life.

Spencer Tracy, so rumor has it, for the last fifteen years of his great career had one stipulation concerning any part he played: no makeup. He had to be able to just drive to work, walk on the set, and do it. There was something, he indicated, unmanly about the life of a male star. The primping, all of that. He couldn't take the phoniness anymore.

Wonderful true Stallone story. He was doing an action flick (no surprise so far), and a major paper sent a reporter to do a long piece on him. This was post-*Rocky* but pre-*Rambo*, when he was relatively new to superstardom. Now you must know this: stars do not do their own stunts. (Except, bless him, Burt Lancaster.) For many reasons, mainly two: 1. They stink at them, and even if they're vaguely competent, they're not in a class with stuntmen. 2. Insurance. Stunts are dangerous. If a stuntman gets hurt, that's obviously a terrible thing, but there are other stuntmen. If a star gets hurt, there goes your schedule, your budget, possibly your picture, conceivably your career.

Anyway, the reporter—who knew *nothing* about movies, which is standard—was witness to Stallone causing a ruckus. Why? Because he insisted on doing this terribly dangerous stunt. Now the director's stunned and trying to head off what may be a career-ending day for him, because if Stallone does the stunt and gets hurt, who's going to trust him again? "Sly," he is saying. "Come on, guy!" And Stallone's saying that he can do the damn thing, and the director says he knows that, hell, Sly could do it better than the stuntman, but there's the problem with insurance—

—Screw the insurance.

—Sly, hey, come on, guy.

Finally, with the reporter watching it all, Stallone moodily agrees to the chicken director's beseeching, goes off to do the interview. The reporter, naturally, reported on Stallone's bravery.

Now why would an international figure like Sylvester Stallone go through the masquerade? He's got as many fans as any performer in the world, he's been well paid, he can write (*Rocky I*), he can direct. He's doing it because he was still trying to cling to the pretense that he was what he seemed on screen.

He's reformed his physique into a thing of beauty. His hairstylist should get a Pulitzer. (Take a look at him in his early work.) But Stallone cannot bring down battalions—explosives experts do that. He can't whip Mike Tyson. He's just this New York kid with a lot of drive, the talent to go with it, who caught lightning in a bottle. Eventually, I wouldn't be surprised if, like Tracy, he started taking parts that didn't need makeup. Something's eating at him anyway.

And if I've dealt with men here, it's probably because there are so few female stars today, and not many of them attended the festival. But the falseness is, if anything, more true with women.

Women don't look the way they look in movies. Ingmar Bergman met Garbo. Not the kid Garbo, the mature one, but she still took his head off. One of the two most glamorous actresses since sound. (I'll get to the other in a second.)

And then he saw her close up—

—saw her mouth in close-up—

—the lines, the terrible vertical lines—

—over and out.

. . . it was dark, creeping toward morning. The man drove as quietly as possible up to the dark house, turned off the motor. Inside was his quarry . . . the most desired woman in the world . . .

. . . he was skilled at getting into the place. The man was expert when it came to his work, and he was working now. He moved quietly to the bedroom, pushed open the bedroom door . . .

. . . the most desired woman in the world was there . . .

. . . asleep . . .

. . . just a negligee . . .

. . . he took a breath, moved in on her, reached down, grabbed her with his small hands . . . she fought . . . he expected that . . . didn't faze him . . . he lifted her . . . she fought . . . the most famous breasts of the twentieth century pressed against his body . . . he did his best to ignore them . . .

. . . chalk . . .

. . . that was the body's color . . .

. . . stone . . .

. . . the body was heavy as stone . . .

. . . he dragged her across the room . . . her eyes were open

now . . . her mouth was open now, going "don't . . . don't
please . . ."

. . . he was relentless . . . he had his job to do . . . she sagged
toward the floor . . . the move surprised him . . . she slipped
from his grasp . . . thudded down . . . he bent, lifted her, his
hands grazing her breasts now . . .

. . . they had no life at all . . .

. . . as he lifted her and held her very tightly so as to
be sure she wouldn't fall again, he was aware of what he
dreaded . . .

. . . the smell . . .

. . . the constant, building smell . . .

. . . vomit . . .

. . . her body had vomit all over . . . her breath smelled of
liquor and who could count the pills . . . her breath smelled
like a coroner's office . . .

. . . always did . . . at least these mornings . . .

. . . he dragged her into the bathroom, managed to get the
shower going strong, forced her under the spray, held her
there, and kept her there until some life came inside her skin,
some tone returned to her muscles . . .

. . . then he took a giant towel, wrapped it around her,
turned off the shower, carried her out of the house to his car,
put her in the back . . .

. . . and drove her to the studio where the hair and makeup
people might get their fingers on Marilyn Monroe so she might
only be a few hours late for the morning call of her greatest
success in her most glamorous role. . . .

Tell that to the thousands at the steps of the Palais. Talk about
what it was like getting Monroe to work when she was still at
her peak. Explain to them that Presley was such an incontinent
husk he had to wear towels as diapers.

They don't want to hear that.

And you know what? Neither do I.

I know glamour doesn't exist.

I know it's all horseshit.

But I need it.

I want my morning fix of stardom. I want to believe now what I did once. I'm just like the people by the stairs. Hell, I *was* the people by the stairs, staring up.

Redford just standing there.

Now, the left hand rises. A wave. He turns, starts up the red carpet toward the Palais door.

The crowd became silent, all their eyes on him. He was leaving them. Going someplace so splendid, where fountains were golden, champagne always poured, the music, such sweet music, never stopped.

Redford stopped.

At the highest Palais stair. And turned one final time to face the thousands. A last generous wave. A quick perfect smile.

Then—

—then he was—

—alas—

—gone.

Murmurs. Not angry at all. He had been so splendid for them, worth the hours of standing there, definitely a three-star stop.

Little children were removed from shoulders. From somewhere, a dog got loose, did its best to run. A collective sigh. He was gone. Yes. True. He had been wonderful, all they could have hoped, but now he was the past. Again, the collective sigh. But not a morose sound at all. Not one of sadness. Yes, one of life's great experiences had just ended.

But remember: Richard Gere is coming tomorrow.

12. THE OCEAN FLOOR

THE SECOND JURY MEETING, three days later, was not a happy occasion. We talked about five films, none of which I'll go into. The one I liked best I noted was told badly. The one I liked least, my comment was, "Bring back *The Big Blue*."

The jury showed some interest in a greenish-tinted Polish film about a punk who kills a cab driver for no reason, but the murder takes, oh, fifteen minutes. The press group at eight-thirty was laughing through the last part of the murder.

As we got ready to leave for the day, a definite panic had set in. We were halfway through and *nothing*. We told ourselves things had to improve. What we didn't say out loud was what if these that we'd seen so far were the best Cannes had to offer?

It was an awful feeling. We wanted to fall in love, but not only were the ladies ignoring us, they weren't even coming to the dance. I think it's safe to say that we all felt like the old joke that goes: "We had a beauty contest in our town, and the girls were so ugly that nobody won. . . ."

AT 1:45 ON THURSDAY AFTERNOON, this scream startled everyone in the jury box. I think it's safe to say that few of them
wanted a repetition of such behavior.

The jurors, the way the seating was set up, had two rows
in the auditorium reserved for them and their guests. And at
the formal evening showings, that's where they sat. But for
the other shows, there was a special place that actually belonged
to the city of Cannes. It was in the center in the rear, had its
own private entrance and waiting room with couches, chairs,
etc., and was the place where guests of the city or executives
in the city hierarchy watched movies. We were allowed there
during the day, as, usually, few honchos were around. It was
a pleasant perk. You were separated from the riffraff, could
stretch out, feel good about yourself.

It was from here, as the movie *Pelle the Conqueror* was into
end credits, that the scream came. George Miller, at the next
meeting of the jury, commented on the behavior, felt that it
must not be repeated, since it was obviously committed by a
fool and clearly didn't enhance anyone's reputation for either
intelligence or impartiality.

I totally agreed with Miller. I more or less had to (since I
was the fool who screamed). George was sitting near me, and
when I stood and let fly, his head spun pretty good. I knew
the jury was supposed to just sit there and show nothing. I

knew we weren't allowed to give any indication of how we felt about a flick, since no one was supposed to know anything until after the final day's voting.

I couldn't help it. I'd just lost my heart.

Pelle the Conqueror was a lot more than one of the films of the decade. It was the sixteenth film I'd seen at Cannes, and I was giving up hope. I'd gone that morning, as always, ignorant of what I was to see. The first half hour was okay, but at the hour mark we were picking up the pace, *Pelle* and I. (I didn't know it then, but it was 150 minutes long; seemed like 40.) Now, at the ninety-minute mark, I've laughed a lot, cried only once, and I'm thinking, Shit, keep it going, you haven't made any mistakes yet, don't fuck it up, *please*, and when we were into the story two hours, I wasn't aware of it, I was just riveted. But Paul Newman said that the last fifteen minutes are the most important of any movie, and how were they going to end it, were they going to get soppy, or pseudotragic, or what?

They ended it beautifully. Everyone was dead silent in the packed place. Twenty-four-hundred media folk staring at that gorgeous screen. And when it ended, I clapped. I'm not much of a clapper, I like to listen instead, gauging the audience, but I couldn't have cared less about the audience now—and I didn't care what the critics would eventually say. What I'd seen was half a step down from a masterpiece—

—and I had to acknowledge that.

So the scream.

I had no idea it was even in there that day. But suddenly out it came, ripping past my throat into the giant darkened room, making heads turn all over the place.

Let 'em.

The scream went higher and higher. My throat began to hurt.

I could deal with that later.

Finally, I sank back into my seat, just exhausted. The credits ended, the lights came on. I looked at Miller near me, just as moved as I was. We exited the jury box, paused. Then he said it: "It's really the greatest mystery, isn't it? When a story works."

No argument. He had it with *Mad Max*, me with *Butch*. It's the most stunning magic trick the movies have. When it happens.

But why does it happen? That's the goddamn eternal mystery, the quest that sends so many writers 'round the bend.

Pelle is a Danish film that is not just better, it's different, the difference being this: it's the first rite-of-passage *epic* I can remember. Most rite-of-passage movies (or books: *The Catcher in the Rye*) are relatively short. Here is the outline of the movie as it's listed in the official program of the festival:

> Swedish Lasse and his nine-year-old son Pelle emigrate to Denmark at the end of the last century. They get the ungrateful job of cattlemen on a farm, where they are treated like slaves. Pelle lives through many humiliations and witnesses several tragedies. Through these events, he develops a strong urge for freedom and preserves his zest for life which is kept alive mainly by his father's boundless love and his close relationship with the farmhand Erik, the only person who dares to rebel against the authorities. In spite of many disappointments and disillusions, Lasse still preserves his dream of a more dignified life. In the end, Pelle revolts, and leaves to conquer the world.

Ho-hum, right?

Some Swedish kid on a farm in Denmark close to a hundred years ago. *That's* exciting?

Believe it. But just reading the outline, it doesn't sound like anything special. Even adding in that Max von Sydow plays the father in perhaps the greatest work of his great career, on top of which the boy who plays his son already understands pain, it still doesn't come alive.

It's in the telling that it breathes.

Stanley Kubrick once said that a really good story is a miracle.

And what's a really good story? Oh, something that begins

with an interesting premise, builds in a logical yet surprising way, comes to a satisfying conclusion.

Sounds so easy.

But you can't hold it in your hands.

Let me give an example of truly atrocious storytelling. The other movie that day was a monster from Chile, a political "thriller" called *Cisco*. Cisco is the name of a city in Chile— we're in the future, folks—and the plot is about people in a politically oppressive system trying to leave and find freedom. (Please bear with me, this won't take long.)

Know this: the first five minutes of a movie are *essential*. You're introducing your people, setting up your world in an *interesting* way—not *one second* can be wasted.

Lights out, roll of drums, hold your stomachs: *Cisco*.

Credits—shown over a map of South America. Also some corny, anthemlike music.

Now a voice-over. (Note: the voice-over—that's the use of a narrator to tell the story—can be a fascinating device. Billy Wilder in *Sunset Boulevard* even has William Holden's character do the voice-over, and his character's dead.) But what you don't do is *just* have the voice-over at the start. *Cisco* just has the voice at the start, then totally abandons the device.

And what the voice tells us, portentously, is that things are tough getting to Cisco, even tougher getting out. While he's giving us this info, we see clumsy shots of people walking or taking a boat to get to Cisco, and we know that's where they're going, because when we don't see shots of people, we see maps (again) and dotted lines showing us our destination.

(We just wasted *a minute* on this.)

Opening sequence: a cop talks on the phone saying that two blank American passports have been stolen from some couriers. If anybody gets them, they can just fill in their own photos and leave town on the one plane that flies in and out and no one can stop them. So now some obvious shots of police rounding up some suspects, shooting others who try to get away.

(Another minute.)

Now, a scene with two rich old folks watching the suspects

get herded into the police station. A sleazy guy explains (again) that these blank passports have been stolen and look out for thieves in Cisco. Then the sleazy guy leaves the rich couple, but not before stealing the guy's passport.

(Yup—another minute wasted on that sucker.)

Now, the next big sequence—the commie villain flies into town and meets the local authorities, who are buffoons. Oh, by the way, he says, any news on those two stolen passports?

(That's their third mention.)

(In six minutes of snooze.)

Can't you just feel how terrible this junk is? You haven't met anyone important. You've been told and told again the one frail piece of data you should have. This entire six minutes could be easily compressed into thirty seconds of good stuff.

But you know what?

It couldn't work better.

How can I be sure?

Because *Cisco* isn't *Cisco*, it's really the opening of *Casablanca*, one of the great pieces of storytelling in all of American films. (I just changed the visa to a passport, the Nazis to commie bad guys.)

Academically, *Casablanca* has no chance of working. None.

But it does.

Why?

After *Pelle* was done, a group of us—Miller; the two Elenas (star and translator); Robinson, the English critic; Müller, the Dutch cinematographer—went to La Mère Besson for lunch, and just talked for hours, trying, in various languages, to figure it out.

Why did we cry?

Why did we care so?

At the end, this little kid walks alone across this vast icy terrain, going off without his father, without friends, no money, nothing. And it's a triumph. A few minutes earlier, his wonderful, weak, loving, drunken father says good-bye to his greatest pride in life, wishes him well—and doesn't try to stop him. He knows the kid might die. We know the kid might die.

But the kid knows different. He's eleven, sure, but nothing's going to bring him down. He's seen such suffering his two years on this farm, and he knows there's got to be better.

Out there. Waiting for him. Big deal if he has to walk across what looks like the frozen Sahara—*it's waiting for him*. And somehow his confidence makes us confident too. We sit, profoundly moved, knowing something wonderfully *right* has just been given us.

We sat at the restaurant for hours, babbling our way, trying to find the heart of the artichoke. The movie worked. On every level, *Pelle* worked.

But dammit, why?

Why?

Maybe the Shadow knows.

I sure don't.

All I do know is this: story is where we all begin. Forget all the crap the intellectual critics (contradiction in terms) spew at us. If you don't care about the story, if you're not hooked, screw the rest. Critics didn't begin wondering what the symbolism was in *The Little Engine That Could*. They weren't fascinated by the alliterative wordplay.

They were like all the rest of us—they were rooting for the train to get the toys over the mountain.

Now we progress from that point, obviously, but this much is still true: narrative is only a piece of string, and it's where you choose to cut it that's essential.

Where *you* choose to cut it. I might pick a piece farther along, or earlier. No one is right. There is no right way to tell a story, only your way.

And I'm glad it's a mystery, because if the computer schmucks ever figure it out, then anyone will write wonderful stories, and if anybody can, nobody will.

And that, folks, we don't want. We need our storytellers. Somebody's got to keep us alive through the dangerous night when the flames are flickering and the wolves howl. That's all, by the by, that storytellers do.

Not a bad occupation, truth to tell.

But in case you're wondering why there aren't better scripts, better stories, better *thinking* that goes into a project that will probably cost upward of fifteen million dollars . . .

It has been written elsewhere that most stars are very bright but, for the most part, equally uneducated. Whatever truth the observation may contain, it needn't be limited to performers. An amazing number of powerful and very successful people simply do not read a lot other than the grosses in *Variety*. If they have to read a book, they don't, they read "coverage," a Hollywood invention. Coverage is a synopsis, occasionally written by someone who is literate. There are often two kinds—very short—

> *War and Peace*
> by Leo Tolstoy
> Yarn concerns a love triangle set against a European war involving Napoleon. Expensive but has potential to be another *Zhivago* with the right director.

—and very long. (I've seen coverage of over thirty pages. Please note the word *seen*—I will, I hope, go to my grave without ever actually reading any coverage.)

The following story is, at best, only an okay one, because it is so ordinary, no matter what you might think.

A small publishing house recently reprinted several novels by John O'Hara, dead these twenty years. A leading book critic was so pleased, she wrote an entire column about *Hope of Heaven*, a thirties Hollywood novel. The review was, to put it mildly, a rave. Soon the publisher got a phone call from a famous Hollywood producer. They went through the standard intro bit. Then the producer got down to the meat of the call.

"Read the O'Hara review. Fantastic."

"We never expected anything of that kind; we're thrilled."

"Do you own the movie rights?" the producers asked.

"No. We just publish the book."

"Do you know who does own the rights?"

"Sorry, I don't."

"Well, do you have O'Hara's phone number so I can get in touch with him myself?"

One final point about the story—if you had said to the producer, *"Asshole, he died in 1970!"* he wouldn't have been embarrassed at all. Why should he be? O'Hara hadn't had a hit in years. . . .

IT WAS DURING THE third meeting that the battle lines became clear.

We had seen seventeen of the twenty-one films in competition, and what I began to realize was that Gilles Jacob orchestrated the festival in the sense that he didn't fire his heavy guns, or what he thought they might be, till after the halfway point. The most talked-about film of the fortnight, *Bird*, was due the following morning. The other final three were, at best, long shots. *Bird* aside, we were going to know the contenders before the third meeting closed.

There would be, I knew, two. One, clearly, was *Pelle the Conqueror*. Not only was it too splendid to ignore, the lunch after made me positive that at least half the jury looked at it as a possible winner of the *Palme d'Or*.

The other contender had to be the American movie *Miles from Home*. I thought it was eccentric, different, original. I also was aware of my American bias. After I saw it, I ran into Barry Norman of the BBC and Roger Ebert, the most famous film critic we have, thanks to television, plus his outlets in both New York and Chicago, his home base. (Ebert, the only film critic ever to win the Pulitzer Prize for movie work, has written a lovely book about Cannes, *Two Weeks in the Midday Sun*, and I consider him the eminence [not so] grise of the festival.) I was gagged, but they weren't. I asked what they thought.

Ebert liked it. A lot. But he's also American.

Norman felt the same way Ebert did.

Buttressed, I thanked them and went on my way.

Miles from Home is not, repeat not, a farm movie. Not any more than *Butch Cassidy* is the story of a couple of cowboys. It's about these two brothers (Richard Gere and Kevin Anderson) who've been brought up on a farm and early on lose it to the banks through no real fault of their own.

It's about, as their production notes put it, "how two brothers react to losing the family home and the effect this economic and emotional stress has on their relationship."

They go slightly crazed—there's a *Bonnie and Clyde*–like feel to some of it. They burn buildings, rob banks, become, in their world, famous. Their adventures darken. It's not a happy ending.

A first feature directed by Gary Sinise, it has some sensational sequences. The bank robbery where it turns out they know the people in the bank is as crazed and exciting as anything the festival had to offer.

I saw it before *Pelle* and was hooked. *Pelle* overtook it for me, but they were the one-two punch, no question. Not that there weren't flaws. In fact, one of the flaws is particularly worth noting.

Weight.

A lot of wise gray heads in the entertainment field believe, as do I, that on your first day of rehearsal your fate is pretty much sealed. The script has to be solid. And the performers have to resonate properly.

Early on in the anguished life of *All the President's Men*, Robert Redford, who produced it and who has not been dumb for many, many years, commented that probably he was wrong for the part he was going to play, young reporter Bob Woodward.

And why?

Because the whole pulse behind that story was based on the fact that Woodward and Bernstein were these two nothing reporters. Not that experienced. Without a great network of tipsters. They fumbled, sure, and stumbled some, but they were pluggers, no one outworked them. And so their inexperience eventually proved no handicap.

They were, in other words, unknowns.

Redford was a star.

So the weight he brought to the part might go against the truth of the story, jar it out of orbit. (But since Warner Bros. had only got involved with the project because he was going to be in it, there was never any doubt that he was going to be in it.)

He made one other point: Bernstein also had to be played by a star. (There were only two thought right: Hoffman and Pacino.) Because if he played against an unknown, as good as that unknown might be, as correct as he might also be, it wouldn't feel right.

An unknown would screw up the balance.

I think that happened in *Miles from Home*. Richard Gere's is a famous face; Kevin Anderson, a brilliant young talent, is as yet known more to his family than to the outside world. And they were both marvelous—I don't think Gere's ever been better.

But there was, I admit, something a bit off-kilter about the endeavor.

Still, it was terrific, I knew it, and I knew the jury felt the same. And it was not, repeat not, a farm movie.

The jury thought it was just another American farm movie, like *The River* or any number of other recent Hollywood stiffs. I tried explaining they were wrong. That this wasn't a movie where the cast stayed up all night picking the crop before the tornado set in.

Sorry.

I put my case with some intellectual accuracy—this goddamn thing wasn't no farm movie.

To all my peers in the room from all around the globe, that's all it was. And they didn't much want to talk about it, because they didn't much like it. *Miles from Home* was dead.

A World Apart was very much alive. And kicking.

I was stunned.

(Though that was not wise—it, along with *Pelle*, had got the loudest and most passionate applause at the screenings.)

A World Apart is an anti-apartheid movie.

> It's based on a true story and takes place in South Africa in 1963. It focuses on the relationship between a white woman, politically committed to the fight against apartheid, and her thirteen-year-old daughter. Set against a backdrop of increasingly violent repression, it chronicles the effects of the breakup of the family, and is, above all, about the child's attempts to come to terms with the political choices her parents have made.

Another first feature, this one directed by the brilliant cinematographer Chris Menges (Oscars for *The Killing Fields* and *The Mission*), it obviously looks great. It's solidly written. (The writer, Shawn Slovo, knew the material—it's based on the story of her life.) And the acting by Barbara Hershey (was she ever really once "Barbara Seagull"?) as the mother, Jodhi May as her daughter, and Linda Mvusi as the family maid is splendid ensemble work.

My problem with it? I thought it was preaching to the converted.

I was never bored and never surprised. The movie's goodness of heart was relentless. It insisted, every second, on being on the side of the angels.

Another problem for me was this: I've done two pictures with Sir Richard Attenborough, and liked *Cry Freedom*, liked it a lot more than *A World Apart*.

But sometimes I don't trust me, especially when I'm seeing

something done by someone I want to succeed. I blot out flaws, raise high points even higher.

Was I doing that here? I didn't think so, at least not at first. But there was a lot of passion in the room for *A World Apart*. So much so that I began to fear for *Pelle*.

I argued against it—tried to be intelligent.

These waves crashed against me. "Bill, you're wrong, it's not about preaching to anybody, much less to the converted." —"Bill, *Cry Freedom* doesn't matter, this is a story that needs to be told and told and told again." —"Bill, you've got to put aside your preconceptions." —"Bill, are you listening to what you're saying?" —"Bill, why are you so stubborn?" —"Bill, why can't you see?" —"Bill—" "Bill—" "*Bill, this is important—*"

I was rocked. I somehow sensed then that we were in for a three-way battle for the prize, *Pelle* and *World* and probably *Bird*.

We talked and argued and all these smart people kept pointing out my errors to me and I suddenly thought, My God, what if they're right? I mean, if enough people tell you you're drunk, lie down. My back was beginning to ache. In a few minutes, I knew there'd be pain.

Then Nastassja Kinski, with her wonderful face and Audrey Hepburn voice, reached across the table toward me and said with such sweet sadness, *"Bill, Bill, you're so cut off, why do you think so much?"*

I didn't know the answer. Probably because of my occupation—it's unnatural, spending most of one's waking hours going into a room alone. I've been doing it for thirty-three years, and I hate my pit. I dread going there, I'd love not to, but I'm afraid that once I stop and find out maybe how easy it is to do nothing, I'll end up doing nothing.

I've never had a real job—college, the army, grad school, and at twenty-four, my first novel got taken. I have had a theory for years and it's this: the trouble with novels is they're all written by writers.

By which I mean, we're not exactly a broad spectrum of any

society you'd want to belong to. Nutballs, most of us. And I truly believe if you took a random sampling of a hundred people across the country and gave them enough to live on and told them whatever they put down would be totally anonymous, what they wrote would not be at all close to what we "professionals" do.

I'll always remember where my mind went when Kinski reached out to me and said those words: I'm cut off because of what I've done with my life, and if I weren't, not only would I be an infinitely happier human, I also wouldn't be getting divorced after twenty-seven years. . . .

A MONTH AFTER HIS TRIUMPHS at Cannes, Clint Eastwood was sitting in his office at the Burbank studios, talking about the week he spent there.

"I'd been there before. With *Pale Rider*. It was an American western, without political overtones, and you don't plan on coming away with much. But they seemed to like it, which is always pleasing.

"They decided what I needed that time was privacy, so they stuck me out on a boat in the harbor. The weather was terrible, the boat didn't go anywhere, and the press was always circling around. I was a prisoner. If I wanted to take a walk, I'd do it at three, four in the morning. This time I stayed at a hotel."

One of the problems the festival has is this: all major studios and most directors of note are afraid to show their movies there. "What if it doesn't win?" is their logic. Which is horseshit. *Patty Hearst* is about to open as I write this, and I don't think too many moviegoers are saying, "Hey, let's skip the Hearst thing, it didn't get any prizes in France three months ago." Gilles Jacob, who selects the films, has commented, "Often when they don't know what to do with a movie, they're happy to give it to us."

Eastwood doesn't share the studio sentiment. "Why not show? I wanted to go with *Play Misty for Me*." (Now, often referred to as *Fatal Attraction I*.) "If it's a good film, go. Jacob saw a rough cut of *Bird* and wanted it. It's an honor to be invited to Cannes."

Bird, written by Joel Oliansky and starring Forest Whitaker as the jazzman Charlie Parker, Diane Venora as Chan, his white wife, is a spectacular piece of work. Different. It runs almost two and three-quarter hours, and if *Pelle* is a rite-of-passage epic, *Bird* is something equally rare—an intimate one. (The only other I can come up with, though wildly different, is *Scenes from a Marriage*.)

Why so long?

"I had to have the music because the music is part of the genius of the man. And while I was preparing it, people, jazz buffs, would say to me, 'Is this going to be another of those pictures where they play four bars and then everyone starts talking?' I told them it wasn't going to be that kind of movie."

Quietly, Eastwood is having one of the remarkable careers. *Bird* is his thirteenth job as a director. He is also, and this is a shock, the most consistently durable popular star in the history of American films. Others—Gable, Wayne, Brando—have been stars longer. But they have all had tremendous dips in their careers. Eastwood is now starting his third decade as an international phenomenon. More than any of his contemporaries, he seems to be heading toward some pleasing destination with a great deal of style.

God knows he was stylish at Cannes. He handled his interviews quietly and well. He quieted the madness of his press conference, talked seriously about how they created the extraordinary sound track, graciously handed out plaudits to his stars, who were nervously seated alongside him in front of the maybe a thousand reporters, the endless camera crews. After close to an hour, a Frenchwoman stood up and berated him for not allowing enough time to the radio reporters. "You should give us more," she said. "You mean make your day?" he replied, getting a good laugh, bringing the conference to a proper conclusion.

He seemed, as he sat there talking, perhaps more proud of *Bird* than any other of his films. Charlie Parker, one of the legitimate jazz legends, was not an easy catch.

As portrayed in *Bird*, Parker was a drunk, a drug addict, a philanderer. All he really had in his corner was the fact that he was a genius when it came to jazz. One of the remarkable things about the movie is this: no apologizing, no excuses, self-pity's been banished. Warts and all, it says, here I am. Like me or not.

Also unusual is what the movie doesn't show. He's a drug addict. But I think there is maybe one shot of a needle in the movie, and he's not using it. He was just a drug addict. Like him or not.

The wife. You know there's got to be a sequence where they get humiliated and turned away from a hotel, a restaurant.

Nope.

It's just about music, the dark lives of musicians, the impossibility of ever having two loves.

All of this directed by this action star.

Who's not really all that tough. ''The night we screened it at Cannes, I went up those stairs—that's an awesome experience—and I waved and went to my seat, but as soon as the lights went down, I waited just long enough to check that the sound was okay, then I snuck out and waited in an office until five minutes before it ended. Then I went back to my seat. I just couldn't have sat there. I didn't have nerve enough. Too terrifying. To sit there and agonize over the choices you've already made after you've seen it so many times—I just couldn't face it. I just need someone to tell me it's okay.

''But at the end, when the lights came up, I was there and they seemed to like it. That was a wonderful moment. Of course, it's always wonderful when they don't throw cabbages at you.''

It was by far the outstanding directorial work of the fortnight. The only stigma being Eastwood and our memories of all those action films. How dare he attempt a serious movie? And bring it off. I believe that if Francis Coppola had directed it, frame for frame, the critics would have put him back on top with Woody Allen. And if Allen had done it, they would have elevated him up alongside Welles.

But Dirty Harry had done the deed. He was the best director. And now it was up to me to bring him home. . . .

GEORGE MILLER WAS LATE, looking for a balloon.

He and I were to be picked up in a festival car by nine in the morning. I was there. He wasn't. I called his hotel. He'd left. Since his place was one block from mine, I was pretty sure he hadn't got lost.

Eventually, he appeared, affable as ever. (I wonder sometimes is it a national law that *all* Australians have to be affable? No Otto Premingers down under? A total absence of Von Stroheims?)

He had been, he announced, *sur la plage*, trying to find a goddamn kid's balloon, because when they had a new pope, they sent up puffs of smoke; when we had a winner, wouldn't a balloon be in order?

There was a certain logic to his search. The festival took this last day with more than a *soupçon* of seriousness.

We were to be out front at nine.

We were to be comfortably dressed, for the day's discussions.

We were to pack our formal wear because we would not be allowed to return to our hotels to change after the voting.

We were to be driven someplace.

The destination of which we were not to be told.

Once there, we would go into a room and begin debate.

We were not allowed to leave the room for any reason other than the calls of Nature.

No working the phones.

In other words, we were locked in with each other till it was done. The logic behind these preparations was simple: there was an international television show that evening before the showing of the festival closing film, *Willow* (not in competition). Just like on the Oscar telecast, no one was to have advance word on anything. So, the secrecy.

I'd been up early, had a bitch of a time packing. Two problems: 1. My cassette tapes. We were always told not to leave anything of value in our rooms. For the first time in my life, I had used tapes (microcassette) to remind me of what might be of interest. I knew there was too much for me to jot down. I had a dozen sides filled, this entire book, in point of fact.

Should I leave them in my room? If they were gone when I returned, I'd have no book. I went to Cannes not knowing if I'd write anything. Now, I was convinced I had to give it a shot. I put all my tapes, along with a few toilet articles and my tuxedo shirt and tie, into a small single piece of luggage. My tuxedo jacket I hung on a hanger.

But not my tuxedo pants. (This is 2.)

I could not fit into my fucking tuxedo pants. If I could have worn a turtleneck, I might have pinned my trousers together and who'd be the wiser? But a shirt? A tucked-in shirt? Not even close. I had eaten myself totally out of my costume.

Solution: I had a pair of dark blue slacks that I could survive in. They didn't match, but in the dusk with the light behind me, I figured I had a shot.

My blue slacks on a hanger with my tuxedo jacket, I tried to guess what lay ahead, who the contenders were.

GRAND PRIZE: (billing alphabetical)	*A World Apart* *Bird* *Pelle the Conqueror*
JURY PRIZE: (another word for second)	Whichever of the above came closest to winning and didn't.

DIRECTOR: *A World Apart* (Menges)
                              Bird (Eastwood)
                              Pelle (Bille August)

ACTOR: Forest Whitaker (*Bird*)
                              Max von Sydow (*Pelle*)

ACTRESS: No favorite existed. In fact, no performance
                              had elicited much comment. Odd. (But even-
                              tually essential.)

Miller and I were driven up into the hills behind Cannes. We were both in terrific moods because we'd enjoyed the Cannes experience so.

Which wasn't at all what I thought it would be when I went. I figured the judges would spend a lot of time together, walking and talking, about I don't know what, great flicks and the movie business in our various countries and mutual friends and maybe even what was going on in our lives.

None of that happened. We saw movies at different times of day. We all had friends there, stopping by the festival. Few of us were comfortable with each other's language. If I saw anyone at all, it was Miller—we could converse and we both loved to eat.

But what was wonderful about it all was not the swirl of it, the familiar faces dotting in and out; it was this: I was learning to love film again.

I have a huge problem with movies: I find it very hard to take them seriously. (These are mostly American films I'm talking about.) We know there's got to be a happy ending. We know, with the sequel craze upon us, that no studio would allow an interesting hero to die. (If *For Whom the Bell Tolls* were made today, no way they'd let Gary Cooper kick at the end.)

Think, just for a second, of a pie. Make that pie the whole of human experience. Well, our movies only concern them- selves with the thinnest wedge. There are heroes and there are villains, but there just aren't any ordinary people.

Shit, all I *know* are ordinary people. Have you met a hero lately? I sure haven't.

But at Cannes, being bathed in one attempt after another, failed or not, to cut a wider wedge of pie, that was a fabulous restorative for me. It came at a great time in my life, and I'll treasure the experience always.

We stared back, Miller and I, as the city and the sea receded below us.

Then a quick turn into a hidden estate. We saw gates being closed. We saw uniformed men.

We saw guard dogs held tightly on lead.

No strolling outside for me, folks.

Up ahead now, the mansion was becoming visible. (Not really a mansion, it turned out. At least not a big one. Florentine in style, it had stunning gardens and giant, deep green cypress trees. The view went all the way down to the harbor.)

The place belongs to the city of Cannes; at least that's what I was told. Functions are held there. Otherwise, it's watched over but unoccupied. It had been deeded to the city by its late owner, a hot painter of the twenties named Jean Gabriel Domerque.

We left our cars, gave our luggage to people waiting to take our luggage, and repaired into a large room, with two purple chandeliers and lots of Mr. Domerque's paintings on the wall. Christianne was there. Gilles Jacob was there. The translators were there.

We sat.

We tended to some minor business.

Then we started talking. About the grand prize, the *Palme d'Or*. Scola felt this was going to be the toughest, so we ought to get it done.

Quickly, if we could.

We couldn't.

It turned out that none of the films had enough for a big victory. Scola suggested a preliminary vote. We wrote the name of our choice on a piece of paper, put the paper in a box, brought the box to Scola. He counted.

It came to 6–4, *Pelle* over *A World Apart*.

But that was just the preliminary vote. We could change our minds, obviously. What was to follow was over two hours of the most passionate movie talk I'd ever been involved in. Because the *World Apart* folks were, if anything, more intense than the *Pelle* people.

Of which I, shrinking violet, was the most outspoken.

There was no right answer, of course. It was, truly, a beauty contest. Were we to select the movie that we would most recommend to a serious friend? Or were we after the flick that in twenty-five years might still be around?

For example: the one classic film I saw in '87 was the last film directed by John Huston, James Joyce's *The Dead*. As long as there're Bergman and Fellini, this baby's going to be alive.

At least I think so.

But no guarantees.

Hope and Glory had a lot of fans that year. *Broadcast News*. *The Last Emperor* won the works. I thought it was dull, ponderous, all those swell things. But it didn't just win in America, it's never stopped collecting ribbons.

And I say *The Dead* is the classic?

Scola made the one genuine criticism of *Pelle*: it smacked of television. Not in content, not in the look, but in the way the narrative unspooled. Did we want to give the grand prize to this kind of movie?

Answer: if *Gone With the Wind* were in the festival, people would say it smacked of television. (In fact, if *Gone With the Wind* came out today as a novel and had the same kind of success, I think it would end up as a miniseries. No studio would have the guts to make a three-hour-and-forty-minute movie.)

Besides, someone said, *Pelle* made me cry.

In rebuttal: Tears are easy. Never trust tears!

Back to television—which is devastating European films. Fewer and fewer people are going to movies. The whole continent's becoming bilingual couch potatoes. And it's not like America—in Europe, the film business is gasping. Is *Pelle* the kind of message you want to send?

Well, what's so great about the message of *A World Apart*? That apartheid is an abomination? You don't stop the presses over that. Besides, *A World Apart* wasn't a contemporary story—the movie takes place back in 1963, thereby weakening the point they wish to make—*it's going on right now.*

What is good in cinema? somebody said. Answer that. What is good?

But for whom, Charlie? . . .

You feel better when you leave *Pelle*.

You feel better when you eat sweets.

A World Apart gives us a conscience.

So does the Catholic Church.

An hour of this.

Half an hour more.

Then: what about sharing the award—a show of hands in favor of sharing the award.

Too few in favor.

(The six of us for *Pelle* had the upper hand, obviously—but the four were implacable. They loved their choice. And if one of the six would just change votes . . .)

When *Cry Freedom* was shown in England, I was told, forty thousand people joined the anti-apartheid movement there.

But that's teaching—you don't make films just to teach, you want to reach the human soul, as *Pelle* does.

Television—

—Propaganda—

—*Television*—

—*Propaganda*—

—TELEVISION—

—PROPAGANDA—

Claude Berri solved it all. The splendid doodler looked down at his notes and said quietly, *Pelle* has the votes. *Pelle* is going to win the *Palme d'Or. A World Apart* will win the Jury Prize.

Grumbles.

Please, from Berri. Let me finish. We have no Best Actress Award that anyone is passionate about. Many fine performances, nothing much more than that. I suggest we also give the Best Actress Award to *A World Apart.*

Which is what we did. The three ladies—the mother, daughter, and maid—shared Best Actress. With two awards—not usual—the *World Apart* people were satisfied. They hadn't won, but it was clear the movie was considered something special. The double crowning showed that.

Pelle had carried the day.

We were tired.

Scola said we might as well vote for actor, so we did. Whitaker for *Bird* had six votes, enough to win. Scola said, "Forest Whitaker is Best Actor."

I erupted. *"Was that the vote?* I didn't think that was the vote. I thought that was the preliminary vote. We had a preliminary vote for movie, I assumed we had one here too."

"I said we would vote for Best Actor, and we did."

"But—"

"Forest Whitaker wins Best Actor."

"You're making a terrible mistake, and I think we should vote again. I don't care if you said it right and I misunderstood, Max von Sydow has been in more great films, with the possible exception of Mastroianni, than any other living performer, and this is his finest work. My God, he plays weak, who ever saw him do that? He's Bergman's hero, the knight, or the killer in *Three Days of the Condor.* This is lasting and different work, and you must take the vote again—"

William Jennings Bryan had nothing on me. Only Max's mother could have been more heartfelt in the man's defense.

The truth? I thought Whitaker was also brilliant. But I knew if he won as actor, my man Eastwood didn't have a prayer for director. The jury would never give two awards to two pictures in the same year. So although I believed every sentence about

Von Sydow, I also had my motives. If Von Sydow won, Eastwood would get director. I was sure of it.

Scola said he was against a revote, but he would consider it. We were all ready to eat the table by this time.

Thank God, lunch. (But during it, I felt nothing but tension wondering what Scola would decide.)

We ate in a large tent set up just below the villa. We were tired, all of us, and all of us exhilarated. Plus, with it all, maybe a trifle sad, because in a few hours it would be over. Unspoken was the fact that most of us would never speak to or see each other again.

People outside the entertainment business tend to assume that people in the business all know each other. I know I tend to. I was surprised when recently Bill Cosby and Eddie Murphy met for the first time.

And I was shocked when, on the first day of shooting of *On Golden Pond*, Katharine Hepburn and Henry Fonda met for the first time. I still can't make that compute, because they were both movie stars *and* Broadway stars. You'd have thought that sometime over half a century they'd have been introduced.

The movies are like one giant Broadway show out of town— you spend a lot of time with the same people.

The rest is silence.

But thanks to the jurors and our meetings, I knew more about movies than I ever knew before. Listening to people in the other crafts talk about those crafts—not your standard screenwriter experience.

Other memories: the unused Majestic pool. At the deep end, a sunning alcove. I was there one afternoon with twelve naked ladies. What added to it was this: just three feet away was a hedge, separating the sunning area from the Majestic driveway. No one that close had the least idea what was ogle-able just beyond the hedge. And just a few feet farther away was the public sidewalk. They didn't know either. So much blessed flesh in such proximity . . .

. . . At Bacon, a super restaurant a few miles from town, something I'd never seen before. Paparazzi in tuxedos . . .

. . . I'd remember my sense of joy on finishing viewing the last flick. We all felt it. We could vote now. . . .

. . . and the teenage girl and boy near the beach. Getting their picture taken by a guy who had a Polaroid camera. He also had a huge snake that he charged you for having your picture taken with. The snake was around the girl and boy. She was panicked. The Polaroid guy raised his camera—the girl smiles—

—oops—out of film—he dashes away to get more, leaving her frozen with the snake at her neck. The snake, it should be mentioned, could not have seemed more bored. . . .

Think I'll forget this? I'm in my bath, prior to dinner, when there's a knock on the door. I know what it is: every evening the festival sends the judges an envelope with press kits for the next day's films and any other data that is necessary. The bathroom door was closed, so I shouted to leave the envelope just inside the door.

The bellboy kept on knocking.

"Leave it outside the door, please."

Knock knock.

"Just leave it, okay?"

Knock knock knock knock—

—the bellboy will not let up, so I rise, grab a towel, go to the door, open it a crack, and say to the bellboy, "Let me have the envelope."

It wasn't the bellboy.

It was Marcus with a C, Karl with a K, and Udo.

Who?

Three young German movie nuts who wanted my autograph. (Some people get Bo Derek.) I snaked out my hand, gave them three damp signatures, and went back to my tub, my opinion of the Majestic security declining rapidly. . . .

Or best of all, the formal screening, starting at ten-thirty, of a film from Portugal, *The Cannibals*. Thousands in formal attire. Lights down. Movie starts. Five minutes in—

—*thunk*—

—thunk—

What no one had told them was *The Cannibals* was an opera. And the "thunk" was the sound the chairs in the theater made when you stood up.

—thunk—

It reminded me of the first time I saw *Marathon Man*. I'd been out of the country when it opened, and as soon as I got back, I went, on a Saturday night, to Times Square.

Packed house.

Pretty classy picture, I thought, munching my popcorn.

Then I noticed something—we're maybe halfway through, and suddenly the aisles are stuffed—

—the audience is fleeing the theater.

I wrote the book, I wrote the screenplay, I don't think it's that bad.

Now, they're flooding out.

I want to shout, "Nothing's *that* bad."

We're into a major evacuation. What did I do? I kept thinking. (What I did, it turned out, was write the dental scene with Hoffman and Olivier. The audience had heard about it, didn't want to see it. The candy stand did big business until the scene was over. Then they all trooped back.)

No such return for *The Cannibals*. The "thunks" became deafening, then ceased to exist. Few were left to leave. Over a *thousand* had hit the road.

Just me and my killer tuxedo trousers all but alone in the sumptuous theater . . .

And I didn't know it then, but I had a bad memory coming up that night, because in the middle of *Willow*, I had the paranoid realization that I hadn't seen my luggage—it had no tag—put into my car. With all my tapes. The entire experience of Cannes. The possibility of this book.

What if they lost my luggage?

I told myself to get a grip. The festival didn't make mistakes like that.

I managed to sit still.

Reflecting on my lack of good luck traveling recently.

What if the Beast of Air France had decided to get back at me for receiving a temporary visa?

Ridiculous.

It couldn't happen.

The luggage would be in my room.

Sometimes I hate my paranoia.

This was one of those times.

Feeling the greatest fool, with *Willow* blasting along, I crept out of the theater, ran down the Palais stairs, past the staring thousands, hurried to my hotel, elevatored up to my room—

—no luggage.

I talked to the concierge in the lobby.

He knew nothing, but he could call the baggage handlers.

They knew nothing.

Outside I saw another jury member.

Yes, his luggage had been returned.

I started back toward the Palais where the limousine drivers were. On the way I met another jury member—no, his luggage wasn't in his room, but he knew where it was—in Gilles Jacob's office. Most of the luggage had been put there.

I got Security to open Jacob's office.

A lot of jury luggage was there.

Not mine.

I was sweating, stunned, as frustrated as I ever wanted to be. I cornered the limousine drivers, tried to talk to them in French.

A joke.

They found a buddy who spoke English.

None of the drivers had seen my luggage.

Had I looked in Jacob's office?

Had I looked in my room?

It had to be one place or the other.

Back to Jacob's office. Sherlock never searched more thoroughly.

Nope.

Back to my room.

Nope.

I guess what I wanted more than anything right then was to get down on the ground, put my thumb in my mouth, and have someone take very good care of me.

"This just came," the concierge said, as I raced back through the lobby. "Could it be yours?" He held out a small piece of luggage.

It was mine. He didn't know who brought it. Someone. It just appeared.

Whoever you are, God bless. . . .

After lunch at the villa that afternoon, we went back to the chandelier room. No one wanted to alter his or her vote. Scola didn't want to change his decision. Whitaker won. And was wonderful.

Eastwood was dead in the water.

Best Director went to *South*—fug—with all that goddamn paper blowing.

When it was over, all the votes and tabulations, we paced around for a little. And what turned out was nobody got everything he wanted, but everybody got something he wanted.

The UN should only do as well.

We had to change then. (In one bedroom.) After that, we took our programs and went to each other, asking for signatures. I felt strained, because what I wanted to write was "I admire you, and I don't admire that many people." But what I wrote was the kind of horseshit doggerel you do, hoping it's remotely clever.

And over it all was that unspoken sadness that we were all about to be tiny spots of each other's history.

Then into cars for the last trip to the Palais.

But in different cars than we arrived in.

As we started off, someone asked the driver why the vehicle change. He said, "Because this is so secret—they wanted it all incognito." A splendid and sensible answer—

—but in front of our cars were these motorcycles roaring

along. Probably what he meant was we were "sort of" incognito, which, like being a little bit pregnant, isn't easy.

I sat back in the car. Whipped. But up. Wonderful experience. We'd helped some careers, hadn't hurt anybody, not a bad two weeks' record.

Of course, I wasn't a judge anymore.

The robes of Solomon had been stripped clean. My wisdom impounded. Prestige vanished. Not to mention the admiration of my fellow man.

After all, everyone admires a judge.

Earlier in the week, I had to get to a press conference, and there was a brute of a guard shoving people away from an entrance. A big guy. Harried. I waited till he had time to catch a breath. Then, quietly, I told him I was on the jury and showed him the proper credentials.

The son of a bitch spit on me. . . .

PART 3

THE

MISS AMERICA

CONTEST

OR

"DO YOU TAKE

PREPARATION H?"

"SHE LOOKS LIKE MISS PIGGY," the voice on the telephone said.

I was four ways surprised.

1. The timing of the call. I was in my office, it was Sunday afternoon, September 11, and I had just returned from Atlantic City. Only weirdos work those hours, so I had expected quiet. But this lady, an old friend, knew a lot about me.

2. She didn't begin with a "hello" or anything resembling a salutation. Just zap—out with it.

3. The anger in her voice.

4. I knew exactly what she was talking about. "She does not," I replied. "She happens to be a lovely young lady."

"Bill," she came back, more ticked than before. "You picked a Miss America who looks exactly like Miss Piggy—HOW COULD YOU DO SUCH A THING? WHAT WAS WRONG WITH MISS COLORADO?"

I started to explain.

Did she not want to hear it. "I'm very disappointed in you, Bill. I expected a lot more from you."

"Listen," I said, "she's a bright woman—tops academically—"

Mistake. *Huge.* "AND WHAT HAPPENS NEXT YEAR? THEY FIND SOME ARMY BRAT WHO ATTENDED THE SORBONNE, SO *SHE* WINS?" Now, a pause. "I'm sorry for shouting. I'm sure you did your best. I'm sorry your best was so rotten. Don't you understand? It's a silly program, but it's *my* silly program. You goddamn men—how would you like it if Pee-wee Herman represented you for a year?''

End of chat.

I hang up, start to unpack my debris, when the phone rings. It's a movie friend from California. ''She blew the jury, that's got to be it.''

''She happens to be a serious girl, deeply religious.''

''All night long I've been going crazy because she reminds me of someone I know only I can't think if I went to college with her or worked on a movie with her or was it high school.''

''Maybe she's a cartoon character,'' I said.

''Oh yeah, right, thanks, Miss Piggy, I was going nuts. I watched it with some friends. Stunned. It had to be Miss Colorado.''

I started to explain.

He was late for a golf game, cut me off—''I'll tell you one good thing—people always wonder if it's fixed. Well, when you pick a winner like you picked, there's no way it can be fixed. I don't think I want to girl-watch with you anymore.''

End of chat.

Ring, ring. A married couple from the Midwest. ''Well, I'm sure you had your reasons,'' the guy said.

His wife said, ''Bill, may I be frank?—I don't give a shit about your reasons.''

Downhill from there.

I called my answering service for messages. ''I saw your picture on the TV show last night,'' the operator said.

''You like the program?''

Long pause. ''The truth?''

''Yup.''

''How could you do that to Miss Colorado?''

I'd been away a week. There were few messages.

But people sure found me that Sunday afternoon. I've never felt so much like Elsa Maxwell. One berating call after another. Finally, I decided to go get some coffee. In the elevator, a guy looked at me. ''You was on that TV thing last night.''

I allowed as to how that was true.

"You're a schmuck, you know that? Nothing personal and all, but you are some fuck-up." The elevator opened in the lobby. "Have a good one," he said, hurrying away.

I brought my container of coffee back to my office, stood staring out the window at what once had been the East River. (Correction: It is still the East River, and it's still sludging its slow way along. When I first rented my place, I had this lovely sweeping view of it. Now, what I see are these hideous apartment buildings. I think, by the by, that New York has cornered the world market on failed architects. You know, you're last in your class at grad school, you're banished to Manhattan. Every time I see the splendors of Chicago, I'm struck anew, as they say, as to how we have destroyed what could have been a lovely island to inhabit.)

Anyway, I'm standing there, sipping my coffee, when the phone goes yet again, but I just let it ring. The service could handle the bitcher. No one wanted to hear the explanation anyway.

The truth is simply this: we have a new Miss America, and she won it fair and square. But if you woke one November morning and found that Harold Stassen had beaten both Bush and Dukakis, and was now president fair and square, you would not be amiss in wondering if perhaps there hadn't been some teeny-weeny blips in the voting system.

There were blips enough for all this year in Atlantic City. . . .

BEFORE I GET TO THE GAFFES, I feel, for probably no logical reason, that the reader should be alerted to the following: the me in Atlantic City was a different model from the Riviera fellow. Not a noted improvement; he just had a slightly altered world view. Or, as a grammar-school teacher would on occasion query, "Which Billy has come to class today?"

Reasons for the change? There are three: legal, medical, and social.

1. The First Thing We Do, Let's Kill All the Lawyers (W. Shakespeare)

The subject under discussion here is divorce lawyers, or, to put a neat point on it, finding one you can live with. As an endeavor, it rates with root canal or being trapped in a Troy Donahue Film Festival.

Because, of course, the shawl of failure is over you when you set out. (And is never taken off.) Plus this: you know your story is different, and you want to explain so that he or she will grasp the desperate uniqueness of your situation and why you need world-class tending. But the lawyer comes at it from a slightly different perspective: you are the snooze of the world, you are conveyor-belt standard, there is nothing new about divorce under his or her sun.

I went to see both a his and a her; to my amazement, liked
them both. And for purely sexist reasons, chose the man. I
have been surrounded by women all my life, and felt now I
wanted a man if it came to guns firing across the water. (Always
the words of my English friend echoed, arm draped over my
shoulder: "It's going to be awful, Bill, it's going to be so awful
you can't believe it, you'll be wishing it was only a nightmare
before you're through. . . . You'll be wishing for death before
it's done. . . .")

Ilene, for her part, also went shyster shopping (an unkind
phrase but shoot me, I like the alliteration), and liked none of
them. No, not this one, wrong, bad feeling about that one,
sorry, couldn't stand this other one.

Then, tra-la, clearing skies.

We are sitting home having drinks one night (no, that is
not a misprint. Through it all, we continued to live in the same
apartment. Lawyers tell you to do that. Sometimes it can go
that way for years. You probably didn't know this, but if you
look up the word "awkward" in the *Oxford English Dictionary*,
the first definition reads, "Two divorcing adults living in the
same apartment because of legal advice.").

Anyway, Ilene says, "I found someone I really like," and I
am, of course, pleased, because the show, at last, can get on
the long and winding road, when she says, "But you've got
to okay it," and I say, "Why?," and she says, "Because you've
already seen her, it's the woman you didn't take."

(. . . of all the gin joints in all the world . . .)

The thing is, of course, that I have confided in this woman.
Nothing top secret. (In point of fact, there isn't that much
about our divorce that's remotely unusual. A fly on the wall
would have gone buzzing off, bored.)

Still, it was a coincidence, and it had to be dealt with. I called
my guy and explained. He thought a moment, then said,
"Fine." I said, "She's reasonable, this woman? You've met her
then?"

He had indeed. What it turned out was this: *my* lawyer was
my *wife's* lawyer's *divorce* lawyer.

2. Medical: Chasing the Turn

I had seen the eye surgeon who was to attempt to fix my hated cross-eyed, producing-double-vision problem before Cannes, but he needed to check me again, before surgery, to see if the condition was deteriorating. "I don't want to chase the turn," he said, which meant nothing to me but referred to the amount the eye turned in.

The gist of it was this: the operation would be a crapshoot. He would have to guess as to just how much to strengthen or weaken the eye muscle. If he guessed wrong, I could end up cross-eyed the other way, and nobody was much in favor of that.

He was a brilliant and good man. He promised nothing.

But I was so excited at the possibility of success, I forgot to get nervous. Surgery was June 7. Just before they wheeled me in, they took my blood pressure—

—120 over 80.

I felt like a kid going to a ball game. I was so blasé when the doctor came in for a last-minute pep talk, I realized I wasn't really sure which eye he was to work on. I assumed the right, the damaged one.

Nope, he said. The left.

I then heard myself asking was he sure he had the correct eye?

We both better hope so, he told me.

Then they wheeled me away.

So excited was I about the possibility of looking normal again, I'd blocked out everything. Like how it feels when you come out of anesthetic. And how it feels when the anesthetic wears off.

The pain part had completely slipped my mind.

You know how when you have a strep throat, when you swallow, it feels like broken glass? Well, it felt like broken glass when I blinked. And it was all so swollen and blurry, I couldn't tell if the surgery had been a success or not.

The next three days were just shit.

Because I realized the goddamn pneumonia, which caused the problem in the beginning, had dogged my life for fifteen years now. Fifteen years since I'd had a business lunch in midtown, come back to my office, started to go for a swim in the basement pool of my office building.

Except I realized as I started to undress, it was too cold for that.

An hour later, I was at home in bed, perspiring like crazy.

A couple of hours after that, I was in New York Hospital. My internist didn't know what I had, didn't think it was serious, but he was going to be away for the weekend (this was a Friday), and better safe than sorry.

Saturday morning I woke up in the hospital, turned on the tube high on the opposite wall, buzzed for the nurse.

She came. "Breakfast?" she asked.

I shook my head, indicated the TV set. "There's a ghost on the picture," I said. "There's a double image—could someone come fix it, please? Or get me a different set?"

She smiled. "I'll be right back," she said.

And so she was. But not with a television repairman. Rather, the doctor who was on duty. "Trouble with the television?" he said.

"It's Saturday, there'll be sports on. That ghost makes it tough to look at."

"Ghost."

"Whatever you call it—see?" I pointed. "It overlaps. You see two of everything."

"Two of everything, right."

Then he was gone.

Probably you don't know what it's like to be a star. I know I don't. We just work our way along, anonymously doing our best to make it intact till morning.

I was a star that day.

I suspect not one medico working the corridors failed to come in and smile at me. And chat me up. Over and over—

—because, you see, the TV was fine. Something had gone wrong with my eye overnight. The nerves, the muscles, one, both, I was never really sure.

But—roll of drums, please—I had developed, purely for their pleasure, an *unusual symptom*.

Well, if you're a young doctor, that's gold.

They'd come in, fiddle around for a bit with my chart, ask about my fever or what ached and how was my stool—

—and then, the biggie: "Now what's this I hear about your eye?"

It got maddening. But I was punchy with the fever, and managed to survive with surly equanimity till Sunday evening, when two hotshot young student surgeons decided to give me a spinal tap.

With *no* authority, understand. The fuckers.

They had this hooked needle they need to zap into my spine, and Ilene was in the room with me, and I said, "Look, I have a bad disc, my spine's not right, L 3 is all screwed up. I don't want any spinal tap, don't do it," and Ilene told them it was true, all true, about my back—

—but it couldn't have mattered less to the hotshots.

They tried to get the needle into my spine, but they couldn't, which didn't stop them from trying again, only now my spine was beginning to bleed.

And just like in the movies, the cavalry came to the rescue. My doctor arrived from his weekend away, there was a good deal of blessed chewing out, and the hotshots were, like Romeo, banis-shed.

I left the hospital, got well, got caught in a snowstorm, got sick again, got very weak, finally, except for my eye, recovered.

With one unoriginal new thought: I had a wife and two young daughters and not much money in the bank, and I could die any day just like everybody else.

I got crazed those next years. I wrote *Marathon Man* and *Magic* and the screenplays to *Marathon Man* and *Magic* and *Stepford Wives* and *Waldo Pepper* and *All the President's Men* and *A Bridge Too Far*. All this in twenty-four months, give or take, and then I took the money and made one giant investment; then, of course, the company I made the investment with hit the shoals and tried to screw me, and I went around for months whipped and, amazingly, broke. Eventually, settlements were reached, but I wasn't with my girls as I should have been, as I wanted to be. But I felt I had to do it, I felt I had to shelter them for when I died, Ilene, too, for my passing. And it wasn't bad work, what I turned out, it was all work I wanted to do—

—but sometimes, oh do I want those years back.

The third day after my eye surgery, I went to my office and tried to make-believe I was a writer.

Joke.

I ached, the blinking was a constant hurt. Finally, I did something I don't think I ever did before in my office.

I slept.

I lay down just to stretch out for a second and the second was over two hours and when I woke in the darkness something was missing. I couldn't figure out what.

I lay there, blinking, blinking, trying to find the handle.

And then I got the gestalt—

—it didn't hurt to blink anymore.

I got up, hurried to the bathroom mirror. The swelling was down. The raw redness was milder. I stared and stared at myself.

Kept staring at the center of the mirror as I inched my head to the right. No problem. But then, there shouldn't have been a problem, I'd always been able to do that without the disfigurement. Hesitation. Then, still keeping my eyes focused at the mirror center, slowly, as slowly as I could, I moved my head to the left, kept moving it left, waiting for the double vision to happen.

My eyes didn't cross. After fifteen years, I at least felt the goddamn pneumonia had slipped from my body.

My eyes did . . . not . . . cross.

One of the better moments of my life.

3. Social: "Are You Dating?"

"Are you dating?" the voice on the phone said. A movie friend. (Aside: movie friends are different from any other relationships I know.) I liked this guy. Funny, bright, interested in things beyond the grosses in Westwood. But—

—an essential one—

—we'd had a *hit* together.

And even though I, as has been previously reported, liked this guy, I also knew we would not be chatting each other up if our flick had bombed. Somebody once said to me, "Never underestimate the insecurity of a star."

I believed that then and do today.

Only it's more than that—everyone in the picture business is amazingly insecure. I don't know Steven Spielberg, but I'll bet that even he got the shakes when *Empire of the Sun* went down the tubes.

I know and know well one of the top dozen directors out there, and he freaked out when his last movie *did well*. Why? Because he was ignored in the reviews. And suddenly he realized that all the years he thought he was marching at the head of the parade, he was only there because he happened to be going the same direction the parade was going, and that only for a little while.

He was not what he thought he was: essential.

The hot studios today are Disney and Paramount, and they're smart as hell. But a top producer said, when I was extolling their brightness, "You're an ass, Goldman—they're only hot for one reason: *it's their turn*."

I guess I believe that too.

What makes the movies such a breeding ground for panic attacks is this: you can't predict public taste three years down the line, and that's what studios try to do. And directors. Stars.

Writers too. The dumbest question ever asked me was by a whizbang hotshot *New York Times* entertainment nerd back in the midseventies when I was on my hot streak, and the question was, verbatim: "Guys like you and Puzo, what is it you know?"

People in other businesses do know at least a little something. If you're the head of Bloomie's, you absolutely can bank on the fact that if you open the store, someone will wander in.

Tell that to the folks who gave us *Ishtar*.

This happened to me. Moss Hart wrote a wonderful bestseller called *Act One*, and I went to see the movie at an East Side theater at the noon show, paid for my ticket, bought my popcorn, wandered into the theater—

—and I was the only one there.

Five hundred empty seats.

Well, it was too much freedom of choice. I could not enter the room. Dumbstruck. This is not a half-hour before the show either.

I wandered to the nearest pay phone in the basement, called up a friend, and said, "You'll never believe this, but I'm at the Trans-Lux and—"

—and there was a knocking on the booth door. It was the one usher, and he said to me, "The movie's about to start."

Scared of Jack the Ripper jumping me, I went in alone and sat there the next two hours. Just me, myself, and I.

The movie business differs from its peers in that there is simply no continuity of affection. John Travolta had the hottest two films back-to-back of any new star in history—*Saturday Night Fever* and *Grease*.

Then someone turned off the faucet.

That "someone"—if you want to know—is *you*.

"I guess I am," I said. (I was answering the question, "Are you dating?" in case you've forgotten, which you must have, because I did.)

"You interested in seeing someone?"

I gave the same answer as before. Mindlessly. Because, in truth, I was trying to remember when I had last "dated" a woman before Ilene. And what was it like.

Hell, what was the *world* like?

Want a few points of reference? *Eisenhower* was president.
Sandra Dee was the biggest young box-office star in the world.
The Beatles hadn't gone to Germany. *To Kill a Mockingbird*
headed the best-seller lists. *Psycho* hadn't been released yet.
The big song of the year was "Itsy Bitsy Teenie Weenie Yellow
Polkadot Bikini."

"Bill? You there?"

I was somewhere, all right. Fighting my way out of my time
warp. I said, "Sorry, phone slipped, tell me about her."

"Well, she's no kid."

"Just so she's younger than I am. Has she got any?"

"Any what?"

"Kids, kids."

"No. No problem there. Really nice lady. Recently divorced.
I think you ought to give it a shot."

I gave it a shot. And you know what worried me as I was
dialing her number? (Let's call her June. She must have been
a June Allyson type twenty-plus years past.) AIDS? Herpes?

Guess again. *Table manners!* I used to joke with Ilene that
the reason I'd never divorce her was I couldn't deal again with
having to worry was this the right fork or not.

Turned out not to be a major concern. "Look," June said,
"we may hate each other. Why don't we just take a walk and
have coffee?"

So we took a walk, had coffee, I saw her to her door, she
invited me into her place for a nightcap. She had short blond
hair, no discernible figure, a good face. We sat on opposite
ends of her couch.

"This is all new?" she said.

"Oh boy."

"You'll do fine."

"From your lips."

"Really. You will. But can I give you some advice?"

"Please."

"Allow yourself time to get over your divorce. It took me
time. I've been divorced two years, but the first half was rough.
I'm fine now though. Your wife leave you?"

Nod.

"My husband left me, so I know the anguish you must be going through. How humiliated you must feel. But believe me, give it time, it goes away."

I nodded again. The truth was, I didn't feel humiliated or anguished, but she was a pro, I didn't argue.

"It really does go away, Bill. I pray you believe me. A year ago, I felt just crushed. But guess what came back: my self-esteem. I think I'm pretty great."

I asked for a refill.

"You don't talk much about your situation. You're ashamed. I understand."

"Make it a light one, please," I said.

"You'll learn to talk without pain, Bill. It was hard for me too. You see, I was a legal secretary, and my husband was a brilliant young legal student. But he wanted to be a stand-up comedian. He was terrible, but of course I never told him. I encouraged him to do whatever he wanted, and naturally he grew up and was one of the most successful lawyers around. For twenty years." She gave me back my drink, sat on the couch again, smiled. "You won't believe me, but a year ago I would have found talking like this painful."

"But you gave it time. Like you told me to do."

"You got it."

Silence.

And now she's starting to cry. "One year ago, I couldn't have gone on like this."

I managed to say, "But your self-esteem came back."

"*Exactly!*"

"That's really great, June. I hope mine does too."

"Oh it will." Sobbing, at this point.

"If I give it time."

Now, she can't even get any words out.

I give her my hankie.

"He came to me . . . one day . . . and he told me . . . he told me we were finished forever . . . out of the blue. . . . I told him . . . I said, 'You'll get tired of her, whoever she is' . . . and he said, 'There's no her, I hate my life, I want to be a stand-up comedian' . . . and I said, 'At your age, are you crazy?' . . . and he said, 'Rodney Dangerfield was older than I am before he got successful' . . . and I said, 'But *he's* funny. . . .' That was the last thing I ever said to him. . . .'' She bent over and put her face on the couch.

I went to the bathroom and brought her a towel. She sopped it for a while, then got control of herself. "I don't know where *that* came from," she said.

"Don't fret it."

She shook her head. "That was embarrassing." A deep breath. "I promise you it'll never happen again."

"It wasn't embarrassing at all."

"I used to cry a lot before my self-esteem came back." Then she was crying again. "I could take being left . . . for a younger woman . . . I think I even could have taken . . . if he'd left me for a man . . . but to be left for Rodney Dangerfield . . ."

She cried at me until she was dopey with fatigue. I walked home feeling in a weird way relieved. My next date had to be better.

What my next date was, was quicker. A really attractive, really successful businesswoman. Set up by another business-woman I know here in town. "Gorgeous and brilliant and single. A bachelor's paradise."

I called her, asked if she wanted a drink. (Let's call her Faye—Dunaway would have played her in the movies.)

"I'm not one of those chickenshits, Bill—let's be ballsy and have dinner. You like Italian? I like Italian."

I suggested one of my favorites, Sistina.

"Sistina," she said. "Sis*tina*? Why would I want to eat there? I've got a much better place." She named it. "I'll book, they know me. Nine-thirty, I work late."

I arrived early, as always. She arrived on time and was great-looking in her business suit and attaché case. Damn near my height. "You must be Bill," she said.

We shook, sat, ordered a drink. The waiter came by with menus. "Don't need 'em."

Then she ordered for herself.

Then she ordered for *me*.

Then she ordered the wine.

Then she said, "A lot of people find me aggressive at first."

Cowering in fear, I managed to say I didn't see how such a thing was possible. . . .

All in all, not an uninteresting summer. . . .

19. WHY IS TONIGHT DIFFERENT FROM ANY OTHER NIGHT? (1)

WHEN I SAID EARLIER THAT the Miss America Pageant "clutched me to its bosom," that was true but only sort of. Meaning that this year was going to be different from all the preceding contests. I'm going to usually call it a contest, but they don't. One missive I got from Atlantic City referred to it as the "1989 Miss America Scholarship Pageant." More often they'll say just "the Pageant." And it well may be that.

Except I want to know who wins, therefore "contest."

In the past, the girls came to Atlantic City, tap shoes aglitter, and worked their buns off to impress the panel of judges. The judges marked the fifty-one lovelies, and the top ten were selected to work their magic on the tube. These same judges then made their final picks from the ten they had selected, and the winner emerged.

I assumed this would be the case in September '88.

Wrong.

On with the new.

I first realized this in a letter I received from Leonard Horn, a really bright lawyer and the recently named chairman of the board and chief executive officer of the operation. (Horn had been involved in other capacities for years.) He's passionate about the event. Passionate and sincere. He wrote me in April.

> . . . it is my earnest goal to make The Miss America Pageant
> Program more visible, more relevant in today's society and more
> involved in the public service issues which are compatible with
> the Miss America Pageant and in which Miss America can have
> a decided beneficial influence. Miss America is and continues
> to be an ideal for millions of young women throughout the
> country and we can prove its validity by demonstrating the
> number of contestants who have gone on to achieve prominence
> in all of the professions.

Having said this, he dropped the shoe.

> This year the Miss America Pageant will introduce a new
> judging system in which two panels of judges will be used. The
> first panel will judge the preliminary competitions from Tuesday
> through Friday. The second panel, made up of national cele-
> brities, will judge the final competition on Saturday night. Both
> panels will be introduced on the Saturday night telecast.
> "I would be pleased if you would join our distinguished panel
> of judges who will select Miss America on the Saturday night
> telecast. This would require your presence from Friday after-
> noon, September 9th, through the crowning on television at
> midnight on Saturday, September 10th.

I found myself, if you will, most unexpectedly, in what once
was referred to as a quandary.

For decades, my two favorite television shows have been the
Academy Awards and Miss America. I can definitely tell you
why the Oscars are so blissfully awful: the by-laws insist that
all the awards be shown. Which is why we have to sit there
for the "Best Black-and-White Animated Short Subject" when
all we really care about is THE STARS. Is Goldie still with
Kurt? How tacky will Cher be this time around? Did Marlon
really send up that Indian girl?

And Sally Field with her "you really like me" aria. You
think Neil Simon or Woody Allen could come up with something as dazzlingly horrendous as that?

Never. Not even close. Not on their best days.

Of course, Miss A. has had her share of great moments. I remember one (out of so many) when a just gorgeous middle-western blond girl stood on the stage and for her talent told a fishing story.

And now, I would be there. Actually in the arena.

Except for this damn double-panel thing.

Which should I pick? The preliminary panel or the celebrity panel? (I immediately decided to call them the "Grunt" panel and the "Cute" one.)

The Grunts arrived on the Monday before the Saturday show and interviewed *all* the ladies. *Live.* And attended the three preliminary evening performances, judging away. They were, in other words, *involved.*

But they didn't get to pick the winner, just the final ten.

The Cuties were to arrive on Friday (though some didn't make it till the next morn). And look at *taped* interviews—of the ten finalists. Then attend the TV show that night.

Snooze.

But they got to pick the winner.

What to do, what to do?

I tried an end run, asked to be on both.

Shot down.

Horn said it wouldn't be possible. Probably because of the possibility that I might "influence" the Cuties if I were also one of the Grunts.

What to do, what to do?

Really, it was no contest. I chose the Grunts. At least that way I'd get a sense of how things worked.

Or didn't.

Horn claims the two juries were his idea, though I suspect NBC, which televised the show, wasn't unhappy. The reason for the double panel? The only reason anything ever happens on network television: ratings. The Miss America Show, once a wonder, was that no more. And the pageant was having increasing trouble getting anyone you've ever heard of to spend a week in Atlantic City. One day was a lot more likely.

Plus the celebrities would give a sense of authenticity to the proceedings. Nothing could possibly be fixed, in other words. (The contest has a legitimate paranoia about that kind of thing. But let me tell you this, from the bottom of my heart: it is so honest you could throw up.)

Plus plus: celebrities would, in theory, bring viewers. (I didn't buy this last somehow. I did not believe that thousands of people across America were saying to each other, "I'm staying home Saturday night, you bet—Deborah Norville's judging the Miss America contest.")

I was a Grunt then, and proud of it. I didn't realize the difference, at that time, the double panels would make. And I'm still not totally sure whose idea it was.

But I do know this: the Edsel was better.

MYRTLE MERIWETHER OF SHINGLEHOUSE, Pennsylvania, has been, for me anyway, a vastly overlooked figure in our national obsession for trivia. She's never once been mentioned, to my knowledge, in either *USA Today, People, Us,* or any of the supermarket tabloids.

Myrtle won the first beauty contest held in America.

This was not Miss America but rather "Miss United States," a competition held in that world-renowned pleasure dome Rehoboth Beach, Delaware. This, it should be noted, was in 1880, forty-one years before Atlantic City crept into our daydreams.

Although I'm sure they had their share of trouble in those early years—remember the business about "15 points for Head Construction?"—I do think it is actually possible to judge a beauty contest.

Ask me to name some lookers. Go ahead.

I closed my eyes, and here is the trio that first appeared:

1. Bardot in *And God Created Woman*, walking, just walking either toward or away from the camera, take your pick.
2. Ursula Andress emerging from the water in *Doctor No*, wearing the white bathing suit.
3. Anita Ekberg in the black dress, meandering in the fountain in *La Dolce Vita*.

You are welcome to disagree with me. You are allowed to say that I'm wrong—but you sure can't say I'm crazy. You may prefer Grable or Garbo or Derek or Monroe, and I will support your right to choose.

The point is this: it's only a matter of personal taste. *We're in the same ball park.*

What the Miss America contest did in 1938 was totally throw any attempt at logic out the window. Madness made its entrance then, and is still there over half a century later. What happened of course, was this—

—they began grading *talent.*

At first glance, why not? What's so hard?

It isn't hard. What it isn't is possible.

Question: Who is the greater film *star*, Schwarzenegger or Olivier? Only one possible answer: Arnold. Remember, the key word in that query was "star."

Question: Who is the greater film *actor*, Schwarzenegger or Olivier?

Different operative word now; still, my guess is that since we are comparing one of the most popular stars of the eighties with the actor of the century, Olivier wins the unanimous decision.

But don't be so sure.

No, I don't want to see Schwarzenegger's *Hamlet.* But would you have wanted to see Olivier's *Terminator?* Schwarzenegger's Heathcliff will not bring me panting to the box office. But I would also not have been present for Sir Larry cleaning out the bad guys as Conan.

I think, and I'm serious, that if you had asked Olivier, he would have, if pressed, picked Schwarzenegger. (He was amazingly uncertain about the worth of his movie work.) But I'm also pretty sure that Schwarzenegger would throw you through the window if you didn't pick the Englishman. And I would agree with him. Olivier is the greater film actor.

But it's a horse race.

Shifting fields briefly: Who is the greater athlete, roundballer Michael Jordan or stickman Wayne Gretzky? No question, they are the two most talented athletes of the decade. You can haggle, but I would suggest Gretzky, because Jordan has not taken his team to a championship, whereas the Great One has, several times.

But so has Magic Johnson, so is he greater than the Great One? I would argue he is not, because even though they are both the greatest passers of their era, if not any, Gretzky is also an amazing scorer, whereas Magic is only very good.

Try this one: Who is the greater athlete, Gretzky or Babe Ruth? They both led teams to glory. They both were remarkable offensive machines. But Ruth was also a great pitcher (Gretzky, to compare, would have had to be an all-star goalie as well). And, final nail in Gretzky's coffin, the Babe revolutionized his sport, whereas Gretzky only refined his.

Now all these answers are, of course, mine only, and you're free to say I'm wrong. But not to worry: *we're still in the same ball park.*

But we're not if I ask you this: Who was greater, Babe Ruth or Jascha Heifetz?

Jesse Owens or Mikhail Baryshnikov?

Wilt Chamberlain or Bobby Fischer?

The addition of grading talent not only separates the Miss America contest from its peers, which are only about looks, but also from sanity.

You cannot judge whether this trampoline girl from Kentucky is better than that ventriloquist from Wyoming or that warbler from Maine.

You know how people are always in polls answering how they just love Mozart when what they buy is U2? Well, often that's what happens when you're trying to judge the impossible: you go for, you should pardon the expression, "class."

And that is why, with its insane double juries, locked in place, the most amazing creature became Miss America my Grunt judge year. . . .

ONE OF THE WEIRDNESSES of the contest is this: at each higher level of competition, the quality of the judging gets worse. As the ladies move from local to state to Atlantic City, they are continually at the mercy of "experts" such as myself, who know next to nothing. There are, believe it, wonderfully skilled judges who really understand stuff like "grace" and "proportion." But they tend not to be well known, and as the stakes rise, they get ground in the dust.

The pageant people understand this anomaly, of course, and do their best to be of service. Between my being accepted and my arrival in September, I was sent information, both print and video, intended to escort me through the maze.

The Tape

The Miss America system of judging is contained in a twenty-five-minute videotape entitled "And . . . the Winner is . . ." The moment I unwrapped it, I slapped it into my machine, got pen and paper ready, let it run—I was feeling the need for all the help I could get.

Because I wanted to do it right.

Because supposedly eighty *thousand* girls enter the damn thing each year.

That's a whole bunch of daydreams.

Some lives were going to be changed.

Maybe even for the better.

I had to learn as best I could how in hell you go about judging a beauty contest.

On the tape, the voice referred to the winner as "America's Most Admired Ambassador."

Maybe . . .

The voice went on, explaining that the fifty-one girls came "straight from the heart of America in the most American event of them all."

Maybe not . . .

More voice: the Miss America Pageant is "The greatest promotional scholarship program for women in the world."

With nothing in second place, say I. If their own figures are to be believed. Because at the local, state, and national Miss America Pageants, over $5 million in scholarships is available annually. (There are strings on a bunch of them. Still, 5 million is a lot of dollars, and a lot of the contestants are in the contest for the scholarship money. True.)

Now, something kind of touching on the tape: a bunch of Miss Americas, from 1982 back to 1933, are shown, both as they looked in their sunshine year as well as now.

Time really etches on us, that we know, but I think it deals the pretties the deepest lashes. Because it's out there, this horror, and when they were babies, everybody cooed, and when they were in high school, they went to the proms, and when they were in college, if they bothered to go to college, they bitched that no one really wanted to know them for the deep creatures some of them were—

—and coming closer was this mean-spirited thing that had always before played in other yards.

Nothing wrong with wrinkles. Or weary eyes.

As long as they're on other faces.

Personally, I feel no sympathy for the rich or the beautiful.

Which doesn't mean they don't suffer. . . .

Only the Miss America contest isn't into beauty, that we know. The talent emphasis is what makes it different. Just how different I didn't realize until the tape began explaining the special qualities needed to be Miss A. herself. Words came on the screen, designating what was needed. And it didn't surprise me that the lead word was "talent."

Guess what was second in line? I mean this. Close your eyes and do a little brainwork. I'll give you fifteen seconds or so, during which time I'll tell you briefly what happened on my next blind date—

"Intelligence."

Okay. So far, we're looking like this:

> Talent
> Intelligence

The third word is . . . ? (A hint: it's two words.) And those words are . . . ? Another hint. The initials of the two words are O and A.

Got it? You know something? You don't. You aren't even remotely close. Not one person in the civilized world could possibly be remotely close. Take all the time you want while I explain what my next blind date said when I asked her out to dinner. She said, after I introduced myself and said so-and-so told me to call, this woman said, after I asked where she wanted to go for dinner—wait for it—she said, *"I'll book the restaurant, you book the limousine."*

> Talent
> Intelligence
> Olympic Ability

I stared at the screen, wondering how I could be so stupid as to make two other words seem to say Olympic Ability, pushed the "rewind" button, stopped, pushed the "forward" button, waited. There it was again.

> Olympic Ability

Anybody who has the least notion what that might possibly mean, Villard Books has my address.

I am now getting pretty sure that "pretty" is on the horizon. What else could a girl possibly need beyond talent, intelligence, and Olympic ability?

> Talent
> Intelligence
> Olympic Ability
> Energy

I assume these are in descending order, since talent is first. I know it's not alphabetical. And now I am getting very curious as to where looks might rate. Next? You think?

You think incorrectly.

> Talent
> Intelligence
> Olympic Ability
> Energy
> Communication

I no longer have expectations. Maybe the next crucial ingredient in the pie will be this: *Overweight*.

> Talent
> Intelligence
> Olympic Ability
> Energy
> Communication
> Poise

Attractiveness, to put you all out of your misery, was rated seventh and last.

Of the individual needs, that is. Because following the seven came the added fillip that it was the best composite of all the attributes as decided by the judges.

In other words, you could maybe get away with being dumb if you rated sensationally on Olympic ability and were energetic as hell. Or something.

Feeling slightly less knowledgeable than when I began, I let the tape run on. And it became immediately clear how the pageant actually did feel about talent. Because we judges voted in four distinct categories: talent, swimsuit, evening gown, and interview.

And talent counted for precisely half.

Swimsuit, evening gown, and interview were weighted one sixth each.

All the contestants were to be scored individually, with ratings ranging anywhere from 1 to 10, using whole numbers only. Swimsuit judging primarily pertained to "how well the contestant has maintained good physical fitness." (I had visions of a female Schwarzenegger knocking 'em dead in her Jantzen.) The evening gown wasn't an evening gown, it was an "onstage statement of the contestant's personality," and we were to pay particular attention to their "arm swing and hand position."

By now I am a lot more confused than when I turned on the VCR. I don't know beans about hand position, and worse, I don't know anybody who knows anything about it, either. I mean, I'm good at research; people I know are used to me calling them and asking weird questions, so I would not have been the least embarrassed phoning some acquaintance and segueing into arm swings through the ages. But no one came even remotely to mind.

Next I am hit with criteria for judging the interview. In no order, they are: first impression, personal appearance, personality, mental alertness, validated opinions, speech, vocabulary and grammar, responses in context, style, and emotional control. (Which I think meant no sobbing.) But I'm not sure of much of anything anymore.

And then we're suddenly in the major leagues. Talent. The voice gets lower, slower, and I hear:

THE DISPROPORTIONATE SCORING IN THIS PHASE OF THE COMPE-
TITION DEMONSTRATES THE PAGEANT'S CONCERN FOR EXCELLENCE
IN THE PRESENTATION OF TALENT.

Why the concern?

THE POSSESSION OF TALENT ASSURES THAT PAGEANT WINNERS,
LOCAL, STATE, AND NATIONAL, WILL BE MULTIDIMENSIONAL YOUNG
WOMEN.

And then, blessedly, the voice let me quit fretting about how
I would do.

THE TALENT COMPETITION IS NOT TO BE COMPARED WITH PROFES-
SIONAL PERFORMANCES ON TELEVISION OR ON THE LIVE STAGE.

Their advice on instrumentalists was, I feel, next to
Shakespearean.

CONSIDER THE CONTESTANT'S ABILITY TO PRODUCE THE CHARAC-
TERISTIC SOUND OF THE INSTRUMENT. . . . *TO PLAY THE IN-
STRUMENT IN TUNE* [emphasis mine]

I watched the rest of it with the same joy I'd always watched
the program. If playing an instrument in tune was something
a judge had to be told, I'd do okay.

Fiddlers fiddled, a girl wrestled with a saxophone, another
hacked up an opera aria, several danced—ballet, jazz ballet,
jazz ballet with batons.

Bliss.

As the tape came to an end, I knew I needed the one same
thing I'd always had watching the tube: someone to care
for. . . .

I didn't know it then, but the answer was already in the
mail.

The Fact Sheets

The voice on my tape told me that the panel would meet with each of the contestants for a private interview. Know this: when the pageant uses the word "private," it doesn't mean what we mean. The girls, from the moment they arrive, all wet and virginal, until their day of departure, are never alone with a (gasp) man. Not even if said fellow is her father. (Believe that.)

The voice went on a bit further:

> THE BASIC TOOL FOR CONDUCTING THIS INTERVIEW, THE CONTES-
> TANT'S FACT SHEET, IS A RÉSUMÉ OF PERSONAL CREDITS AND A
> GUIDE FOR GETTING TO KNOW THE CONTESTANT. CUES TO PERSON-
> ALITY AND ABILITY ARE GIVEN.

When the envelope arrived, I was obviously curious, since my suspicion was that the interview might prove to be the hinge that ultimately swung the contest toward one contestant or another. (Which turned out to be entirely true this year, as will, alas, be shown.)

The first sheet I read belonged to Miss Alabama. (This bunch was in alphabetical order. The underlining is mine, indicating stuff I thought either might be of interest in questioning or somehow unexpected.)

MISS ALABAMA 1988

Jenny Lee Jackson	Age—21
Auburn, Alabama	Date of Birth—October 5, 1966

PARENTS Mr. & Mrs. Paul Jackson
EDUCATION High School—Lake Braddock Secondary School—
1984
College—Auburn University—Senior (Marketing)
Social Sorority—Alpha Omicron Pi (National)
Special Training—Classical piano—14 years; classical violin—
7 years; ballet, tap & jazz—5 years; and harpsichord

MISS ALABAMA

SCHOLASTIC AMBITION She would like to attend graduate school to obtain an MBA.

TALENT Classical Piano

HOBBIES Cross-stitch, scuba diving, water-skiing, aerobics, jogging & peoplewatching

SPORTS Varsity track & field, intramural softball, volleyball & football

STATISTICS Height—5'8½"   Hair—Blonde
           Weight—125   Eyes—Blue
                                            Complexion—Fair

SCHOLASTIC HONORS High School—Homecoming Queen; State High Jump Champion of Virginia; Winner of National Piano Playing Auditions—College Prep Class—2 years; Superior ratings in National Federation of Music Club Festival & National Guild of Piano Teachers

College—Miss Homecoming Finalist; War Eagle Girl; Official Hostess of Auburn University

OTHER ACCOMPLISHMENTS Numerous awards in music for both piano & violin; member, Auburn University Marketing Club; Concert Mistress, High School Orchestra & Regional Orchestra; Bach Festival participant; modeling school; Braddock Soccer Club (national champions); Certified Scuba Diver

EMPLOYMENT Summer Camp Counselor; Nautilus Trainer; Health Instructor; Pro Shop Sales Manager

FAMILY Father is a computer software scientist; mother is an interior decorator. She has one sister, Karen, 26.

OTHER FACTS She has always been fascinated with people. When she was six and her family was in Europe, she sneaked out of her room and her parents found her later entertaining a Dutch couple who didn't speak a word of English. When she had a chance to sit in the President's Box at the Kennedy Center, she sat in every chair, so she could say she had sat in the same chair as President Reagan, whom she admires. She also participates as a volunteer in Special Olympics every year.

FUTURE AMBITION She would like to get an MBA and get some marketing experience with a big firm, hopefully in the cosmetics industry. Eventually, she would like to own her own business.

LOCAL PAGEANT SPONSOR Miss Auburn University Pageant

STATE PAGEANT SPONSOR The Birmingham News Company, Birmingham

I studied Miss Alabama for a while. And the truth is, you *can* kind of get a picture of the girl. (Not as much as if the girls—and they should do this but they don't—wrote the fact sheets themselves. My guess is the state pageant heads are the creative ones here. Too bad.)

Anyway, you notice things on a second reading that you miss first time out. What jumps out is stuff like in high school she was a piano teacher, homecoming queen, and state high-jump champion. Not your everyday combo.

What you miss early on is stuff like what's listed under "Special Training." Fourteen years of piano, seven of fiddle, five of dance, and last, unadorned, harpsichord. Did she just start harpsichord? A lot of girls when they enter the contest start, in panic, to try to find a talent, so you'll see notes like, "Voice, 2 years."

But you don't learn harpsichord for the Miss America contest.

And no years listed. Did she just get a yen to pick up a Renaissance instrument?

Interesting.

What's more interesting, which couldn't be known, was that in college she was only a Miss Homecoming *finalist*.

Want to know why that's interesting? Because this lady, it turned out, was the one genuine gasper in the whole contest. Just achingly gorgeous.

And she wasn't homecoming *queen*?

What are they growing down at Auburn?

I decided to remember Miss Alabama.

Many was the hour I spent cramming over the fact sheets. There was a lot of oddball stuff. Trivia heaven.

One girl had visited "more than 23 countries."

What is that? Is that "24 countries"? If it is, why didn't whoever wrote it write, "has visited 24 countries"?

Another had a "4.25 GPA on a 4.0 scale."

Another (one of my all-time favorites) had this as a hobby: "reading Clive Cussler novels."

Nothing against Cussler, but he's not that prolific. Reading Agatha Christie, fine. Erle Stanley Gardner, yup. Don't ask me why, but I sensed this girl was not a bibliophile.

"Could bench press 100 lbs. when she only weighed 100 lbs." A lot of the girls were into this kind of weight work. I suppose the two biggest hobbies were this and collecting Madame Alexander dolls.

As I said, some of the girls tend to get into talent training in the very recent past. For some reason, I suspected this girl had a more genuine interest in music: "Oboe—12 years; piano—15 years; voice—2 years. Also plays organ, flute, piccolo, guitar, saxophone, bassoon, trombone, trumpet, tuba and various percussion instruments."

(Whew.)

How about this for a hobby? "Collecting poetry."

How about this for a hobby? "Designing refrigerator magnets."

Think you're well-rounded? "Special Training: Piano—3 yrs.; flute—3 yrs.; ballet—6 yrs.; jazz—12 yrs.; gymnastics— 7 yrs.; art—18 yrs.; photography—3 yrs.; graphic design—4 years; staging—1 yr.; and public speaking—5 yrs.—"

—and her talent? "Popular singing."

But where oh where was the one for me?

Not that I would be unfair or unduly biased, but the basis of more things in life than we want to think about is just this: *rooting*.

The locations manager on *The Princess Bride* used to bet on beauty contests. (It's legal in England.) He claimed he won, and we hooted and scoffed until the year we were working there and he was actually heard to say, "Hmm; Miss Trinidad and Tobago looks like a winner to me."

So he bet on her. (He had all kinds of mystic reasons—it was the right time for this continent or that one—I think Miss World was the epic under discussion.) So he put his money on Miss Trinidad and Tobago—*and she won.*

I'm not like that—I don't bet. If I can't work up enough passion without bread being on the table, it's not a good day for me.

I'd studied forty-odd before I found her.

Turn the page and meet Miss Utah.

MISS UTAH

M I S S   U T A H   1 9 8 8

Sophia Christine Symko   Age—21
Salt Lake City, Utah   Date of Birth—February
                                          11, 1967

PARENTS Dr. & Mrs. Orest Symko
EDUCATION High School—Skyline High—1984
College—University of Utah—Graduate (Physics)
Honorary Sorority—Phi Eta Sigma National Honors Society
Special Training—Piano—17 years; ballet—8 years; & jazz
dance—3 yrs.
SCHOLASTIC AMBITION She has completed her Bachelor of Science
Degree in Physics and is currently pursuing a Master's in
Physics.
TALENT Piano Solo
HOBBIES Reading science books & articles, dancing, general read-
ing & collecting postcards
SPORTS Snow skiing, mountain biking, hiking and aerobics
STATISTICS Height—5'7"   Hair—Blonde
             Weight—115   Eyes—Brown
                                          Complexion—Fair
SCHOLASTIC HONORS High School—Officer & Tutor of National
Honors Society & awarded most valuable member; received
highest superior ratings in State solo & ensemble piano festivals;
awarded Outstanding Science Award; performed as soloist in
Concerto Nights
College—Honors at Entrance Scholarship; graduate in physics
with honors Cum Laude; Homecoming Queen; Officer of Phi
Eta Sigma National Honors Society
OTHER ACCOMPLISHMENTS Performed in local recitals & piano
competitions; performed in Snowbird's Summer Art's Piano
Festival concert; member of Nordstrom's Teen Board
EMPLOYMENT Research Assistant at the University of Utah in
the NMR Imaging Research Group; pianist for School of Ballet
West & other local ballet companies; Aerobics Instructor
FAMILY Father is a Professor of Physics; mother is a housewife.
She has one sister, Martha, 19.
OTHER FACTS Born in Oxford, England; volunteers at Holy Cross
Hospital & as a music instructor for second graders at local
elementary school (Lowell); 2½ Physicists in family; comes
from a family of music lovers

<u>FUTURE AMBITION</u> She would like to complete her Master's Degree in Physics and then to pursue a career in medicine.
<u>LOCAL PAGEANT SPONSOR</u> Miss University of Utah Pageant
<u>STATE PAGEANT SPONSOR</u> Miss Utah Scholarship Pageant, Inc., Orem

Why was I smitten?

Well, if you were a feeb, a klutz, a total social outcast when you were young, guess what—that never leaves you. Just like you never stop being—part of you doesn't anyway—young.

And wouldn't you like to rewrite that horrid record book?

Would it be so terrible to meet someone who was pretty obviously no dummy? (A cum laude graduate in physics who was already working on her Master's—this at twenty-one.) A beauty queen. Who liked to read and ski, and in her spare time was a good enough instrumentalist to play for the School of Ballet West.

We didn't have a whole bushel of them at Oberlin.

Of course, all I had of Miss Utah at this time was book knowledge. In person, she might have a face like a foot. (In point of fact, she was stunning. With an impeccable figure.) And she might clutch and hit a bunch of wrong notes when she did her piano solo. (When the time came, she may have played better, but not often. She was the most talented girl at the contest. By a lot.)

Break, heart . . .

"POINT AT ONCE," the guy said. "I cannot stress that too strongly. *Point immediately*. Is that clear?"

Nothing was really clear to me right then. Monday, September 5, and the Grunt jury was having its first meeting, the night before the competition was to start, and this expert judge was telling us how to do it, but all I could think of while he talked was that when I was a little boy growing up back in the thirties, we were told *never* to point, it was rude.

My mind was also full, at that moment of many things, mainly Atlantic City itself.

And bird droppings.

As you drove to Atlantic City from Manhattan, when you first see it what you think of is this: an Arab country. More precisely, the capital of some Arab country that has just stumbled on oil.

Because what you see as you stare across several miles of marshland is this low, flat, tattered place with these close to a dozen phallic fingers rising toward the autumn sky. These fingers—the casinos—are not just startling as they rise from the flat earth; they are also amazingly tacky.

I had thought Las Vegas was amazingly tacky, but Vegas is Venice in comparison. Understand this, and it's not my opinion, it is fact: Atlantic City could not, underlined *not*, be more dreary, depressing, or dreadful.

In the August '88 issue of *Money* magazine, American cities were rated, the ratings all trying to isolate the best places to live. Number 1 is Danbury, Connecticut. Joliet, Illinois, is fiftieth, and if you know anything about that place, you know we are not talking about Valhalla.

Well, the ratings go all the way down to number 300. Guess what is the worst place to live in America?

Would I lie to you? Not only is Atlantic City the dregs, it is getting worse—in '87, it was only number 297.

The populace is fleeing—nearly a quarter gone from '70 to '86. Yes, it attracts the most tourists in the nation—almost 32 million—but they don't stay long—eight *hours*.

Eight hours is plenty long enough.

Why? Pick your poison. Poverty. Homelessness. Despair. Crime. The FBI estimates Atlantic City has the worst crime rate against property in all of America.

But for me, the blinding awfulness of the place is because of the genuinely startling contrast. You walk the boardwalk and look at the hotels and their glitz and you walk into the hotels and of course you don't expect a tasteful casino.

You *do* expect money flashing, and that they have.

Twenty-five-dollar minimum bets sometimes at many of the tables and the tables are full.

And then—

—and only if you have courage—

—if you walk out the back of these hotels, the side away from the Atlantic—

—you are in a bleak, boarded-up slum.

I've never in any country experienced the like. My office is in Manhattan, in Yorkville. If I walk a mile uptown, I'm in a slum.

If I walk half a mile, I have to be at least a little careful.

But across the goddamn *street?* Just outside a building where millions are rolling, the lushes and the panhandlers idle, the muggers wait.

And I truly believe this: nobody cares. As long as the tables and the slots are occupied, it's "what, me worry?"

Atlantic City is, say I, the Masque of the Red Death.

Of course, it wasn't always. There is the bruited memory of Atlantic City as the American Monte Carlo, playground of the very famous; it wasn't that either.

What it was, was this: the lungs of Philadelphia.

In 1852, a Philly hustler led a bunch of what we would now call "venture capitalists" to the world-class beach of lonely Absecon Island and indicated that "this was the place."

A place for what? they wondered.

A beach resort for Philadelphians was the general idea. Build a railroad spur, put up a few hotels, and *voilà*.

Within two years, the train from Philly rumbled down the track. The first census, in 1860, listed the population at 687 souls. Here's how it took off after that:

1870	1,043
1875	2,009
1880	5,477
1890	13,037
1900	27,838
1910	46,150

The first boardwalk was built in 1870, only eight feet wide and not that long. But it was a success because it kept the sand out of hotel lobbies and made a pleasant stroll a possibility.

Pleasure is what Atlantic City always wanted to be about. And it was a glamorous place for the lower and middle classes who trained there on sultry city afternoons. But it never got the rich and mighty.

The place always had to hustle, which was why, in 1921, in an effort to extend the tourist season, what is now the pageant was born. (Just as the film festival was set in May in Cannes to try and get their tourist season started earlier.)

And the city staggered along, more good times than bad, until it was hit by a lot of plagues, perhaps most notably after World War II, cheap air travel: Why go to Atlantic City when Europe was possible?

Gambling was supposed to save it, but gambling has done only what it always does: made some rich men richer. Sure, the casinos provide employment, but precious few of those jobs go to locals. Or to local intellectuals.

Example: I got there early on September 5 for the first Grunt meeting, checked into Trump Plaza, decided to find whatever books I could on the city and its history:

>   ME
>   (in the lobby,
>   to a passing
>   bellman)
>   Excuse me.
>
>   BELLMAN
>   (young and smiling)
>   Hey, I'm here to serve you.
>
>   ME
>   Could you tell me where the
>   nearest bookstore might be?
>
>   BELLMAN
>   (a long pause; then—)
>   A bookstore?
>
>   ME
>   Umm-hmm.
>
>   BELLMAN
>   (another pause; then—)
>   You mean porn, right? Dirty
>   stuff?
>
>   ME
>   I sort of meant a real
>   bookstore.

BELLMAN
Porn places are just out back.
  (shaking his head)
Real bookstore, real bookstore . . .
  (smiles)
Sorry, can't help you.
  (and off he went)

If I have given a somewhat negative view of the town thus far, I don't mean to indicate there aren't bright spots. The White House sub shop makes as good a non-deli sandwich as anyplace in the hemisphere. It's a limited menu—just sandwiches and potato chips, nothing that requires utensils—but at least five thousand people a week wait in line there, as they have for forty-some years, so you figure they must be doing more than a little something right.

I also like the boardwalk. The first one was narrow and short and in no way impressive. The present version is the width of a four-lane highway and miles long, paralleling the ocean behind the glitzy hotels. The view from the boardwalk, looking toward the water, is splendid. (Aside—there are benches for resting set up at various intervals. And what's loony is the benches don't face the sand and the water, they face the backs of the horrid hotels. It would be like sitting all day with your rear toward the Grand Canyon.)

Most of all though, I'm a sucker for the rolling chairs.

They seat two across, and they're supplied with cushions and robes for when it's chilly. And best of all, they're supplied with a man who pushes you along the boardwalk—no poohbah ever had an easier time of it.

The people who push you all have their stories. It's brutal work for them, up to eighteen hours a day, and the first days their legs cramp and ache terribly. Most of them are young, they sort of have to be, and many of them come from across the world to make some quick cash. The rental rate from the owners is about sixty bucks per chair per day, and on a decent day, they can clear a couple of hundred dollars. Valhalla for them was the night of the Tyson-Spinks fight, when the town was jammed and the fight short—ninety-one seconds—leaving a lot of people with a lot of time to kill. One rolling-chair pusher reputedly cleared a thousand dollars that night, and is still spoken of with wonder by his peers.

The following took place the afternoon of my arrival. The chair pusher was American, forty, well fed, red-cheeked, and absolutely serious. His attitude was professorial. As we passed a hotel/casino, he looked at it, I thought longingly.

> ME
> Do you gamble?

> ROLLING-CHAIR MAESTRO
> You could say that.

> ME
> Why are you smiling?

> THE MAESTRO
> I don't want to seem con-
> ceited, but I'm the most
> knowledgeable crap player in
> America.
> (beat)
> Maybe the world.

> ME
> Wonderful.

> THE MAESTRO
> I wasn't always great—it's
> like anything, you have to
> work your way to the top.
> I'm only on top now because
> of my system.
> (beat)
> I won forty thousand dollars
> last week.

ME

That's amazing.

THE MAESTRO

You're probably wondering if
I won forty thousand last
week, how come I'm pushing
and you're riding.
   (I nod)
I did it without money. I just
stood there and used my system without really betting and
came out forty ahead.

ME

What happens when you use
real money?

THE MAESTRO

Oh I always lose then.
   (beat)
For a very good reason—I get
away from my system when I
bet for real. I pushed a psy-
chiatrist last year, and we
talked about it. It's my personality—I get anxious and
lose my discipline. I stop betting my system. But when I
play my system, I always
win. . . .

I left him, bought an ice-cream cone, walked slowly back to
the hotel to get ready for the first meeting. The boardwalk
was pretty full. An awful lot of very old people moving slowly.

And I didn't bump into any of them—

—because what I was thinking was how much better my life
was than before Cannes started, when that car collided with
my knee, when my eyes crossed, when I wore my accursed
shades. Life, at that moment, seemed so on the upswing I

didn't even mind my clumsiness at being messy with the ice-cream cone, letting the vanilla drip onto my wrist and hand. I took a paper napkin, started to wipe it away—

—God, I'd been a slob. I'd really spilled a lot of the cone.

Dab dab. It wasn't Häagen Dazs—

—a goddamn *bird* had dumped on me.

My entire right arm was redolent of birdshit.

"Poise," I told myself. Important for contestants; judges too. Filled with what I hoped was *savoir faire*, I lumbered back to my hotel room.

Dab dab dab all the way home. . . .

We met from eight to ten in the evening, in one of the hotel's conference rooms. Maybe twenty-five of us there. The other panel members, pageant executives and volunteer workers, NBC Standards and Practices people.

Leonard Horn, the head of the pageant, spoke very clearly about what he wanted and what our job was.

Horn believes in the pageant fiercely and in what it represents, and it bugs him that outsiders might think of it as a joke or just a parade of a bunch of dumb bimbos. (My choice of words.) Because, he said, the image is false: they are a terrific bunch of young women.

(I didn't know it then, but he's right.)

He explained that with the double-jury system this year, everything was different. But our job was absolutely clear: *give them ten girls, any one of whom could be Miss America.* Not just a girl with some talent, who might or might not be attractive. But one who could serve as a role model for her generation.

Then Karen Aarons, administrative officer of the pageant, spoke briefly. (She is lovely, by the way, but then, all of the pageant people are nice. And I don't mean Stepford wifelike either. Just a decent bunch of folks all interested in their common cause.)

What we were doing, she explained, was just this: *we were interviewing someone for a job.*

And what was that job?

Well, she would have to deal with her first press conference after the pageant. And another the following morning, Sunday. And then off to New York for television and more interviews on Monday.

That was the kind of year it would be.

Did you see the movie from Frank Deford's novel *Everybody's All-American*? In it there's a scene in an empty football stadium where Jessica Lange, the prettiest girl in college, is all upset and cries to her love, Dennis Quaid, because she can't be in the Miss America contest because it would mean a year's separation from him. (Not one for the time capsule, by the by, since Lange, who is gorgeous and a wonderful dramatic actress, is twice too old for the part. And Quaid, who's also fine in the flick, is a tad long in the tooth for a college senior.)

Forget all that: the point is a valid one. Miss America busts her chops during her year. It's been estimated that the prize brings close to $200,000 in all to the lady. But it's earned.

The girl works every other day, several times a day, personal appearances, public-relations work for the sponsors of the program, talking at schools, hospitals, on and on.

She is always, always *on*.

The day she isn't pressing the flesh is spent mainly in traveling from one city to the next.

Always with a chaperon, usually an elderly woman. (There are two of them, and they alternate months.)

Never, God forbid, with anyone who might cause talk.

It was here that I first realized one of the great schisms of the whole affair: the television people and the pageant people have entirely different goals. The TV folk could care less how she does traipsing from one town to the next. The pageant organizers want her to be talented; of course, but her skill with a xylophone is not such a must when she's chatting up Rotary Clubs.

In other words: TV wants the ten finalists to be whiter Whitneys or less ethnic Barbras. The pageant wants the finalists to be ten Jane Pauleys.

Now, an expert judge was telling us, "Point at once. I cannot stress that too strongly. *Point immediately.* Is that clear?"

Someone asked a question then, and in answering, the expert made it clear that when he said "point," he did not mean with your finger, he meant "score."

"Don't let your first impression betray you."

In other words, the minute the interview or the bathing suit twirl was over, write your reaction. Give the lady her points and on to the next.

"And study your notebooks."

We had been given notebooks upon arrival. They were red ring binders and set up so that when you opened a page, the girl's photo, a black-and-white 8½" × 11" glossy, was on the left, her fact sheet on the right.

The other members of the Grunt jury were far more familiar with this kind of thing than I was. None of them household names, they mostly had some connection with the pageant. One was married to a recent runner-up and had judged before. Another had helped with the California contest for twenty years. A third had come in third thirty years before. I was one of only two who'd never judged before. I had years of catching up to do.

I got back to my room and *Monday Night Football* was on, but did I watch? Actually, I didn't. Because we had seventeen girls to interview coming up at half past eight the next morning, and since they were going to be at their best for me, how could I be less than prepared for them? (Every so often, I admit, I flicked on the set, clocking things.)

I woke the next morning at 5:45. Went downstairs. Nothing much was open in Trump Plaza except this odd place that I only went to this one time, but it was a restaurant that served coffee and eggs and bacon—

—plus, naturally, Chinese food.

I took a tray and went up to where there was this gangrenous-looking display of vittles. And don't get the notion that I'm finicky.

As I stood there, a chef came up and said to a busboy, after making a sweeping gesture toward the edibles: "Throw this shit out before it kills somebody."

Just like Paul Bocuse . . .

NAME OF PAGEANT _____

AN OFFICIAL PRELIMINARY OF THE MISS AMERICA PAGEANT

SCORE SHEET

PRIVATE INTERVIEW

_____   Group   Day or Date _____

NUMBER	TITLE or NAME OF CONTESTANT	POINTS

_____

Signature of Judge

The contestants appearing NOW are to be scored for PRIVATE INTERVIEW with NO relation to their other qualifications.

10 — A
9 — B+
8 — B
7 — B-
6 — C+
5 — C
4 — C-
3 — D+
2 — D
1 — F

The point scale is 1 to 10. 1 is the lowest possible score and 10 is the highest possible score a contestant may receive.

·Every contestant MUST be given points.

If you make any change or erasure on your score sheet, please initial such change or erasure. When you have finished, hand your score sheet to the Chairman of the Judges Committee.

THE INTERVIEW IS EVERYTHING.

From a percentage point of view, of course, that's nonsense. It rates the same only as the swimsuit and the evening gown, all three together equaling the talent score.

But that's only math.

Because the way the girl strikes you in the seven-minute interview affects everything else she does. Did you like her? Then guess what happens when she walks toward you in her swimsuit? Right, her hips slim down.

It's like having a home team in football.

The fifty-one girls are divided into three groups. (For those after the arcane, the groups are named the Alpha Group, the Sigma Group, and the Mu Group, which, if said quickly, sounds like some kind of Chinese morsel, and which, this year, was by far the best of the three.)

The reason for the division is because of the live shows. If the ladies were selected at random, you might have twelve opera singers one night, seven accordionists the next. (I realize I am making what is truly simple unduly complicated.)

Here's the deal: The three nights preceding the finals, there are what amount to duplicate shows performed on the stage of the Convention Center. And each of the three groups does something different. Here, for example, is the Alpha Group's schedule:

Tuesday morning	Interview
Wednesday night	Talent
Thursday night	Swimsuit
Friday night	Evening gown

The timing of the interviews this year was simple: the Grunt jury talked with all fifty-one girls before the Wednesday night performance.

It didn't used to be that way. Before, you'd interview some, watch an evening's show, interview some more the next morning, watch another show that night, etc. What happened was this: the girls who were interviewed first had a huge advantage, because the jury knew who they were. Over one twelve-year stretch, nine winners came from the first batch of interviewees.

Much fairer now. But the jury got *punchy*. The first day, Tuesday, we did thirty-four interviews. We did fine for the first seventeen, broke for lunch, went back for more.

Well, we all lost it, it turned out, after interview number twenty-eight. Precisely, all seven of us. God knows how we got past the last six without giggling, but we did.

Because although each of the contestants was special, unique, all that, when they keep coming at you one after the other after the next, it's like you're chatting up Huey, Dewey, and Louie. (Show-biz anecdote. One of the unhappiest men I ever met Out There was a very nice fellow who, for his sins, was directing segments of *Charlie's Angels*. There was, as all of us who like to dish are well aware, a remarkable amount of tension on the set. One of the trio of yummies was always called, by the crew and when she was out of earshot, Hate Jackson.

I'm having dinner with the director and some friends of his, and he had once wanted to do theater. Had done theater. Off-Broadway, etc. But mouths to feed are not without import, so here he was, Suffering. His friends would ask him zapping questions, just to get him started. Like, "Well, was it Chekhovian today?" "I'm writing a paper on Symbolism in Female Detective Agencies, can I interview you?" And he would say,

"You're not funny. That is not a funny question. Not to me. Not anymore."

Anyway, let's say this was a line of dialogue for a *Charlie's Angels* episode:

> ANGEL
> I think it's about time for us
> to split up, go downtown, see
> what we can see.

Well, no go. It would end up like this:

> FARRAH
> I think it's about time for us
> to split up—
>
> KATE
> —go downtown—
>
> JACLYN
> —see what we can see.

It was referred to, at that time, as Huey, Dewey, and Louie dialogue. End of show-biz anecdote.)

The first interviewee, Miss Delaware, entered the hotel conference room at 8:54, nine minutes late, not her fault, but just as we were about to hit the ground running, someone realized that our voting ballots had not yet arrived.

Until that matter was cleared up, a dozen of us and more milled around the room:

The Grunt jury, all seven of us. We were at two tables, right-angled, facing a chair where the grillee would sit.

A cameraman and his assistant. They were to videotape the girls in the chair; your basic close-up. Maybe you'd get down to her shoulders. But essentially, the talking-head shot we've all come to know and detest on the tube. These two were behind the jury, where the two tables met.

Also present was a pageant executive, who would lead the girl into the room, introduce her, then lead her out of the room when she was done.

There was another pageant executive who would time the interview; he was out of the girl's eyesight, but faced us, so he could signal when there was a minute left, thirty seconds, etc.

An NBC Standards and Practices executive, I suspect to make sure there wasn't a hint of hanky-panky in the judging.

Finally, a sweet, remarkably elderly man, who, if I have it right, had seen every pageant. Considering the first one was in 1921, he should immediately write a book detailing his diet. This was a lovely, spry gent. The book would be a cinch bestseller.

Eight fifty-four, and suddenly Miss Delaware was there.

I was blabbing away, talking about Jerry Lewis. (I don't usually do that.) It must have been about that great moment in his telethon when he couldn't find the pitch. Did you see it? Fabulous. He starts to sing a song, which he does better than I ever expected, and he's confident, finger-snappy, looks slim and trim, opens his mouth—

—oops, he can't get the note from the band behind him.

But he's a pro, so he simply goes up to where he thinks the band probably is.

At the same moment that the band changed notes too.

He shifts again.

But they're too quick for him—they're switching again.

One of the fun things in the arts is when something goes wrong live. Talk to any actor who did live TV, and you're on the floor with stories about doors that don't open, props that weren't there, and sound effects—gunfire ringing out before anyone's come close to pulling a six-shooter.

You just get helpless with laughter, which is what I did watching Jerry Lewis, and probably I was trying to describe to my peers the great madness of the moment—it went on with

half a dozen note changes before he turned to face them and
begged for some cooperation—

—Miss Delaware sat demurely down.

She was in an equally demure turquoise dress. ("Not great
dress," my notes say.)

My notes also say, "Door in wrong wall," which was true
and I'll explain it. Ideally, the door should have been placed
so that she could see the jury as she entered, get a sense of
place and what we looked like as she was led to the chair. It
would have been a little quick confidence-builder.

Well, this door was wrong. What she saw as she was led in
was the table with the guy who had been coming since 1921,
the timer, and the NBC exec—

—and what she must have been thinking was, *That's* the
jury? Then a head turn to the left would be executed, and there
we were—

—but she was already thrown; a small and unnecessary
hiccup had been placed in her path.

I have to describe now how she sat in the chair.

Back straight.

Smile on.

Skirt pulled down.

Right hand on top of left hand.

Left hand on right thigh.

We introduced ourselves and began the questions. We always asked in the same order, starting with the person farthest
to her right. I was the seventh questioner.

I looked at her photo and her fact sheet while I waited my
turn.

Her name was of absolutely no importance. (I think that
was true for all of us. We never talked of any of them as if
they had names. To us, she would forever be Miss Delaware.)

She looked like her photo. (A remarkable number of them
didn't look at all like their pictures. Interestingly to me, as
many looked better as looked worse.)

Her fact sheet gave her height as 5'8½", her weight as 123.
I'm not much on weight guessing, but she seemed about the

height she claimed. (A lot of them weren't even close. They reminded me of basketball players who were always 6'10" in high school, but by the time they got to the pros, they'd be 6'8".)

She was the second of three sisters. She was interested in drug abuse. She'd been a lead singer with several bands, and liked art, beachcombing, music, baking, tennis, volleyball, and swimming.

I didn't have a lot of zippy questions written down.

She talked well.

By the time it was my turn, I realized she was skilled at parrying, so I tried to think up stuff she maybe hadn't been asked before. I think I asked her which sister she hated more, the older or younger, and how big a disadvantage she thought it was, being the first contestant into the breach.

She just loved both her sisters; naturally, she loved them both exactly the same. She also thought it was an advantage going first, since she wouldn't have to worry about it as the other girls would.

I watched her closely, comparing her to other women I knew her age, or had known, and she seemed like neither a daughter nor potential date. Very smooth. Very polite. Probably didn't need to use deodorant—they almost all came across like that.

And thin.

Not a pudge in the carload.

She was just finishing her feelings on the death penalty— she didn't believe in it—

—and gone.

The seven minutes were up. Amazing. Finger-snap fast.

I marked her on a scale of 1 to 10, hesitating only a little—

—because Miss Missouri was entering the room, looking at the old guy, the NBC guy, the timer guy—

—*That's* the jury? her somewhat surprised face read.

Then she was in the chair.

Back straight.

Smile on.

Skirt pulled down.

Right hand on top of left hand.

Left hand on right thigh.

Small (5'3"). Slender (100 pounds). Blue dress that accentuated her shoulders. Much prettier than her picture. Nice smile. Sincere.

And now I had the glimmerings of something.

Miss Washington came next.

The panicked look at the aforementioned trio.

The first sight of us.

Into the chair.

Back straight, smile on, skirt pulled down—

—right hand on left hand.

Left hand on right thigh.

That was the thing—they all sat that way. It's really uncomfortable. Go ahead, try it. That weird hand posture must have started decades back and become the only way to get through the interview. They must have been told—"DON'T MOVE YOUR HANDS, WHATEVER YOU DO."

And were they good at obeying orders.

Then my glimmering became fact. *They were all so practiced.* Drilled and taught and schooled. There was somewhere a proper way to become Miss America, and they all knew it and they all did it. Some judges asked the same questions over and over, some of us varied our attack.

I realized soon it didn't matter what the question was— they'd all been asked anything we could ask them. What mattered wasn't their reply either—it was what, if anything, they projected.

One contestant, seventeen and six feet tall, got a *huge* laugh when she answered this question: "What's the greatest environmental concern you have?"

Her answer: "All the hair spray the girls are using this week."

Okay, it's not Billy Crystal, but it worked when she said it. Something was alive and ticking there.

That's not fair. They were all more than a little alive. Most just wouldn't let it show.

Grading them, which I thought would be a problem, turned out not so. You learn amazingly quickly what to look for, what you find appealing. I scored them all 7—a B—at first and in pencil. Then, after I'd seen maybe half a dozen, I shifted some up, dropped some down.

But the first group, the Alphas, were, I confess, kind of dreary. Not great desert-island companions.

Except, of course, for Miss Mississippi. Here are my notes jotted down during her interview:

> "Looks like Miss America."
> "Smart enough."
> "Definitely a finalist."
> "Oh, boy."
> "QUESTION: CAN A GIRL BE THIS SEXY AND WIN?"

For this was indeed a package. A green-eyed blonde with a body that didn't seem to ever want to end. Nothing flirtatious about her. She was just sexy.

I couldn't ever remember a Miss America that was remotely sensual. You don't want to bed down with them so much as make sure they've had their pablum that day.

As I watched Miss Mississippi glide out of the room, I realized it might be hard for her to win, and that all those people who say it isn't a beauty contest?

They're right.

The second group, after lunch, began with Miss Florida. She had, I thought, the best photo of all the contestants; she just kind of popped out at you. But when she walked in, did the by-now-obligatory take at the nonjury, and sat down, I realized she was not as attractive as her photo. These are my notes taken during her seven minutes in my life, as the interview went on:

> "Not as pretty as her picture."
> "Actually, speaks wonderfully well."

"The truth is, she does resemble her picture."
"Just a charming young woman."
"Self-possessed, funny."
"*Much* prettier than her picture."

I suppose what wins the Miss America Contest more than any other thing is poise. Unfortunately, I do not pretend to know what the word means. But it's like "star quality" in the movies.

Something hits you.

Miss Florida was a cinch top tenner. And probably, depending on the events of the next three days, the new Miss A. As she walked out of the room, we all just sat there, we Grunts, and looked at each other. At the other end of the table, one of my peers just said, "Wow."

The next lady to be followed closely was Miss Minnesota. Why?

Credentials.

A classical violin player who went to Stanford. Not your ho-hum entrant. Certain things were clear about her in the chair. *Real* bright. Chunky. Self-possessed. Not a lot of humor. At one point, she said this: "Yes, even though I attend an affluent school, I thank God I come from Minnesota, where people still have VALUES."

The teeth ached at the sentiment. But I felt then that she would have made the most dedicated Sunday School teacher in the history of the Western world.

Them kinds win.

Soon after Miss Minnesota's exit, Miss Alabama was in the room.

She was the lady who had the first fact sheet I studied, included before. The high-jumping harpsichordist. She sat and she talked. She wore a blue suit. Not a bad choice if you're a blue-eyed blonde. She was soft and sweet, and I listened and nodded, and probably she was halfway through her time before, swift fellow that I am, I realized she was simply gorgeous. Her picture didn't begin to do her justice.

She didn't have the kind of startling face that spins us in the streets. Just this kind of quiet, soft-spoken college senior whom you watch and think, Well, I guess the eyes are okay, maybe better than okay, and the lips are good, nothing much wrong with the nose, and the hair's good and—and—

—and, jerk, she's *perfect.*

So she was. The only one in the pageant. There had never been a pageant she wouldn't come close to winning.

So now I'm watching four:

> Florida, with the personality;
> Mississippi, with the sex;
> Minnesota, with the school;
> Alabama, with the face.

And then Gloria Steinem walked in the room, disguised as Miss Colorado.

Have you ever heard Ms. Steinem on the tube, with that deep voice and an almost inflectionless tone and the words come quick and it shouldn't be that riveting but you know as you listen that *you better pay attention or you'll miss something.*

Well, the lady from Colorado was like that. Smart and impressive and *different:* she wanted to be a *talent agent.* Had to be a first. She was assertive but not so she scared you. And a lot more attractive than her picture.

We all babbled along so happily that certain things were never mentioned—that she lived half her life in Japan, that her mother was of Japanese descent, that her father was black.

If the pageant really wanted a bright contemporary woman,

someone who would bring its image out of the previous century, they had to go with this one.

All the way.

Following then, my big five as I saw them in my notebook. Note: The photo on the left, the fact sheet on the right. Check 'em out:

MISS COLORADO

MISS COLORADO

Maya Walker   Age—23
Eagle/Vail, Colorado   Date of Birth—February
                                     25, 1965

PARENTS Mr. & Mrs. Logan Walker
EDUCATION High School—Eisenhower High School—1983
College—Oklahoma City University—Senior (Music Business)
Special Training—Classical voice training—4 years; piano—7
years; organ—1 year; dance—1 year; acting—1 year
SCHOLASTIC AMBITION To obtain a Bachelor's degree in Music
Business, then continue in the field of Entertainment Law.
TALENT Vocal Jazz Standard
HOBBIES Crossword puzzles, reading, singing, movies and pets
SPORTS Jogging, aerobics and weight training
STATISTICS Height—5'4"   Hair—Black
           Weight—105   Eyes—Brown
                                  Complexion—Medium
SCHOLASTIC HONORS High School—Recipient of Bill Crawford
Scholarship; Best Female Vocalist, 1983; All-State Choir—3
years; Student of the Month; Show Choir; Drill Team
College—$4,000 Music Merit Scholarship; Department of De-
fense Tour of the Orient; Dean's Honor Roll; Member of Surrey
Singers; 1 year tuition from Miss OCU Pageant
OTHER ACCOMPLISHMENTS Winner of numerous music contests
for vocal and piano
EMPLOYMENT Professional singer in various resort locations; also
working as a Furrier
FAMILY Father works for Civil Service as Head of Music Branch;
mother is a piano/organ instructor and church organist. She
has three brothers: Michael, 20; Logan, 17, and Kenneth, 13.
OTHER FACTS She was born in Okinawa, Japan, and lived there
for 11 years. Her father is black and her mother is of Japanese
descent.
FUTURE AMBITION She plans to work in the music industry
through her own agency representing various talents.
LOCAL PAGEANT SPONSOR Miss Western Counties Pageant
STATE PAGEANT SPONSOR Miss Colorado Scholarship Pageant,
Inc., Denver

MISS MINNESOTA

MISS MINNESOTA

Gretchen Elizabeth Carlson   Age—22
Anoka, Minnesota   Date of Birth—June
                                            21, 1966

PARENTS Mr. & Mrs. Lee Carlson
EDUCATION High School—Anoka Senior High—1984
College—Stanford University/Oxford University—Senior
(Organizational Behavior)
Social Sorority—Kappa Kappa Gamma (National)
Special Training—Violin—16 years; piano—12 years; choir
and vocal ensembles—12 years; drama—5 years; Julliard Aspen
Music Festival—5 years; and ballet—2 years
SCHOLASTIC AMBITION To obtain a Bachelor of Arts degree in
Organizational Behavior followed by a Doctor of Jurisprudence
at Harvard Law School.
TALENT Classical Violin Solo
HOBBIES Collecting international dolls, traveling, pro football
fan and volunteering
SPORTS Aerobic & anaerobic training, tennis, skiing, Ping-Pong
and biking
STATISTICS Height—5'3½"   Hair—Blonde
           Weight—108   Eyes—Emerald Green
                                     Complexion—Fair
SCHOLASTIC HONORS High School—Valedictorian; Nat'l March
of Dimes Volunteer Service Award; lead role—"South Pacific"
College—Association of Nat'l Outstanding College Students;
chosen for Standard Academic Program/Oxford; Chairperson
of Stanford Sociological Research Project
OTHER ACCOMPLISHMENTS Soloist with Minnesota Orchestra;
selected performer for Isaac Stern and Pinchas Zukerman; winner of Nat'l & State violin competitions; concert mistress of
GTCYS; Julliard School of Music scholarship; scored in 93rd
percentile nationally in law school admissions test
EMPLOYMENT Intern at WCCO-TV in Minneapolis; free-lance
musician; Director of Service Marketing Project at auto dealership; violin teacher
FAMILY Father is Pres. of Chevrolet dealership; mother is a
homemaker. She has one sister and two brothers: Kristin, 24;
Bill, 20; and Mark, 17.
OTHER FACTS 100% Swedish; favorite food is Sushi; has perfect

MISS MISSISSIPPI

pitch; traveled with family on several international church trips to Middle East & Europe; attended Passion Play in Oberammergau, West Germany; American sister to AFS student from Norway; active member of second largest Lutheran Church in America ministered by grandfather for 31 years; featured on Nat'l Children's TV Program "Kidsworld" and on PM Magazine as one of four outstanding youths in MN

FUTURE AMBITION To be first Miss America with a classical violin talent, complete her undergraduate degree at Stanford University and enter into graduate law studies.

LOCAL PAGEANT SPONSOR Miss Cottage Grove Scholarship Pageant

STATE PAGEANT SPONSOR Miss Minnesota Scholarship Program, Inc., Austin

MISS MISSISSIPPI

Carla Haag   Age—23
Hattiesburg, Mississippi   Date of Birth—March
                                    18, 1965

PARENTS Mr. Carl P. Haag, Jr. (mother deceased)

EDUCATION High School—Hattiesburg High School—1983
College—University of Alabama at Birmingham—Graduate (Psychology)
Honorary Sorority—Omicron Delta Kappa
Social Sorority—Chi Omega
Special Training—Vocal training—5 years; dance—5 years; piano—8 years; oboe—4 years; clarinet—4 years; additional vocal training with Rachel Mathes

SCHOLASTIC AMBITION To obtain a law degree at the University of Mississippi.

TALENT Sing

HOBBIES Collecting stuffed monkeys, fiction writing, sewing & shopping for accessories

SPORTS Racquetball and speedwalking

STATISTICS Height—5'6½"   Hair—Blonde
            Weight—105   Eyes—Green
                                    Complexion—Medium

SCHOLASTIC HONORS High School—National Honor Society; Who's Who Among High School Students; Most Beautiful;

MISS FLORIDA

Beta Club; Latin Club; National DECA Finalist Madrigal Singers; UAB Homecoming Soloist; Freshman Homecoming Maid; Who's Who Among American Colleges and Universities; Outstanding Young Women of America

OTHER ACCOMPLISHMENTS American Cancer Society Volunteer; Member of Revelation Gospel Group; Played role of "CINDERELLA" in two separate theater productions; Mississippi Debutante

EMPLOYMENT Worked as cosmetic consultant for a cosmetic firm; worked as a legal secretary; free lance modeling; bank receptionist

FAMILY Father is a convenience store owner; mother is deceased. She has two sisters and one brother: Cheryl, 25; Cacee, 12; and Carl, 19.

OTHER FACTS Spent most of her childhood working on farm; enjoys cooking from old family recipes; won a cheese cooking contest; is a "chocoholic" and aspires to be a soap opera actress.

FUTURE AMBITION To develop a legal subspeciality called "Preventive Divorce Law" which will require degrees both in Psychology and Law.

LOCAL PAGEANT SPONSOR Miss Dixie Pageant

STATE PAGEANT SPONSOR Miss Mississippi Pageant, Inc. & Vicksburg Jaycees

MISS FLORIDA

Melissa Aggeles   Age—24
St. Petersburg, Florida   Date of Birth—November
                                         24, 1963

PARENTS Lt. Col. & Mrs. James Aggeles

EDUCATION High School—St. Petersburg High School—1981 College—The Florida State University—1987 Graduate (BFA Musical Theater) Special Training—Vocal training—12 years; dance training (ballet, jazz, tap, pointe)—11 years; acting—The Florida State University

SCHOLASTIC AMBITION To receive a Master's Degree in Fine Arts from New York University, specializing in classics and film.

TALENT Song/Dance

HOBBIES Watching old movies, cooking and working out

STATISTICS Height—5'8"   Hair—Brown
          Weight—128   Eyes—Brown
                                         Complexion—Medium

SCHOLASTIC HONORS High School—Outstanding Young American; Who's Who in American High School students; Human Relations Committee; Civinette Club Calendar Girl; Captain of Devilettes; Thespian; Superior rating at the Florida Vocal Conference

College—Dean's List; Honor Roll; Hostess of F.S.U. TV Campus Connection; F.S.U. Model Board member; leading roles in all Mainstage Musicals while attending F.S.U.

EMPLOYMENT She has performed the role of Cassie in "A Chorus Line" & Louise in "Gypsy," receiving critical acclaim from local drama & newspaper critics for these performances.

FAMILY Father is a retired Lt. Col. from the U.S. Army; mother is a homemaker & a former professional vocalist. She has two brothers and two sisters: Klaus, 45; Thomas, 34; Jane, 33; and Ruth, 31.

OTHER FACTS Chosen to kiss candidate Ronald Reagan; was a member of the first Miss Florida U.S.O. Show, then toured the Caribbean & Central America with the Miss Florida U.S.O. Show as Assistant Director, Choreographer & performer; was selected for membership in the Miss Florida U.S.O. Sorority (Upsilon Sigma Omega). During her reign as Miss Florida, she plans to implement a program to reduce high school dropouts, with the theme being "School is Cool." This program has been enthusiastically received by the Department of Education for the State of Florida.

FUTURE AMBITION To have a successful career on the Broadway stage and in the film industry through her education and training from Florida State University and New York University.

LOCAL PAGEANT SPONSOR Miss Manatee County Scholarship Pageant

STATE PAGEANT SPONSOR Miss Florida Pageant of Orlando, Inc.

And what, you may ask, of Miss Utah, the homecoming queen, cum laude physics, grad of 21?

Her fate will soon be told.

But first, a few comments about the girls in general. I, who might have been thought of as Chief Scoffer, was eventually won over. The fifty-one broke down like this:

One, as mentioned, was genuinely the kind who could have incepted the plot of a Raymond Chandler novel—i.e., was sexy.

One, as mentioned, was gorgeous.

One, and only one, was dumb. (That's in many ways the most remarkable stat of all.)

Only two were airheads. (They weren't dumb, just uninterested. The kind who would have been happiest playing with their bubble gum at the nearest shopping mall.)

Two were superbright.

Two were time warps—girls who might have won back in the fifties or sixties, when God-clutching was more in style than today.

And nary a one was the kind who dominated the pageant in its first thirty years—would-be starlets. That child, who was of dubious intellectual weight and wanted only to be swept up by Clark or Gary, is gone now.

And in her place: Maria Shriver.

If there was one person that these fifty-one reminded me of it was Shriver, overwhelmingly. Certainly attractive. Unquestionably driven. Bright enough. Willing to work like hell. (Remember that Diane Sawyer, maybe the most talked-about talking head on the tube, was the winner of a national beauty contest when she was in her teens.)

The lovely I mentioned earlier, who told a fish story for her talent? She doesn't get out of the local level today. These may not be wildly contemporary women in the contest now—too many of them are still Small-Town Queens—but they're edging in that direction.

You can tell that from talking to them.

You can tell an amazing amount from talking to them. Even now, as I write this, months after the event, if I look at my notes and the fact sheets and the photo, I can get some sort of image of the girl.

I remember the girl who said that something or other "made things just as worse," then winced as she realized her grammar might have cost her her shot.

And the one who said, "I think Dan Quayle shouldn't be

the nominee, it's an insult to the country." (Most girls, when asked political questions, sidestepped adroitly: "I think one of the great things about America is freedom of choice blah blah blah . . .")

Another meant to say she'd got her foot in the door but what came out was, "I got my foot in the ground floor." And then mightily managed not to giggle.

And the political-science major who didn't know the word "incumbent." Remarkable, because she was a bright girl.

And the pre-med who didn't know what the Hippocratic Oath was.

And the one who swung her hips beautifully when she walked in and out and I know will end up in a life of crime.

But most of all, I remember Miss Utah. Look back at her picture—not a flattering one. We're talking about a wonderful-looking girl.

She had no way of knowing I was her admirer as she blanched a bit, looking at the trio sitting where the jury should have been. Then she saw us, sat in the chair.

Back straight.

Smile on.

Skirt pulled down.

Right hand on top of left hand.

Left hand on right thigh.

So far, okay.

Let me ask you a question—did you ever see a great black comedy called *Dr. Strangelove or How I Learned to Stop Worrying and Love the Bomb*? In it, one of the ninety-five people played by Peter Sellers is a German scientist who has trouble controlling his own hands.

That was Miss Utah's problem.

She was so smart and so lovely and so terrific and so in the wrong pew. When she spoke (and it was hard for her to keep her voice level), she would sometimes want to make a gesture with her hands—

—except she'd been practiced in the art of keeping her hands in that dopey position. But sometimes one of her hands would start to move—

—and then the other one would grab for it, keep grabbing, finally get it, bring it back down to the starting position. Totally beyond her control, her hands were fighting.

She was not a beauty-contest type. Which was really a shame, because I think this year, if she could have made it to the final ten, she would have won, since she so outclassed the winner in all the categories—

—except now, the forty-seventh girl to be interviewed, she couldn't bring herself under control. I wanted to leave my chair and go hug her and tell her it was okay, what was a stupid beauty contest anyway, she'd get a Ph.D. and an M.D. and maybe win a Nobel Prize half a century down the line.

Why had she entered?

Who had convinced her?

Her hands kept fluttering as they struggled for control. Without success.

Maybe five minutes into the interview, I sensed she sensed it was over, her shot. Her energy seemed to drop even lower.

But her hands wouldn't stay still.

That was then and is now my strongest memory of my judging days there—

—those two betraying hands . . .

IF I DON'T GO INTO A LOT of detail on what else was going on during the week, it's because except for the judging work, there wasn't much going on at all. I gambled a little, won less. I ate dreadful meals (except for the White House), usually in company with the other Grunts—we were kind of like the characters in *Make Way for Ducklings*—herded from one Continental cuisine establishment to another.

The fact is, except for gambling, there's nothing for anybody to talk about in town. There's no town. I kept in touch with New York some. The apartment sale was one of those "she's up, she's down" businesses—the deal was good, it was dead, good, dead, none of it comforting.

Ilene and I were in touch not only because we were still living in the same apartment and had the business of the sale to keep track of, there was also the problem with her lawyer.

Her lawyer was going through a midlife crisis. When she wasn't confiding in Ilene, she was yelling at her—

—and whatever her mood, she didn't much feel like working.

Nothing was moving forward. It should have been the most amicable of partings—there were no hidden Swiss accounts to hire truffle pigs to find—but it was *glue*. My social life had picked up—how could it not?—but the ladies were back home, while I was in my room in the hotel with its magnificent view of the room of the Convention Center.

The Atlantic City Convention Center, a building only slightly larger than your average Central American country, is where the television show of the contest takes place. Helicopters have flown inside this baby. Horse races have taken place there.

We are talking, please understand, vast.

And as clunky an edifice as you can hope to find. I imagine the architect must have been a secret partner in one of those Jersey Mafia cement companies. I worked for two years (by mistake, but that's another story) in the basement of the Pentagon—and the Convention Center makes that monstrosity seem as graceful as Brancusi on a good day.

The center is also the place where, for the three nights preceding the main event, preliminary shows are run. These nights are open to the public who want to pay the tariff to see the ladies, on alternating nights, perform in talent, evening gown, and bathing suit. The crowds tend to build. The first prelim audience is kind of scanty, the second less so, the third bigger still, and the TV show pretty much capacity.

I am sure there are many out there who find it hard watching even one Miss America Pageant. In essence, the Grunt jury saw four, the last one only as spectators.

A sinful admission: I enjoyed it. It's like a musical in trouble on the road. They keep the timing pretty much the same as the real show, but they're constantly putting in new numbers, taking out others, trying jokes, pitching them, trying others, pitching them, shifting the mikes from here to there, moving other essential paraphernalia to more advantageous spots, stagehands and TV folk by the bushel, all of them chasing their tails.

And seated right up at the very front, just to the left of the runway, us. The seven Grunts. Licking our pencils. Keen eyes and eager. Anxious to be at least Solomon.

Bathing Suit

There are those in this great land of ours who find this part
of the competition degrading to women.

(Can you believe that?)

And thoroughly sexist.

(I swear.)

Having now judged the bods of fifty-one cuties over three
nights, I can only say this: are they ever right.

Actually, Leonard Horn, the pageant honcho, agrees with
these people and would like to jettison the flesh section of the
competition. But he's also no fool, and hasn't the least idea
how to do it. I don't know your feelings, but personally, if he
ever did, I would never watch the show again. (It's like when
Playboy ran these amazingly pretentious articles by its founder
and creator, numberless pages devoted to the *Playboy* philos-
ophy, the intent of all trying to prove that *Playboy* was more
than a skin magazine; this at a time when we internationally
known intellectuals knew it was nothing *but* a skin magazine.
If they took away the dollies, I would have been in favor of
censoring the rag, on the grounds that *Playboy* without pictures is truly pornographic.)

What is it like when these dear and desperate young things,
shivering in the vastness, trying not to totter in their high
heels, come advancing toward you? All this in attire that has
yet to be worn on any beach in either hemisphere?

Answer: If you're a girl-watcher, A + .*

(The asterisk is there because . . . it's just different.) Let's
say we're at the beach, and we grade away. You like this one,
I say you're crazy, bad ankles; you say ankles are trivial, blah-
de-blah. Nobody's feelings are hurt, nobody even knows what
we're doing if we're surreptitious.

Here, suddenly, there were *consequences*.

Aside that I just, truly, remembered. Among my memorable
ogles I cannot forget the *Butch Cassidy* summer of the late
sixties when I worked at Fox Out There. And that time, some
of the biggies decided it would be nice to have a young-talent

program. So they put a bunch of guys and gals under what I assume were very low salary contracts, and they studied, would you believe, acting.

They ate in the commissary.

Moi aussi.

Now it might not shock you to learn that the men were mostly blue-eyed and model types. And the girls, among them, had mopped up on most of the major beauty contests in the world.

The first day they came in for lunch: silence as they traipsed by.

(Another aside, a historical one. The greatest girl-watching in world history, I am told by a connoisseur, was during the great days of Metro. Lana Turner rated third. Ava Gardner second. Elizabeth Taylor, in her teens, was mistress of all she surveyed. When she entered that large commissary, there was always, day after day, a reverential silence.)

It didn't continue day after day at Fox. After about a week, a producer friend said, of a Miss World or Universe, "Is she getting hairier?" I said I didn't think so. He said, "Well, she's not looking so good to me today."

And he was right.

We had become picky, overdemanding, jaded. If you have a wine-tasting and you rate Gallo Hearty Burgundy against Christian Brothers, fair enough. But if you rate '61 Palmer against '61 Petrus against '61 Latour, three of the great wines of our lifetime, one of them will begin to seem less than glorious. Your palate will have become overdemanding. It's not fair to whichever of the three you're downgrading.

In Atlantic City, we had to try to be, if possible, fair. (I'll deal with fairness now; the other, perhaps more important question was this: what's real? I'll get to that in a sec.)

Fairness begins with this statement: *they are all keepers.* Margaret Hamilton does not get to Atlantic City. Sure, they range from five to six feet in height, from under a hundred to over one hundred and thirty in tonnage.

But they're none of them going to cause you embarrassment

if you have to stroll with them poolside. And they all passed
the criterion we were given: how well the contestant maintained sound physical fitness. (Weight training being very big
now, if their fact sheets are to be believed.)

I rated the five I was following like this:

Miss Mississippi	(the sexy one)	Perfect
Miss Alabama	(prettiest)	Excellent
Miss Colorado	(the modern one)	Excellent
Miss Florida	(personality)	Excellent
Miss Minnesota	(bloodlines)	Kind of dumpy

At least to these eyes. But these eyes can be deceived, especially in Atlantic City, because you simply don't know what's
real.

When we arrived and were given our orientation, the subject
of padding was brought up, and the pageant said, in essence,
it was aware of its existence and wasn't, obviously, in favor of
it, but wasn't in a position to take a position.

I thought it was and said so.

The reply was essentially this: the pageant people didn't
want to get into the problem. They didn't want to hire nurses
and have the girls dress in front of them or some such solution.
They believed in the girls' sense of fair play, and that was that.

I didn't really believe in that and said so.

There are strange things done not just in the midnight sun.
Example: the title of this section came from the following
exchange:

REPORTER
(to contestant)
Do you use Preparation H?

CONTESTANT
(shocked)
Aren't you being too
personal?

REPORTER
(quickly explaining)
I meant under your eyes.

The product, so I'm told, does the same thing under your eyes it does in other parts of the body: shrinks things. The point of use being that if you feel a little baggy, you dab it on and pray for the best. The reason you pray for the best is that it's dangerous—too much and you can burn that extremely sensitive area.

They do a lot of stuff to themselves. Vaseline is now so well known as to be a snooze, but they use it on their teeth and lips so everything stays nice and moist and you can smile for hours.

And they tape their boobs. (Surgical tape is the stickem of choice, and I think what they do is crisscross the stuff beneath their breasts to make them stick out and look perkier.)

They tape their swimsuit bottom so it doesn't ride up when they prance, and of course, one recent winner got a second jolt of fame when it was shown she'd had a fabulous nose job not long before she entered the contest.

But the biggie this year is breast surgery.

Some of my peers and pageant experts feel they can spot it instantly. (I can't.) And the guesses were that maybe only 10 percent had had it, maybe a third. A number of people felt it shouldn't be allowed. I thought, Hell, if they wanted to go do it, go do it. Everybody else is. A hundred thousand women a year are paying over a third of a billion to surgeons. (I gather there is a stylistic difference from one coast to the other. Eastern women are a bit reticent about going from dainty to walloping overnight, whereas Californians want as much silicone as can be funneled in.)

I suppose the main reason I don't care is because, from this judge's point of view, the bathing-suit competition was just this: an acting exercise.

It didn't matter finally if they were in sound physical shape or not. What mattered was the same as in movies: star quality.

Which, as said, cannot be defined, but we do know this: it's somewhere in the eyes.

And that was what you concentrated on as the girls came down the stage toward you. What the eyes said.

Some eyes said this: "This is not a nice place."

Others, this: "Hellllppp."

And: "You rotten son of a bitch, staring at me."

"Sexist bastard."

"Pig."

"I want my mommm-eeee."

But some of them, the best actresses of the bunch, had a slow drumbeat coming from somewhere, keeping them company as they came closer and closer, all the time whispering . . .

"I want you . . .

. . . oh Daddy yes . . .

. . . so bad . . .

. . . oh Daddy yes . . .

. . . just you, Daddy . . .

. . . please . . .

. . . take me, Daddy . . .

. . . take me all the way . . ."

. . . d

      o

        w

          n . . ."

Evening Gown

You all know, I'm sure, that the two most famous lies of our time are "The check is in the mail" and "I promise I won't come in your mouth." For me, you can add a third: "All brides are beautiful."

I have seen panicked brides, angry brides, drunken brides; once (I swear) even a happy one.

What I do believe is this: no woman ever hurt her chances by putting on an evening gown. (With the exception, of course, of women in gowns designed by that sadistic Frenchie, Christian Lacroix. The ones with the bubbles of fabric in all those neat places. I loved it when those society ladies were scabbling over their Lacroix's. They all looked like "What's wrong with this picture?" as far as I was concerned. The over/under on his survival was a bet we all should have taken.)

All the Atlantic City fifty-one seemed at peace and serene as they wafted their ways across the stage. Somebody said to me that what we were seeing was "timeless" beauty.

Which made me ask a lot of people in the beauty business— movie people, model people, casting people—if such a thing existed. And the feeling was this: uniformly, yes. "Lombard would be stunning today, Tiegs twenty years ago." (Actually, Tiegs, who is amazing for her longevity, started twenty years ago, so let's make it forty.)

I know it's their business and I'm just an amateur ogler, but I think they're only at least 200 percent wrong.

I think the ideal of feminine beauty changes, and changes constantly. It's not unreasonable to say, today, that Streisand has "a kind of classic beauty." I think that's true.

Do you remember where you were the first time you saw her?

I do, as a matter of fact. It was on the stage of a Broadway theater thirty years ago, and she was auditioning for a tiny part in a musical I was involved with—

—and I hated everything about her.

I was personally responsible for her not getting the job. But by her extraordinary talent, she has made us see the truth: she's a kind of classic beauty. And we pass that on. Without Barbra, Bette is still working the baths in lower Manhattan.

Do you think Rubens's ladies would be sought after today?

I think Miss America changes too, and not just a little. In the old days, they used to give the measurements of the contestants. Here is a number. Commit it to memory:

25

That was the waist measurement of Margaret Gorman, Miss Washington, D.C., and the first Miss America back in 1921. All right. Thinking caps on. Envision her. I am now going to list five more numbers. Which do you think represents her bust measurement?

34
35
36
37
38

Got your number? The envelope, please. Answer . . . none of the above. Okay? Two more numbers. Which is her bust measurement?

33
39

None of the above again. Ready for two more?

32
40

Enough suspense—she had a *thirty*-inch bust, good people. Three-zero. This, remember, was the enchantress whom the contest declared "the most beautiful Bathing Girl in America."

And this is not a onetime aberration. In the late twenties, Warner Bros. released some facts about the chorus girls in a musical it was making.

"The ideal movie chorine measured in:

32½ inch bust
23 inch waist
34 inch hips

Venus de Milo, with her 28½ inch waist, couldn't get a job as
a script girl on Poverty Row."

Now granted this was a movie press release, but if anything,
it would be glorifying the shapes of the ladies under contract.
Miss de Milo (where does Hollywood come up with those
names?) might not be able to get a job as a scriptgirl, but at
the same time, precious few of their chorines would work these
days in Vegas.

The measurements of Miss America contestants are not di-
vulged anymore, at least not to judges, but they all did fine in
this portion of the contest, in the same order as before, with
Miss Mississippi the class of the field, Miss Minnesota bringing
up the rear. But no complaints about any of them.

So does the ideal of beauty change? I say, as I've already
said, that it does. You may feel differently. It's not as important
an argument as can peace break out in the Middle East, but it
is a lot more accessible.

One last thing on the subject. I was discussing this with
some homosexual friends, and after a lot of chitchat, they
tended to agree with me. Then one of them said this: "But I
don't think beauty changes in men."

He went on to explain that Michelangelo's "David" is still
a touchstone, as were so many of the ancient sculptures. I offer
this only as something that's kind of interesting.

And who else but me and Suzy tells you these things? . . .

Talent

How talented, as Mr. Carson might inquire, are they?

Those of you who've watched the show over the years already have your answer. But remember, you're only seeing
the, you should pardon the expression, cream. These eyes have
seen 'em all.

And the answer, of course, is: "not."

But you have to add this: nor should they be.

Major talents don't need to enter a contest like this. They're
already out there on the road, working. These are basically

college kids, and a lot of them are here for the scholarship money, which is a lot. At all levels, the pageant, as noted, claims over $5 *million* is available each and every year. And for the girls here, it can be a bundle.

Miss America	$30,000
First Runner-up	17,000
Second Runner-up	11,000
Third Runner-up	8,000
Fourth Runner-up	6,000
Other Semifinalists	4,000

The reigning Miss America at this time has been entering this contest for years, never quite getting to the national level till last year. But she'd put herself through college with her winnings.

Not only are we dealing with performers noted for their limitations, another factor must be added in: they're pooped. I'm amazed they can open their mouths or move their legs at all. Because in the ten days they're in New Jersey, they are constantly involved with trying to make the television show less of an embarrassment than last year's.

The Friday before the Saturday telecast—and this is not an unusual schedule—they didn't have to arrive at the Convention Center till half past seven. That's in the morning. They rehearse all day. The final preliminary show starts at nine. That's at night. So by the time they've been released from active duty, they've put in close to an eighteen-hour day.

The production numbers are kind of what you might call great bad art. It's not till you see them over and over that you realize the stupendous problem facing the choreographer, that problem being mainly this: the girls mostly aren't long on grace.

Three decades past, I was involved in the unsuccessful salvaging of a Broadway musical. The star of the musical, a splendid and acclaimed renderer of the Bard, had agreed to attempt the switch with three strikes against him: 1. he couldn't sing, if by singing you mean coming close to carrying the tune; 2. he couldn't remember his lines, not because of any memory problem but because he hadn't done a part in which lines were rewritten in many years; 3. he couldn't move. Exaggeration. He was perfectly ambulatory. What he would not do was move in rhythm.

We solved number 1 by giving him as few songs as possible, and those only with chorus singers to help him find the notes; number 2 was improved by putting signs up out of the audience's view with his new lines written out; number 3, though, was just a bitch. The final solution was this: have him just kind of stand there smiling while other people, dancers, moved around him. You would be amazed, if skillfully done, how well this works. Now, when I say "just kind of stand there," I don't mean impersonate a statue. He'd smile and wave and sometimes do spins—only he wasn't spinning, he was being spun by his dancing partner. All he had to do was keep smiling and stay upright.

That's sort of what they do on the Miss America show. You've got fifty-one mostly untrained singers and dancers and not enough time to do anything. So mostly, they just kind of smile and stand there while the seven or eight real dancers the program hires go mad with activity. (If you'll watch closely next year, you'll discover that during the numbers some of the contestants always seem to be in positions of importance. That's because the choreographer, desperate, grabs any that can do anything and sticks them up front.)

This year, the best number was the Sondheim song from *Follies*, "Beautiful Girls," because it was a number constructed in the musical for the girls to just mostly stand there and smile and walk around. I think it should be in the show forever.

The girls do it great.

My five didn't do so great, but no one threw fruit at them either.

. . .

Miss Mississippi sang a medley of "Alexander's Ragtime Band" and "Here's to the Band." She looked, as always, startling. And did okay.

Miss Florida, the personality kid, sang and danced something called "Showstopper." Adroitly.

Miss Alabama, the beauty, played, alas, "The Warsaw Concerto." (I think that piece was composed with shows like this in mind. Like the guy who gave us "Lady of Spain" must have had a soft spot in his heart for bad accordion players.) But if her choice of music wasn't inspired, she played it well.

Miss Colorado, the modernist, did a jazz vocal of "Night and Day," and was, I felt, the only singer you might have actually gone to a club and paid money to hear sing.

Miss Minnesota played something entitled "Gypsy Airs" on her fiddle, and you knew you weren't listening to Itzhak Perlman, but she nailed the notes dead-solid perfect.

I figured all five had to be among the ten finalists.

And the one I had given me heart to?

Well, Miss Utah hadn't hidden her nerves during our Wednesday morning interview. And she didn't look happy that night when it was her turn to wear a swimsuit for me. (Terrific figure. You just knew, though, that she really didn't want to be traipsing around in the chill air dressed like that.) And the next night, she still wasn't at ease in her evening gown.

Now, Friday night, the last night, late in the show, she came out and sat on the piano bench and played something called "Spanish Melody." And I knew, watching her, for the first time, it didn't matter anymore. She was back where she'd been since she was four, on the damn bench with the grand in front of her—

—and she just let fly.

About two minutes later, she stood up, and you know how there's applause and then there's *applause*?

Well, this was *applause*!

For the first and only time, there was actually a stunned

audience clapping like hell, turning to their neighbors, saying, "Did she really play like that?"

She did. She stood there for a moment in the sound, this stunning, bright, talented creature, with no chance at all.

Woulda, shoulda, coulda . . .

25. GREAT MOMENTS IN TELEVISION OR "TELL ME ABOUT THE HOSPICE"

Moist, they stood there, clutching each other's hands, the brunette wearing black, the blonde in blue, and they tried to keep their smiles working, but it was almost too great a task, not surprising considering the freakish events they had just been through. It was late, later than anyone possibly figured, Sunday morning now, and the contest was approaching the most remarkable conclusion in its history.

Gary Collins, the host, stood beside them, and color was slowly returning to his face. He had just faced the death of all ceremonial masters, had done well enough but was still scathed.

> COLLINS
> Now, there are two.
>   (pause)
> Just two.
>   (pause)
> I mentioned earlier tonight
> ninety thousand are involved
> in the pageant, and it's come
> down to two. One of you is
> going to receive a seventeen-
> thousand-dollar scholarship.
> You will also be Miss Ameri-

ca's standby. First Runner-up
is still pretty sensational.

It is and it isn't. Only the most arcane of trivia freaks can
tell you who Miss America of the year before last is. But no
one breathing keeps track of the first runners-up. (Except
maybe Suzette Charles, who replaced Vanessa Williams after
her fall. The scuttlebutt on Miss Williams, by the by, is that
until *Penthouse*, she was as good as any winner ever. Hard-
working, gracious, bright—not to mention having an actual
talent for singing. Her new success as a pop vocalist surprised
no one in Atlantic City.)

Collins's voice now has genuine weight. Maybe it was because he knew that nothing awful could happen to him anymore, he'd emerged from the fire. Maybe it was the moment
itself, but sitting in the huge Convention Center, you could
feel the crowd getting a collective case of dry throat.

> COLLINS
> But now . . .
> . . . one of you is going to
> have her life changed . . .
> . . . dramatically . . .
> . . . forever . . .
> . . . from this moment on . . .
>
> IT WILL NEVER BE THE
> SAME.

What he said was cornball, yes, but true. I've been a New
York Knickerbocker season-ticket holder for I'm not even sure
now how many years, but rarely have I rooted harder than I
did at that moment.

I've watched the TV show forever, never alone; sometimes
Ilene and I would have people over and we'd grab paper and
pencil and the one who picked the winner would get something
of no value whatsoever.

Great good clean malicious fun. You'd just sit there staring at the screen waiting for mistakes in taste. Or for some panicked singer to lose the tune, a dancer to stumble.

Make it sadistic fun.

Guilty.

But there's something so, I don't know, something so just heartwarmingly tacky about the enterprise. Ilene was coerced by her sorority sisters when she was at SMU (ye gods) to enter, and she was runner-up to Miss Dallas and still counts it as one of the more empty and embarrassing experiences of her life.

I don't think there's much of anything on the tube except the Oscars that so brings out the beast in all of us. Because in your living room it's easy to deride them, all fifty-one—

—they're all so *good*. They all believe in all those *virtues*. And *you* know, it's all so *false*. They aren't, all fifty-one, sweet. They can't, all fifty-one, love their parents. They're not, all fifty-one, virgins.

But year in, year out, they smile out at you and fib, and year in, year out, I sit at home and throw popcorn at the screen.

But it's different when you're there.

You want them to miss the banana peels. You've seen them sweat, caught the lip tremble, the quick panic when they've goofed. They're children, that's all, with nutball fantasies, and this one, the nuttiest of them all, they can only approach this the one time. So what you want is a minimum of embarrassment, a lot of justice triumphing.

Next year, back to the living room.

For now it was the Convention Center, packed and cavernous. The Grunt jury reached the place on time, were seated up front not much before 10:00 P.M., when the program was to start.

Great seats.

A+ seats.

But not where we'd been stationed the night preceding.

The Cute jury was there now. The Celebs. We never met them, by design or not, I don't know.

I peered across the runway at them. Some of them looked

like themselves, some of them looked worse. Stories about their behavior had been popping all day. You couldn't not hear them. From bell captains, room clerks, TV personnel. One of them threw a screaming fit because of having to stand in line when they checked in. Another spent almost all the day lying in bed in her suite with creams on, so her face wouldn't crinkle in public. One member, who was a drunk, accused another member, who had been a drunk, of being a drunk.

Yum.

Personally, all I wanted from them was that they wouldn't screw up. By which I mean, vote logically, sensibly, properly. By which I mean, of course, that they agree with me.

The TV show began promptly at ten with the soon-to-be-departing Miss A., Kaye Lani Rae Rafko, telling us that the crown meant a bunch more than it did in the old days. Because the winners now represented "the New American Woman," who, as well as being bright and well educated, was also "ambitious."

Intriguing, kind of. Ambition didn't used to be something women admitted to. Except maybe in hopes for your children.

In the Convention Center, things got off quickly and cleanly. The contestants sang a song, in the middle of which they each got to go to a nearby mike and announce who they were, state, school, etc. Then it was the Grunt jury's turn to be introduced (via videotape) and thanked for doing our chores so nobly and well.

Then the top ten finalists were announced.

This is always the first big surprise moment of the show, and the pageant does its best to keep it as secret as possible—the pageant people don't want the Unlucky Forty-One to know too soon, in case they decide to walk through the program or, worse, walk out on it.

We knew, of course, the night preceding. After our final judging was done Friday night, we got together with some NBC people and were told who the top ten would be. No big surprises. We also knew who was going to grab it all. There could only possibly be three.

MISS ALABAMA: The Prettiest
                        A decent serious pianist
                        College senior (Auburn)
                        High-jump champion (Love it)

MISS COLORADO: The Feminist
                        Good scat singer
                        College senior (Oklahoma City)
                        Wants to be an agent (Love it)

MISS FLORIDA: Best Interview
                        Best picture
                        Okay-plus singer/dancer
                        Master's student (Florida State)

The other two I'd been following had fallen out of it. Miss Mississippi, the bombshell, was just too sexy to win it all. And Miss Minnesota, the one from Stanford, just wasn't attractive enough or appealing enough to have a shot. Final ten, sure— she'd won talent her night, just about assuring that. But there was never a beauty contest in the history of the world she could be favored in.

The top three were just the class of the field. Miss Alabama had such classical beauty and enough talent and a terrific figure. The only weaknesses were two: she didn't sparkle and she was from the South. (Maybe it's just me, but there seemed to be a reaction setting in against those antebellum sweeties who had dominated the pageant for so long.) The only negative against Miss Colorado was also her strength: a contemporary lady. Miss Florida had no flaws. No overwhelming strengths either, but often the winner here is like a student who gets straight "B"s, whereas those who lump "A"s and "D"s get left behind.

I figured it had to be Miss Colorado. The pageant had done

so much talking about wanting to get on with the future. Well, here she was, all dolled up and in their own backyard.

Miss Florida was the first one announced.

Followed by Miss North Dakota, a ballet dancer who goes to Juilliard and who had no chance.

Miss Mississippi, looking illegal, followed her.

Then Miss California, a very thin woman of twenty-six who just might make a fortune as a TV pitchwoman. And who had no chance.

Miss Minnesota. No chance a-tall.

Miss Hawaii, and if there was an outsider contender, she was it. Stunning. No Miss Hawaii had ever won. She was a professional-type singer, not surprising since she had been a professional singer since her teenage years. A negative was that she was a college freshman. Why a negative? Probably because she was twenty-six years old.

Miss Oklahoma, an opera singer from the Great Plains, with zero chance.

Miss Louisiana, a ballet dancer with a slim outside shot— she might have won back in the fifties, when her type was more fashionable. Also, again, a southerner. I'm getting a bit tense now—where's my girl?

Now Miss Alabama. Growing more stunning by the hour.

And last, there she was, my very own Miss Colorado.

I studied the ten of them standing there, smiling as the applause drenched them. Not a bad bunch. I felt we'd done, as a jury, our job, which was to give them ten, any of whom could be Miss A.

Well, we gave them nine. Miss Minnesota had more chance than I did. But not that much.

Then, from the stage, Gary Collins said, "But now the pre-liminary panel has done its job, and we begin three brand-new competitions in Swimsuit, Evening Gown, and Talent."

Then a little slip of the tongue happened that was a harbinger of future weirdnesses. "Here's how each competition is going

to be rated in the final score," Collins read. "Talent will count
fifty—uhh—forty percent, excuse me."

Doesn't seem like much, granted, but suppose for a minute
you're captain of a Super Bowl team and you trot out just
before game time for the flip of the coin and there you are
along with the other captain and the referee, and just before
he flips he looks at you both and starts to chat.

> SUPER BOWL REF
> Good luck, guys, and oh, one
> little thing, did anybody go
> over the few scoring changes
> with you?

> YOU
> (stunned)
> *Scoring* changes?

> OTHER CAPTAIN
> (an offensive lineman)
> Duhhhhhh.

> SUPER BOWL REF
> Here's the deal, guys—for
> this game and this game only,
> we've decided to put a little
> historical perspective into
> play. So today, the touchdown
> will count two instead of six,
> and the field goal will count
> five instead of three—

> YOU
> —but that isn't fair—it's not
> what got us here—

> SUPER BOWL REF
> —right you are, heads or
> tails?

OTHER CAPTAIN
(sucking his
thumb now)
Whahhhhh.
(and as his tears
pour down—

Fade Out.

To put a little historical perspective into this book, field goals once did count five and touchdowns two. And if you think that's ancient history, you are wrong. When Alfred Hitchcock was born, points after touchdowns counted *four*.

You can't change the rules during the Super Bowl. But the Miss America contest does its equivalent. Blithely.

Brief refresher: for the Grunt jury, scoring went like this:

Talent: it had been 50 percent for us. Now, for the Cuties, it had dropped to 40 percent. But, in truth, since none of the contestants was, is, or ever will be the kind of talent you'd pay to hear, they could drop it a lot more. The need for talent is truly only important for the tube—you don't get ratings with a bunch of girls explaining how to pack a suitcase (that happened, I swear). The fact is, what the pageant needs is someone who can *talk*. Who can be charming in the face of the mindless months ahead. They don't bring their trampolines on the road.

Swimsuit: had been 16⅔ percent for us, now up to 20 percent.

Evening Gown: Do you remember earlier when I was giving the virtues that Miss America had to have and how baffled I was by that old favorite, "Olympic Ability"? Well, Evening Gown not only went from 16⅔ to 40 percent, it also had two new traits added—one being personality.

Fine with me.

How you judge personality in an evening gown is not something I know a lot about, but if they say it belongs, it belongs.

But what, pray tell, is "Expression"?

That was the other trait the judges were to factor in. "Evening Gown, Personality, and Expression," Gary Collins said.

Incredible.

But still nothing compared to what had happened to the value of the most important element of all, the interview. It had just plain disappeared.

Zee-ro.

Still, I figured my big three would have done well. Some of the other ten might not have made it with this new and whacko system, but the trio, yes, absolutely.

"Now, let's meet the celebrated members of that panel," Gary Collins said.

He introduced the first.

> COLLINS
> Twenty-five movies, star of
> three NBC television series,
> *The A Team, Banacek,* and
> *Doctors' Hospital.*

Okay, I ask you, who is it? (Answer below.) Next biggie.

> COLLINS
> One of America's most popu-
> lar and glamorous stars, star
> of *Green Acres,* who is also
> chairman of the board of
> (blank) International, the
> inimitable—

Okay, think a sec. Who's this one? (Answer next to previously noted celeb.)

(George Peppard and Eva Gabor)

Did any of you get them?

How about the next one? "Stage, screen and television personality, starring as Leland MacKenzie on NBC's *L.A. Law.*"

Or: "Anchor of *NBC News at Sunrise,* backup host of the *Today* show, you see her on NBC's *At This Hour.* Meet—"

—who?

Next Collins talked about someone we all know and love so well.

COLLINS

The editor of *Parade* maga-
zine, author of *The Greatest
Risk of All*, recipient of the
Tree of Life Award from the
Jewish National Fund—

I will give a free subscription to *Collier's* magazine to anyone who answered Richard Dysart, Deborah Norville, and Walter Anderson.

I was appalled. The whole reason for the cockamamie double-jury system was because they couldn't get famous people to survive in Atlantic City for one week.

Now, looking across the runway, it was evident the pageant couldn't get *anyone* for more than twenty-four hours. These weren't celebrities; they were a bunch of NBC employees, or would-be employees. Not only that, they hadn't met the girls—they'd seen taped interviews, head shots only. If that's all we'd seen, Miss Utah would have won, says I, because no one would have been able to notice her hands.

Still, I was sure that they'd agree with me. My God, anyone with the least talent for girl-watching *had* to agree with me. *Because I was right.*

(But deep inside, my stomach was starting to churn.)

· · ·

The show itself went slickly. Only a few giggles and teeth-clenchers. Swimsuit was a triumph for the lady from Missis-sippi, all in white. You'll have to take my word that this one is a gift from above. And while she's walking toward the Cuties, vamping them, that mystical drumbeat had never been as urging:

"I want you . . .
. . . oh Daddy yes . . .
. . . so bad . . .
. . . oh Daddy yes . . .
. . . just you, Daddy . . .
. . . please . . .
. . . take me, Daddy . . .
. . . take me all the way . . .
. . . d
    o
     w
      n . . ."

Well, while those intellectual thoughts are going through your bean, up onstage, Mary Ann Mobley, co-MC and wife of Gary Collins, is reading this, in a kind of haughty tone: "Carla Haag is working toward her law degree. She already has a degree in psychology."

Law degree? Who cares about her law degree? I want juicy stuff. I want secrets revealed: *How do you get to look like that?*

The talent competition, the heart of the show, went well. There were no embarrassments; all the singers could at the very least carry a tune, the dancers knew where their feet were almost all the time.

Of my three, Miss Florida and Miss Colorado were a hair down from the preliminary nights, while the stunning Miss Alabama played the piano faultlessly.

I was looking, suddenly, at a dead heat.

Any one of the three and I was a most happy fellow.

Evening Gown (including, don't forget, the mysterious "Expression") was the last competition, and the girls were asked a question, unrehearsed, to show, I guess, if they could think on their feet. Some could.

COLLINS
(to Miss California)
Only twenty percent of eligi-
ble voters under the age of

twenty-five exercise the right
to vote; in your opinion,
why?

MISS CALIFORNIA
(a poised, absolutely
blank look; then—)
Well, I'm not sure I quite
have the answer to that one,
Gary—
(louder)
—but I would like to tell the
people of America that it's vi-
tal that we get out and
vote. . . .

In other words, I don't know but do it, whatever it is.

Miss Minnesota, who went to Stanford and played the fiddle,
did not disappoint me. She is a God-Clutcher, and I'm not
partial to them—I still hate the Dallas Cowboys more than
any team in sports because when they were terrific they always
insinuated that it wasn't because they had more skill but because they were being Watched Over. From On High. They
never failed to trumpet their churchgoing habit. (Later, when
their drug habit became known, and the team began being
called not "America's Team" but "South America's Team," I
didn't mind it much. I guess I just don't like or trust people
who seem to say, "If only you loved Him as much as I do,
you could step up a class.")
    Anyway, she was asked this:

COLLINS
There's much discussion of
the influence of the media in

the political process; how do
you feel about this issue?

       MISS MINNESOTA
Well, I feel that every individual has their own decisions
and their own rights—and I
feel that being brought up
with a moral background—
and I was lucky enough to
have a lot of values—and that
I would feel strong enough in
my own decisions that the
media would not disrupt any
of my decisions in the political
realm.

Loads of smiles with that one along life's journey.

Then it was finished, the officials were tabulating off to my
right, and Gary Collins, a handsome figure all week long,
courteous and in control, smiled out at the masses alongside
the ten finalists who stood hand-holding in a line.

My three were on the outsides. Miss Colorado at the left
end, Miss Alabama beside her. Miss Florida farthest from me,
on the right.

Did they know what I knew? I wondered. That it was down
to them. It wasn't just me, of course; the whole Grunt jury,
at least those I'd talked to, felt pretty much the same.

Up front, Collins held his mike, awaiting his cue.

       COLLINS
Well, the suspense is building.
  (looks at the girls)
What about it, top ten—
nervous?
  (he smiles)

Anybody want out?
(they laugh, he laughs
—but oh, are they
anxious for time to fly)
Which of these talented ten is
going to be Miss America,
1989? Well, there's no moment like the present. While
you at home still decide, let's
see what our judges have
decided.
(and now, at last, the
big walk for the results)
May I have the decision
please?

Just before a reply, I stare at the retiring Miss America, the
nurse, Kaye Lani Rae Rafko, the Michigan girl with the Ha-
waiian first name. She was very popular. And apparently had
done a wonderful job for the pageant. Now, she was going
back to nursing.

What was she thinking as she watched Collins standing by
the Cute jury? I met her my first day in Atlantic City. She
was tall, and attractive enough, but what you liked most about
her was the eyes. There was intelligence in them; she was
clearly a bright young lady. As we were introduced, standing
in the boardwalk sunshine, I stuck out my hand to shake hers—

—only she didn't stick out her hand back.

Do you know those toys—ducks, I think they are—you buy
in the dime store and you stick them on the rim of glasses full
of water and they bend over, take the water, go back up straight,
then bend over again, sip more water.

Well, she bent like one of those ducks.

It was an instinctive move—she bent, gave me her cheek to
kiss. I kissed it. She stood back up straight. I remember thinking then, Where did *that* move come from? Not nursing school.
My God, how many cheeks had she kissed in the months
preceding, and then—

—and then Gary Collins, all elegance and charm, said words
I hadn't thought possible:

> COLLINS
> You have a *what? A tie?*
>   (stares at the audience)
> Do you believe this?
>   (back to the officials)
> Can you give me some idea? . . .
> just . . . an *inkling?* Will we
> be finished before midnight?
>   (big laugh)

Collins stands there, smiling as the crowd roars. Because he
is a pro and the pageant people are too, so he knows something:
this is a blip. It's happening, sure, but no big deal. Do a little
tap dancing and it's done. He decides to go chat up the girls.
First in line is my maiden, Miss Colorado. And she is great.
Gets the biggest laugh of the night.

> COLLINS
> What was your favorite part
> of the competition?

> MISS COLORADO
>   (like a shot)
> Oh, lunchtime.

Briefly now, a few comments about dramatic time and real
time. When you watch something on the tube or in a theater,
time better move its ass. In real life, if I stand on the curb,
hail a cab, and get one *right away*, that's great.

In dramatic life, if you shot that, it would mean a rush for
the popcorn machine. It might take a minute for me to get
into the taxi, and that's not allowable.

Take this year's contest. When the girls introduce themselves and tell where they're from and their schools? Well,
they're on camera just short of *six seconds* each. The parade

in the swimsuit? Fifteen seconds of airtime per girl. Same with the evening gown. You watch them with great care in your living room, but it's a blink, no more.

Well, when Miss Colorado made her "lunchtime" joke, Collins had been left dangling slowly in the wind for *sixty-five* seconds.

And counting.

But he still had his *savoir faire* on. As he must. He's still clinging to his truth: *this is a blip.*

He makes a sweet line about how funny the girls are after the competition's over, glances back to the officials—

—nope.

He goes to Miss Alabama next. Then to the girl beside her. He assumes all of them are going to try for careers in show business. "I want to try to be a corporate attorney," the third girl says.

Two minutes gone now. One hundred and twenty seconds.

Another glance at the officials—

—nope.

> COLLINS
> (trying for jovial)
> They're still working on the
> tie.

He moves down the line. How many of you are new to pageants? Two raise their hands. Now, he's by Miss Minnesota and asks if she'd have done anything different. She says she would have answered her question better.

Another glance—

—nope.

I don't know what it was like in your living room, but being there, I kept looking around knowing I had to try to commit every morsel to what was left of my memory, because something was very clear to me by now—

—this was no fucking blip, man; this was Krakatoa.

It was along about here, and this may have been my imagination, but Collins's hands were still steady, only his color began to close in on that of his tuxedo shirt.

He leaves the top ten, goes to a nonfinalist, and she immediately asks him if he remembers her name, which is not what he needs to hear along about now. He asks her if she can spell her state without looking down at her sash. She tells him he's been watching David Letterman again. (During all of this, he was smiling—but his handsome face, and this wasn't my imagination, began to seem definitely skull-like.)

After 250 seconds, Collins turns and plods back to the officials.

> COLLINS
> Guys, that's it.

—nope.

It isn't.

They haven't got it figured yet. Collins stands there. Maybe his knees sag, maybe they don't.

> COLLINS
> Can you give me four out of
> five?

—nope.

They can't.

Collins talks briefly with a judge, explains that he is, in front of God and everybody, dying, and then goes wandering across the Sahara-like stage in search of his wife.

Mary Ann Mobley, who was Miss America three decades back, greets him with this:

> MOBLEY
> You're dying well, my dear.
>   (good laugh)
> You know, when you're mar-
> ried twenty-one years, you

don't often get to see them
suffer—it's *wonderful*—and
on national television.
(more laughs, but quieter)

Now, Collins, who I assume applied for hazardous-duty pay
afterward, let the mask drop. Wiping his forehead, after another glance at the officials—
—still nope, it seemed to him forever, nope—

COLLINS
(plaintively)
I thought they had this problem *solved* . . .

—nothing was solved.

Three hundred and fifty seconds gone now. He turns to his
still-so-pretty wife and says, "Thirty years. How do you feel
tonight?" And she answered, "I'm very proud. I'm very proud
to be alive."

That was the last laugh of the night.

Every time Collins clocks the judges and the officials, so do
I. And from just across the runway, the panic is palpable.
There's not much frantic movement, but there's activity. People are showing each other papers, people are conferring, heads
are spinning. I was aware that the whole thing was not handled
by computers, but even if you licked your pencil tip every time
you added up a column of numbers, how could it take this
long? Little crazed bursts of applause bubbled up from behind
us. A few people shouted this and that. No one in the place,
I think it's safe to say, knew whether to shit or wind his watch.

On the stage, Collins and Mobley, who had performed above
and beyond with their ad-libs, decided to get serious. And
began thanking people. Sitting there, I didn't know why anybody needed thanking—a good chewing out seemed more the
order of the day—but off they went.

MOBLEY
I look at these contestants on
the stage, and I feel nothing
but pride. For the states, the
homes, the families that produced the caliber of young ladies that I see on the stage.
  (a deep curtsy)
I salute you, states.
  (the audience is forced
  to applaud)
I salute the parents.
  (less)
I salute the young ladies for
what they're making of their
lives.
  (little)

Now, as Collins keeps glancing over for his salvation—
—of course, nope—
—I wondered how paranoid he was. Did he think it was all
some kind of cosmic practical joke they were playing? Did they
really have the answers? Was all this public humiliation a
payback for some evil committed years before?

During these looks, his wife is as game as any contender,
going on about daughters are friends of parents by choice, and
congratulating the parents, whom she'd already just saluted.

Clearly, the good lady was running out of people to thank.
My God, what if she thanked the old folks a third time?—

—trying to stop it from becoming the Gong Show, Collins
stared at the camera and began some similar palaver of his
own.

COLLINS
(poor bastard)
We would also like to pay our
respects and a bit of a tribute

> to the thousands and thou-
> sands of volunteers . . .
>> (blah blah, ending with
>> a salute to—)
> . . . the volunteers, the state-
> pageant directors, and all the
> people who make this pageant
> work.
>> (beat—)
> And of course the millions of
> people watching on television.

He saluted us too, and he's getting, I thought, a little wild-eyed and the audience can't stand to be asked to clap again so now shouts of "Kaye Lani, Kaye Lani" build, and Collins turns to the reigning Miss A., who has been standing there kind of smiling and clapping throughout the carnage.

They chat briefly.

And then Collins, who has really won my heart by his efforts, makes one of the great requests in television history.

> COLLINS
> Tell me about the hospice.

A word of explanation perhaps is in order: Kaye Lani is a practicing nurse. But she doesn't work for your ordinary GP. She works for the dead and the dying. In other words, what he was saying was this:

> COLLINS
> Give us a few words on ex-
> tinction.

And she does.

On the Miss America program.

After a delay that had now gone on over five hundred seconds.

KAYE LANI
I'm going back to school in
the spring, to start work toward my Master's degree in
oncology, which is the study
of cancer, with a minor in
business administration.
   (beat)
So that one day *I will* open
my own hospice center for all
terminally ill patients, both
cancer as well as AIDS.

The audience, horsewhipped by this time, bursts into applause. *What were they clapping for?* Cancer? Death? I wasn't
sure of much right then except this: I was just so happy being
there, watching this great fuck-up. I hoped those goofballs
trying to figure it out never got the winner right. I wanted to
be there forever.

I almost was. But they got it. It took them over eleven
minutes, but the officials waved the card, and Collins, very old
by now, grabbed it before they could change their minds, and
started reading.

Zap—the prettiest, Miss Alabama, was fifth. I watched her
walk over, hug Kaye Lani, and she must have been disappointed. She should have been disappointed. There was no way
she was worse than third. Maybe a winner. But the southern-
bias thing had struck. Miss California was fourth, the pitchwoman type, and the opera singer from Oklahoma took
third.

I wasn't really interested. Because the last two, my two,
Colorado and Florida, were left, and they were going to go
head-to-head for the prize, and obviously, it was going to be
the closest vote in pageant history, having taken eleven-plus
minutes to separate the two. Onstage, Collins said, "The two
women receiving the highest scores are . . ."

I wanted Miss Colorado, but either way I felt good about

the week. I'd felt good at Cannes too, when *Pelle the Conqueror* grabbed top spot. Thoughts of that movie came back—of the brilliant kid in the title role, of Max von Sydow as the father, in a career-culminating performance, and how I'd screamed in the movie theater when it ended, how I'd—

"Miss Minnesota," Gary Collins said, stunning me back to bleak reality. The God-Clutcher was still contending.

The entire Grunt jury spun in toward each other, stunned.

"Assholes," one of us said. (I, say I proudly, was that one.) I think it's safe to say we felt betrayed—our work had turned out to be next to meaningless. No one I talked to had particularly warm feelings for Miss Minnesota.

Now, back to the stage.

"And Miss Colorado," Collins finished.

Moist, they stood there, clutching each other's hands, the brunette from Colorado wearing black, the blonde from Minnesota in blue. They were the two shortest of the last ten, not much over 5'2".

It was no contest. Or shouldn't have been. But the Cuties had found the two of them so close as to be equal. (Wrong. The whole tie fiasco concerned second and third. The winner here was home breezing.)

I had said to some of my fellow jurors earlier that evening that my nightmare was that Miss Minnesota would win. They all laughed and assured me it was inconceivable.

> COLLINS
> . . . life changed . . .
> . . . dramatically . . .
> . . . forever . . .
> . . . from this moment on . . .
>
> . . . IT WILL NEVER BE THE
> SAME . . .

Miss Piggy won the crown.

. . .

There was a reception after the program for the juries and the sponsors and any other hotshots who happened to be in the vicinity, and the one word that best set the tone was this: shock. No one could believe Miss Minnesota, the fiddler from Stanford, had done it. One of the Cute jury members, the flittiest, explained his vote by saying that he considered the gown and swimsuit contests trivial, so he only voted for talent, and he liked the fact that a fiddle player was in the top ten.

Gretchen Carlson, for that was Miss America's name, came in a bit later and gave a speech.

About values?

And morals?

Nope. She couldn't have been more gracious or grateful. A little humor crept in too. Probably in a year, when she gives up her title, no one will conceive that anyone else could have been as good.

And you know what? That may be true, because if Claude Berri, back in Cannes, didn't come up with his compromise giving *A World Apart* the female acting award as well as second place, my guess is that there would have been a lot of hurt feelings, and every other award would have been different.

And here, if the craze for ratings hadn't come up with the double-jury system (there was talk that night of changing it for next year, it was so clearly flawed), Miss Minnesota, instead of winning, would have finished ninth or tenth, at least by my reckoning. By knocking out the interview, everything had altered. None of the Cute Jury had been in a room with her, heard her platitudes. What they saw was a fiddler from Stanford; why not give it to her? My guess is that Miss Minnesota won the only Miss America contest in history she possibly could have. But she won it fairly—it was, after all, the only one she entered.

Here, all my life I'd thought beauty was in the eyes of the beholder, when the truth is, it's in the hands of the gods. . . .

. . . returns . . .

I WENT BACK TO Atlantic City yesterday, wandered. It seemed the proper time. The film festival had been in May, the pageant in September.

Now, it was May again.

A year since Cannes came calling. Some of the festival movies played in America. They all stiffed at the box office. *Pelle the Conqueror* got some wonderful reviews; nobody much cared. It went on to win the Oscar for Best Foreign Film; nobody much cared.

It was not a vintage year for Cannes. Remember 1960, with *Ben-Hur* and *La Dolce Vita*, and a Bergman, a Buñuel?

Eighty-eight would not linger in anyone's memory.

Not a vintage year for Atlantic City either. Miss Minnesota is flying from one state to another for her nine guh-zillionth appearance, and she has been an exemplary Miss America, but they're changing the format again—next year (at least tentatively), some of the Grunt jury's votes will be carried over and melded with the Cuties'.

And you know what?

I don't care.

I went back to see *Pelle,* and it was still a wonder—

—but I didn't scream out loud, didn't really care. I did once though. Once I had wanted *Pelle* to win so badly; Miss Colorado too.

Why? I guess I got caught up in the hype. It was, in many ways, a year of hype and glory, and what's so sad is that the bullshit is increasing while the glory disappears. Sometimes it seems to me as if our world is getting buried in bullshit.

I was walking with a movie actor recently. We were leaving the theater and his car was parked four blocks away and the paparazzi found him, surrounded him, began flashing away.

We walked on.

They traveled backward a few steps ahead of him, and he put his head down, his hands jammed into his pockets, and they talked to him, asked him to look at them, asked him to smile, asked him whom he was fucking now.

I dropped back a bit, watched it all. They wouldn't stop. Block after city block they tracked him, and they must have taken a thousand shots. I don't know this guy well, he means zero to me, but by the third block I couldn't stand it, I grabbed a camera putz, and he said, ''You touch my camera, and I sue,'' and why was I angry, I couldn't figure it for a while.

Eventually, we reached the actor's car, where maybe half a dozen of the original twenty were still on him. We got in, and they were going at him through the windshield now, when I realized that what upset me was it was crazy, anybody chasing this guy, because he wasn't a very good actor and he wasn't a very big star—

—but he'd had an affair with a famous woman recently, and the way we live now, that's enough.

I can't wait for the eighties to die. The decade of the centimillionaire. The Pig Decade. Sons of the rich buying businesses they don't care about or understand so they can dismantle them at a profit. That's always happened, I guess, but what hasn't is this: now, they're the good guys.

I walked along the boardwalk thinking of the wonderful antidote to hype I'd seen earlier that day from a homeless woman. She had a sign, as so many do now, but hers wasn't a hype sign, not one of these:

I'D HELP YOU IF I COULD. HELP ME. I'M A GOOD PERSON WITH
BAD LUCK. YOU CAN CHANGE THAT. I'M NOT A BEGGAR BUT GIVE
ME MONEY. THANX.

No, hers simply said this:

HOMELESS ETC.

I'd been moved by that, gave her money. I'd been that more
and more lately: moved. A good sign. I remembered Nastassja
Kinski reaching out to me, saying, "Bill, Bill, why are you so
cut off?"

That was changing, because maybe it hadn't been a vintage
year for the festival or the pageant, but it sure had been for
me. They were about changing lives. Mine changed too. A
little. A start. No more limousine-ordering ladies.

I spent some time in London, and the apartment worked. I
flew from Heathrow to Nice (I spent a few minutes searching
for the Vision, but I didn't find her. I did spot the Beast of Air
France, stalking along the corridors, smoking as much as I
remembered. She didn't quite remember me, though, but she
did look at me for longer than necessary, and for a blink I half-
expected her to say in her dulcet Von Stroheimish way, "*You
are a schtupid American, you haff no veesa, and you vill neffer
get to Cannes.*"

But she just walked on by).

I wore my tuxedo last month, and it almost fit, no popping
Ralph Lauren studs to torment me. I look back on that guy
with a kind of relief. He was such a panicked figure, setting
off for Europe alone.

We still know each other, and on bad days we meet and nod
in inevitable recognition, but on the whole he is receding, or
rather, I'm leaving him behind.

Dusk on the boardwalk, and now, even though I didn't know
it, the two events were going to meld again for me, as they
had when I saw the MISS PLAGE sign a year ago. Because this

glorious song that moves us so began to become audible, played
on some kind of electric organ . . .

> *uh . . . may . . .*
> *zing Grace . . .*
> *how sweet the sound . . .*

And it was a sweet sound. I turned, trying to locate the
music maker. I found her. She had the most radiant smile and
she was lying on her stomach on a kind of four-wheeled
stretcher, there on the boardwalk. The organ was in front of
her as she played the notes—

—played them with her tongue, for she had neither func-
tioning arms nor legs. People all but stood in line to put money
in her bucket, and they smiled at her, and believe me that this
was not unsettling, because she was playing the hand she was
dealt as well as anybody could. That, I think, is what washed
over all her listeners.

Of course, I went back in my mind to the contortionist on
the steps of the Palais at Cannes, jumping off the table, hitting
his head lightly on the cement walk, then staring at us, de-
manding money, almost none of which came.

I hadn't thought of him for half a year perhaps, and he
brought back a lot of festival moments. I hailed a rolling chair,
got in, asked the young guy pushing me to just walk for a
while.

I didn't know it, of course, but a movie moment was about
to happen, movie moments being things that take place on film
that we nod at and accept but that are totally impossible in
everyday life.

I asked him where he was from.

"Nottingham," he replied. His accent very strong. He explained that this was his third year, that he played soccer over
there, so his legs didn't mind the hours on the boardwalk.
When he wasn't playing soccer, he'd gone to school, had just
graduated. I asked what he majored in.

"Cinema," he said.

And then he explained how he imagined he'd go to the BBC now; then, eventually, he'd become a movie director. He was so self-assured—he would need that—and we moved further along the boardwalk as it got darker. I imagined the pirate ship in the harbor because he was complaining about how hard it was to see all the movies he wanted to see in Nottingham, so he went to Cannes; he'd just come from there.

"Cannes?" I said.

He explained to me that it was a film festival held in May each year in the south of France.

"Where do you stay?" I asked.

I was truly from Mars. "Stay?"

"What hotel?"

"I sleep on the beach." And then he explained how he snuck into cocktail parties and the like for sustenance and he wrote a little movie journal at his school and that got him some accreditation so he saw a lot of movies with the press, used his ingenuity to fake his way into whatever else he wanted.

"They have a staircase at the Palais—the Palais is where the films in competition are shown. Fabulous."

"What's so special about a staircase?" I wondered.

"Well, it's hard to explain, but it's a wide staircase, you see, and they put down a red carpet, and the important people, the stars and directors of each movie, they walk up the staircase on this red carpet, and the crowd—thousands, mind you—goes bonkers cheering." He paused before he said this next: "They'll cheer for me someday."

I wished him joy, but my mind was moving back a bit, because this had been my second movie moment within weeks. Not that many days ago, it had been early evening, and I left my apartment in New York—yes, my home is different; we sold our old place, each bought new ones—and got into a taxi, asked to be taken to an address where a ladyfriend lived. We zoomed down Park Avenue, and in the East-fifties, a woman stepped into the street, right arm raised, hailing a cab. I stared at her so carefully as my moving angle changed. She had no idea she was being watched.

It was Ilene.

She had just come from her divorce lawyer, where she'd signed the legal-separation papers. I'd already signed. We were unhooked at last.

She got into her cab, her driver made a turn, the two cars separated, she, I hope happily, heading for her new life, me, I hope happily for mine. . . .

WILLIAM GOLDMAN wrote his first novel, *The Temple of Gold*, when he was twenty-four. He has written over a dozen since then, many of them—*Boys and Girls Together, Marathon Man, Magic*—national best-sellers. He wrote the novel and screenplay *The Princess Bride* and won Academy Awards for *Butch Cassidy and the Sundance Kid* and *All the President's Men*. In 1985 he received the Laurel Award for lifetime achievement in screenwriting. His nonfiction includes *The Season*, a book about how Broadway works, and *Adventures in the Screen Trade*. He has been a sports fan since he saw Joe DiMaggio hit a double off the centerfield wall in Chicago's Comiskey Park.